Kwame Bediako and African Christian Scholarship

african christian studies series (africs)

This series will make available significant works in the field of African Christian studies, taking into account the many forms of Christianity across the whole continent of Africa. African Christian studies is defined here as any scholarship that relates to themes and issues on the history, nature, identity, character, and place of African Christianity in world Christianity. It also refers to topics that address the continuing search for abundant life for Africans through multiple appeals to African religions and African Christianity in a challenging social context. The books in this series are expected to make significant contributions in historicizing trends in African Christian studies, while shifting the contemporary discourse in these areas from narrow theological concerns to a broader inter-disciplinary engagement with African religio-cultural traditions and Africa's challenging social context.

The series will cater to scholarly and educational texts in the areas of religious studies, theology, mission studies, biblical studies, philosophy, social justice, and other diverse issues current in African Christianity. We define these studies broadly and specifically as primarily focused on new voices, fresh perspectives, new approaches, and historical and cultural analyses that are emerging because of the significant place of African Christianity and African religio-cultural traditions in world Christianity. The series intends to continually fill a gap in African scholarship, especially in the areas of social analysis in African Christian studies, African philosophies, new biblical and narrative hermeneutical approaches to African theologies, and the challenges facing African women in today's Africa and within African Christianity. Other diverse themes in African Traditional Religions; African ecology; African ecclesiology; inter-cultural, inter-ethnic, and inter-religious dialogue; ecumenism; creative inculturation; African theologies of development, reconciliation, globalization, and poverty reduction will also be covered in this series.

SERIES EDITORS

Dr. Stan Chu Ilo (DePaul University, Chicago, USA)
Dr. Esther Acolatse (Duke University, Durham, USA)
Dr. Mwenda Ntarangwi (Calvin College, Grand Rapids, MI, USA)

Kwame Bediako and African Christian Scholarship

Emerging Religious Discourse in Twentieth-Century Ghana

SARA J. FRETHEIM

FOREWORD BY
ELIAS K. BONGMBA

PICKWICK *Publications* · Eugene, Oregon

KWAME BEDIAKO AND AFRICAN CHRISTIAN SCHOLARSHIP
Emerging Religious Discourse in Twentieth-Century Ghana

African Christian Studies Series 13

Copyright © 2018 Sara J. Fretheim. All rights reserved. Except for brief quotations in critical publications or reviews, no part of this book may be reproduced in any manner without prior written permission from the publisher. Write: Permissions, Wipf and Stock Publishers, 199 W. 8th Ave., Suite 3, Eugene, OR 97401.

Cascade Books
An Imprint of Wipf and Stock Publishers
199 W. 8th Ave., Suite 3
Eugene, OR 97401

www.wipfandstock.com

PAPERBACK ISBN: 978-1-4982-9904-6
HARDCOVER ISBN: 978-1-4982-9906-0
EBOOK ISBN: 978-1-4982-9905-3

Cataloguing-in-Publication data:

Names: Fretheim, Sara J., author. | Bongmba, Elias Kifon, 1953–, foreword.

Title: Kwame Bediako and African Christian scholarship : emerging religious discourse in twentieth-century Ghana / Sara J. Fretheim ; foreword by Elias K. Bongmba.

Description: Eugene, OR : Cascade Books, 2018 | Series: African Christian Studies Series 13 | Includes bibliographical references and index.

Identifiers: ISBN 978-1-4982-9904-6 (paperback) | ISBN 978-1-4982-9906-0 (hardcover) | ISBN 978-1-4982-9905-3 (ebook)

Subjects: LCSH: Bediako, Kwame. | Theology—Africa. | Christianity—Africa, Sub-Saharan.

Classification: BT30.A4 F74 2018 (print) | BT30.A4 F74 (ebook)

Manufactured in the U.S.A.   04/16/18

To my Dad, for the life-long encouragement to pursue "wild ideas," and to my Mom, for reading my work with a critical eye and unfeigned enthusiasm. I am because we are!

Contents

Foreword by Elias K. Bongmba | ix
Acknowledgments | xv
Abbreviations | xviii

Chapter 1
Kwame Bediako in Perspective | 1
    Bediako: On the Page and in Person 2
    A Historical and Biographical Approach 13
    The Problematization of Gender and Ethnicity: Ongoing Challenges 18

Chapter 2
The African Christian Study of African Religions:
An Emerging Discourse | 23
    African Christian Scholarship: Fresh Perspectives, New Methodologies 24
    The African Study of African Religions 28
    Methodology: The Great Divide 35

Chapter 3
Reading, Writing, 'Rithmetic, and Religion: Nineteenth-
and Twentieth-Century Mission and Colonial Contributions
to the African Christian Study of Religions in Ghana | 58
    Nineteenth-Century Missions: Sowing the Dragon's Teeth of Education 59
    Colonial Education: 1919–1950 70
    Missionaries and Colonialists: Motivations 77

Chapter 4
Seeking First the Political Kingdom: Politics and the Study of Religion in Ghana | 82

    Independence and the Study of Religion in Ghana 83
    Church and State: Politics and Religion in Ghana 97
    Bediako in Context: Student Days 103

Chapter 5
"Down From What Tree?" The Unexpected Influence of Négritude Poetry on Bediako's Christian Thought | 109

    Négritude: Like a Woman Born to Die 110
    Bediako and U Tam'si: Exploring Unexpected Influences 121
    Bediako and U Tam'si: Areas of Affinity 132
    From Poetry and Identity to *Theology and Identity* 139

Chapter 6
Reading the Akrofi-Christaller Institute as Text: Bediako's *Magnum Opus* | 148

    The Story of ACI 149
    The Masters of Theology in African Christianity: Bediako's Abiding Contribution to the African Study of African Religions 164
    Evaluating Bediako Through ACI: A Critique 180

Chapter 7
Their Past, Our Present: Bediako's Abiding Significance for African Christian Scholarship | 191

    One Part of the Story Comes to an End: Kwame Bediako, 1945–2008 192
    African Christian Scholarship as Emerging Discourse 192
    Bediako: Relic, Relevant, or Relative? 197
    Future Directions for African Christian Scholarship 202
    Concluding Remarks 205

Appendix A
Current Scholarship Engaging With Bediako | 209

Appendix B
The Akrofi-Christaller Institute's Master of Theology in African Christianity | 212

Bibliography | 215
Index | 227

Foreword

SARA FRETHEIM INVITES READERS to this work focused exclusively on the intellectual legacy of Kwame Bediako, a scholar of the humanities whose theological imagination and creativity have received critical appraisal from scholars around the world. Bediako completed doctoral degrees in France and Britain before returning to Ghana where he served in various positions with the Presbyterian Church and later became the Founding Director of the Akrofi-Christaller Institute, where he and his wife, Gillian Bediako, embarked on a fascinating experiment in African-centered theological education. During his short life, Bediako's scholarly activities included teaching and lecturing around the world; extensive writing and publishing; and service to theological and other academic institutions, editorial boards, and mission organizations. In recognition of these accomplishments, he was elected to the Ghana Academy of Arts and Sciences.

Bediako made an early exit from this life but remains a prominent figure in African Christianity, its discourse, practice, theology, and vision, because of his attempts to appreciate and incorporate African realities into his scholarship and image of African Christian thought. Fretheim's book is an essential full-length study of a scholar whose journey in the Christian tradition began when he studied the work of Tchicaya U Tam'si, a *Négritude* poet from the Congo. Bediako saw in the *Négritude* movement, whose key thinkers included peoples of African descent, not only a quest for identity and sense of belonging to the human community at a time when slavery, the slave trade, and the colonial project had sought to eviscerate that identity, but a yearning to assert the will to *be*, a drive for intellectual, political, and economic freedom. The protest poetry of U Tam'si, which became the subject of Bediako's first doctoral thesis, was the catalyst for a transformation of identity, but more importantly for Bediako, a conversion experience and the beginning of his Christian identity and journey. In-depth analysis of his *Négritude* scholarship and its residual impact upon his Christian thought is a key contribution of this book. As Fretheim demonstrates, engagement with Bediako's theological writing must begin with his earlier Negritude scholarship, from which clear lines of continuity may be drawn. Bediako navigated a personal and global commitment to his faith which was born out of a passionate commitment to the *Geisteswissenschaften,* towards an evangelical and ecclesial theological commitment which unashamedly reclaimed Christianity as an African Religion which needed a multi-disciplinary and pluralistic vision to restore a distorted African identity and build the ecclesial community of the future.

Fretheim tells this story and much more, because she gives readers a critical portrait and appraisal of Bediako and his place in Ghanaian and African ecclesial and theological culture where for Bediako, being a Christian cannot be divorced from his Ghanaian and African roots. Fretheim brings the *einfühlung* of a former student at the Akrofi-Christaller Institute and that of a scholar of African Religions and Christianity, situating Bediako in the history of the Presbyterian Church and its mission and educational services, and in the political and intellectual history of post-colonial Ghana, where culture, politics, and the African personality led the quest for freedom, championed by many Ghanaians and their charismatic first President, Dr. Kwame Nkrumah. Fretheim then takes the reader through the poetry of U Tam'si, who embraced Négritude, which was championed by the Senegalese poet, Leopold Sédar Senghor; Martinican poet, Aimé Césaire, whose epic poem *Cahier d'un Retour au pays natal* gave birth to the term *négritude;* and Leon Damas of Guyana. Fretheim discusses the importance of the movement as a critique of rationalism, a recovery of African personality, and a revolt against the European domination of Africa and the African Diaspora, which sought to broaden and strengthen Trans-Atlantic nationalism as it attempted to recover and reinstate black identity and personality as well as usher in a new political vision. Fretheim addresses criticisms of the movement, including its focus on race, which some claimed came at the expense of genuine liberation, as well as its birthplace, Paris, the heart of the beast; and the criticism that *Negritude* largely reflected the views of assimilated African intellectuals, a point which Jean-Marc Ela echoed when he argued: "Any appraisal of the problems of faith organized narrowly around the recovery of the past will never allow us to stand beside Africans as they ask their questions of today. . . African Churches must resist the temptation to link theological reflection to the 'authenticity' that appears today as an ideology masking the stalemate of the ruling classes that are prey to the increasing difficulties of underdevelopment."[1] Yet it is the protest ideas and language of *Négritude* that turned Bediako to the Christian tradition and shaped his views on several tenets of Christian doctrine and theology, bringing him into dialogue with a diverse group of thinkers who could not be any more different from Sigmund Freud and Frantz Fanon, on the one hand, and Francis Schaeffer and A.W. Tozer on the other, with the last two signaling his Evangelical theological position even as he relished what he described as the "surrealist mysticism" in U'Tam'si's poetry. According to Fretheim, what brought U Tam'si and Bediako together was the search for identity. Yet Bediako ultimately joined in the critique of the shortcomings of *Négritude*, and set out in his work to provide a humanistic vision for the church in Africa that would also include social justice.

Fretheim is correct to argue that Bediako's *Theology and Identity: The Impact of Culture on Christian Thought in the Second Century and Modern Africa* is a significant text flowing from the concerns raised in his *Negritude* scholarship, and one that invites critical reflections on questions of religion and identity. This book is a landscaping approach to the question of identity as it discusses Christian identity in the Greco-Roman world, offers a rather triumphalist account of the gospel over what Bediako calls barbarism; discusses Christ and the Hellenistic culture--analysis animated with a critical examination of the work of Tatian, Tertullian, Justin, and Clement of Alexandria. Therefore, the book studies the contribution of seminal thinkers of the period and how they addressed the question of cultural identity. In the second part of the book, Bediako discusses the legacy of Christianity brought to Africa as a civilization and the identity crisis it created. Africans responded to this crisis of identity in different ways. Here Bediako engages E. Bolaji Idowu of Nigeria, who championed independence for the African Church, and John Mbiti of Kenya, who, unlike Idowu, rejected the notion of indigenization of Christianity and preferred to stress the continuity of Christianity and primal religions while seeking an approach to African theology that would articulate the gospel in light of African existence. He also engages Mulago gwa Cikala Musharhamina (Vincent Mulago), who argued that missionaries wrongly assumed Africa was a *tabula rasa* on which they would install western Christendom while destroying African civilization, contending instead for the revival of the old primitive revelation that would become the flame of Christ for everybody. Finally, Bediako introduces a dissenting voice with Byang Kato,

1. Jean-Marc Éla, *My Faith as an African* (Maryknoll: Orbis, 1988), 171.

the Nigerian Evangelical theologian who presented a deeply conservative view of theology rooted in American Evangelical conservatism. Bediako is critical of his disdainful attitude towards the African religious heritage, which ignored the religious traditions of Kato's people, the Jaba of Nigeria, and even ignored the social context of the numerous biblical texts he cited to promote his bibliology. Bediako is equally critical of Kato's critique of ecumenism, which Kato saw as the movement undermining the absolute authority of the Bible. Bediako concluded the book by issuing a call for African scholars to appreciate the theme of continuity and discontinuity in order to anticiapte and appreciate a future which emerges from a synthesis of traditions. This will give scholars an opportunity to face challenges in a changing society as they embrace theology as indigenization, and promote theology that responds to criticisms that African theologians have merely imposed Greek ideas on Africa, and above all recognize faith as a historical category that should prioritize the African experience.

Fretheim rightly considers that Bediako's *magnum opus* will always remain the Akrofi-Christaller Institute for Theology, Mission and Culture (Akropong, Ghana). Fretheim documents the long journey of this project, recording events, individuals, and especially the Presbyterian Church of Ghana, who provided inspiration, encouragement, and support for the vision that would lead to the establishment of a post-graduate center for African Christian scholarship. The African-centered curriculum is designed to prepare excellent scholars for academia and the growing African church at home and in diaspora in a new global climate. Bediako's pioneering vision emerges in a center for mother tongue theology in a setting that has a distinctly communal feel, different from both universities and seminaries. One significant aspect of Fretheim's work is the critical engagement and appraisal of the goals of the Institute through the thought of Bediako. In doing so, Fretheim underscores not only the relevance of the entire project to African Religions and their place in Africa, but the dynamic interaction they have with other religions, and for relating Bediako's vision to World Christianity.

Fretheim discusses the curriculum of its Master's of Theology in African Christianity, indicating how Bediako's training in *Négritude* literature and engagement with John Mbiti's scholarship shaped his thinking and framing of this flagship program to focus on biblical theology, theological perspectives from other parts of the Christian tradition, African contributions to theology, and as Fretheim calls it, "theology of the living Church," concluding this book with a discussion of Bediako's legacy.

This is an amazing study that should draw critical dialogue and analysis. As a biography, it offers us an account of one individual whose engagement in the humanities leads to a vigorous theological enterprise that has attracted debates and critiques from colleagues across the world. It is an important reminder of the need for greater interdisciplinarity and what I have referred to elsewhere as "epistemological flexibility" in the study of African Christianity.[2] And in tracing competing voices within the study of Religion in Africa, it highlights the significance of African Christian scholars within this discourse. I must add that this is just the beginning of an engagement with Bediako's legacy. He also demonstrated his African-centeredness in other books, numerous articles, and in the significant body of unpublished sermons, lectures, and essays which he left behind. In his important book, *Christianity in Africa: The Renewal of a Non-Western Religion*, Bediako addresses not only the growth of Christianity in the Global South, but offers perspectives on grounding African Christianity in the religious realities of African communities. He called for fresh engagement with lived Christianity because of the work of different church groups in Ghana, where the explosive growth of Pentecostalism enacted a spiritual renaissance in Africa by paying attention to the spiritual world, the power and presence of the Spirit, which he linked to the hard-to-describe expression, "primal imagination." These perspectives reflect Bediako's view that Christianity is an African Religion.

In his earlier book, *Jesus and the Gospel in Africa: History and Experience*, Bediako joined a growing conversation on Jesus in Africa, emphasizing that the African Church needed to look deep in its history and traditions to see Jesus as sufficient for their needs. It is a work which was grounded in an analysis of the Christian experience in Africa, including the cherished African traditions of pouring libations and ancestor veneration, which, as Fretheim discusses, Kwame Nkrumah was not shy to introduce in public ceremonies. Bediako's argument that Christ was not an alien figure to specific religious traditions was what made Jesus Lord for many Africans. The fact that Jesus is Lord from Bediako's perspective called for a rethinking of the notion of primal religions as the grounding for religious life in Africa; an approach that differed from a negative portrayal of the religions of Africa which many Westerners denigrated as paganism. Instead, the reality of African religions was a demonstration of religious pluralism that the Christian tradition could not ignore. Bediako's creativity in this work included a call for a Christian vision underscoring human connectivity with the created order which humans share with other creatures. This would be a prelude to building a world where the spirits remind

---

2. Elias Kifon Bongmba, "Writing African Christianity: Perspectives from the History of the Historiography of African Christianity," *Religion & Theology* 23 (2016), 275–312: 291.

us of that vital connection Africans have with the universe and with their ancestors, because it is this broad connectivity with the cosmos that would strengthen an African Christian identity. Such an identity would flourish in a world where political practice caters to the needs of all people because God liberates in all dimensions of life. Since God liberates all areas of life and society, Fretheim succeeds in her goal of introducing readers to the legacy of Bediako and in doing so invites scholars to further consider not only Bediako but other African scholars, whose work continues to shape theological scholarship on the continent and beyond.

Elias K. Bongmba
Harry and Hazel Chair in Christian Theology and Professor of Religion
Rice University

Acknowledgments

THERE IS AN AKAN proverb that says, *Baanu so a emmia*--when two people carry a heavy load, it does not hurt. The support that I have received from many colleagues, friends, and family in assisting me to "carry" this book to completion allows me to enthusiastically bear witness to the truth of this statement!

This book is a substantial revision of material that I first presented as a thesis for the degree of Doctor of Philosophy at the University of Liverpool in partnership with Liverpool Hope University in July 2015. My research was undertaken under the supervision of Professors Andrew F. Walls and Daniel Jeyaraj, with further generous support from Dr. Andrew Cheatle, all of Liverpool Hope. I am grateful to each one for academic assistance and collegiality, and for helping me to grow as a scholar and a writer. I also return thanks to Ms. Karen Backhouse, Special Collections Librarian at the Andrew Walls Centre for the Study of African and Asian Christianity at the Sheppard-Worlock Library, Liverpool Hope. Working with her and discovering many hidden treasures (and occasionally puzzling mysteries!) in the Centre's collection was a highlight of this period of research.

In his Preface to *Theology and Identity*, which Kwame Bediako originally completed for a doctoral degree under the supervision of Andrew Walls in 1983, he writes, "It is a special delight for me that Prof. Walls warmly welcomed the results of my research, and I wish to record my deepest gratitude to him for his generous commendation of my book." It is an honor to echo Bediako's words of gratitude to Prof. Walls, now a generation later, for his continued support throughout this project, including his generous recommendation of this book. I am also grateful to Elias Bongmba (Rice University) for strategic input during my research and writing, as well as for graciously contributing the foreword.

In terms of institutional support, further thanks are due to the Akrofi-Christaller Institute for Theology, Mission and Culture (Akropong-Akuapem, Ghana). Here, I enjoyed two six-month residential periods of research, as well as continued long-distance collegial engagement. I also express my fond thanks to Prof. Gillian Mary Bediako—"Auntie Mary"—for continued friendship and scholarly support in this and other projects. I am particularly grateful that she granted me generous access to important unpublished materials by Kwame Bediako for this research. Thanks also go to Prof. Allison Howell for warm friendship through the years. To these and all of my colleagues and friends at ACI, I say *medaase paa*!

I am also indebted to those who granted me interviews and/or gave me access to unpublished written and documentary materials, allowing me to add important insights to this research. In this regard, I wish to thank the following: Dr. and Mrs. Alexander and Rosemary Glover-Quartey (Ghana), who generously hosted me in their home in Accra and allowed me to interview them for this project, while Dr. Glover-Quartey also provided further written responses to questions that arose during the course of my research. The Revd. Bill and (now late) Mary Adams (USA) graciously granted me an interview via correspondence and furnished me with a copy of their unpublished account of their years of missionary service in Bordeaux, which included reflections of their interactions with Kwame Bediako. As well, James Ault helpfully provided and granted permission for me to use unpublished transcripts from unused portions of his documentary footage of Kwame Bediako for the *African Christianity Rising* documentary. For each one of these, I am thankful and hope that my rendering of their thoughts and use of their materials will be deemed accurate and acceptable.

In recalling all of the friends in different cities and continents who have supported me through this project, I face an embarrassment of riches and an insufficiency of space! But I wish to especially acknowledge the following: in Vancouver, those friends with whom I have met regularly for feedback and encouragement during this final writing process; in Calgary, the Wolf and Debrey families, with special thanks to Morgan Wolf for extensive editorial support; in Berlin, Jutta and Norbert Kirsch; friends in Aberdeen and at Jesus House Church (RCCG); in Liverpool, the Most Reverend Justice and Dr. Mrs. Maria Akrofi and friends in the Ghanaian community there; friends at the Anglican Cathedral and Frontline Church; and Michele Amico, Sharon Holden, and Maria Duffy, for friendship and generous hospitality towards a stray Canadian ("sorry!"). In London, particular thanks to the Revd. Dr. Daniel

Eshun, for helpful feedback and memories of his own encounters with Kwame Bediako; in Nigeria, special thanks to the Most Reverend Dr. Emmanuel A.S. and Mrs. Biodun Egbunu and family, and in Ghana, to Dr. Dorcas Ini Dah. To these friends, as well as to the many not expressly mentioned, I extend my sincere appreciation for sharing the weight of this load!

I also wish to extend sincere thanks to colleagues at Wipf & Stock for their many and varied efforts getting this manuscript into its present format. I am also grateful for Wipf & Stock's willingness to work with Regnum Africa to ensure that the book is easily accessible in Ghana, from where the research was drawn. I hope that other publishers will follow suit so that scholarly discourse on African Christianity can continue to expand across geographical boundary lines.

My most profound gratitude, however, goes to my family, who remain a deep and abiding source of support, care, and joy. I particularly thank my sister, Erin Fretheim, for checking in and encouraging me daily during intense writing periods; my brother, David Fretheim, for his interest in this project; and finally, my parents, the Revd. Tim and Marcia Fretheim, for unfailingly carrying far more than their fair share of this load with generosity of spirit and without hesitation or complaint.

While so many have contributed so much, in this finished work I alone bear full responsibility for any errors, inconsistencies, or infelicities in the text.

Abbreviations

ACI   Akrofi-Christaller Institute of Theology, Mission and Culture (Akropong-Akuapem, Ghana)

CCG   The Christian Council of Ghana

CPP   Convention People's Party

IBMR   International Bulletin of Mission Research

JACT   Journal of African Christian Thought

PCG   Presbyterian Church of Ghana

Chapter 1

Kwame Bediako in Perspective

O my absurd ancestry! Down from what tree?[1]

—Tchicaya U Tam'si

---

1. U Tam'si, *Selected Poems*, "Summary of a Passion," from *Epitomé*, 37. Adinkra symbols in Ghana are used to communicate social and religious meanings and are traditionally printed on cloth, though they are used in myriad decorative ways to convey meaning. I have used one adinkra symbol at the start of each chapter to support the theme of the chapter and as a way of highlighting Ghana's centrality in this research. Each symbol is referenced first by its Twi name, followed by an English explanation. All adinkra symbols used here have been taken from https://vincenttechblog.com/adinkra-symbols-brushes-shapes-download/ where they are freely available.

The adinkra symbol above, *sankofa*, means "return and get it" and signifies the importance of learning from the past.

1

Bediako: On the Page and In Person

I FIRST MET KWAME Bediako in Akropong, Ghana, when I had the opportunity to study with him at the Akrofi-Christaller Institute for Theology, Mission, and Culture, a postgraduate research center that he founded and directed from 1984 until his death in 2008.[2] It was 2006, and I was nearing the end of a master's degree in Theological Studies in Canada when the opportunity arose to spend a semester at ACI in their Master of Theology in African Christianity program. I had been reading Bediako's work, and the chance to study with him in person was not to be missed.

I was intrigued by his perspective on the role of "mother tongue theology," and his contentious argument that primal religion—a term upon which he insisted—could be viewed as a substructure to Christianity. Similarly, his Christological proposal of Jesus as the ancestor *par excellence* in Akan cosmology provided much food for thought. In person and in his writing, Bediako continually challenged me to reconsider and re-examine issues relating to African Christianity, primal religion, world Christian history; and, more broadly, to methodological approaches to the study of religion in Africa. Some of his views offered intriguing responses to long-held questions of mine, while others raised further queries. But above all, I remained interested in his process and motivations as an African Christian intellectual.

As I began to read others' assessments of Bediako, I was further intrigued by the degree of controversy he engendered and by the wide-ranging scope of respondents. Bediako, aptly reflecting the tensions, interdisciplinarity, and creativity within this emerging African religious discourse, is an ambiguous figure who defies clear-cut categorisation. He has received high praises and harsh criticism from theologians and scholars of religion alike, with his critics and supporters spread across Africa and the West. Indeed, his reach as an African Christian scholar can hardly be underestimated, as Alan Thomson notes, describing him in the early 2000s as "an evangelical theologian who is an increasingly important bridging figure between Africa and the West. He is both director of [ACI] in Ghana, and a director of the Oxford Center of Mission Studies, Oxford, England; as well as formerly being Visiting Lecturer in African Theology at the Centre for the Study of Christianity in the Non-Western World, New College, University of Edinburgh, Scotland."[3]

---

2. Throughout this book, I refer to this institution by its commonly known designations, "ACI" or "the Institute."

3. Thomson, "Learning from the African Experience," 35.

While a majority of scholarship on Bediako unsurprisingly engages various aspects of his theology, a theological analysis is not the focus of this book. Seeing the polarization of some of these responses further confirmed for me that adding yet another theological analysis would not ultimately further our understanding of Bediako's scholarly itinerary. Instead, this book is an intellectual history that examines Bediako in broader historical, contextual, and methodological terms. However, in order to get a sense of where this book variously interacts with and departs from current scholarship, it is helpful to have a sense of the warp and weft of these discussions.[4]

There are many who identify Bediako as a pioneer and trailblazer, one who forged important new paths for African Christian scholarship. British mission historian Andrew Walls, a long-time friend and colleague of Bediako's, labels him "the outstanding African theologian of his generation."[5] Walls notes Bediako's establishment of ACI as one of his most important and enduring scholarly contributions, and has himself continued to support that vision through regular teaching and doctoral student supervision at ACI from its inception through to the present.

Ghanaian Pentecostal scholar J. Kwabena Asamoah-Gyadu describes Bediako as "a colossus, indeed an icon of a scholar in the field of African Christianity," and notes his unique combination of scholastic rigor alongside of his evangelical faith and devotional use of the Bible, often at the start of classes or seminars.[6] From his experiences with Bediako as his teacher and colleague, Asamoah-Gyadu shares that "Bediako constantly planted into those who studied under him the thoughts that first, Christian theological scholarship must always engage with contextual issues."[7]

Nigerian Church historian Ogbu Kalu, in referencing Bediako's efforts to develop affordable African theological publishing on the continent, identifies publishing as "only one of the pioneering ways in which Kwame Bediako . . . has sought to define the theological enterprise in contemporary Africa."[8]

Others engage specific aspects of his theological viewpoints for dialogue and critique, with his arguments surrounding ancestor Christology and primal religion eliciting perhaps the greatest range and intensity of responses. Norwegian scholar Roar Fotland completed an extensive doctoral study analyzing Bediako's Christ-as-ancestor argument. He concluded positively that

---

4. See Appendix A for a detailed listing of current scholarship on Bediako.
5. Walls, "Kwame Bediako and Christian Scholarship in Africa," 192.
6. Asamoah-Gyadu, "Bediako on Africa," 9.
7. Ibid., 8.
8. Kalu, Review of *Jesus and the Gospel in Africa*, 48.

Bediako was articulating "a new concept of Christian ancestors with two categories: divine and human," in which, among the ancestors, "Jesus Christ is the most prominent and is the only divine ancestor."[9] In Bediako's approach, Fotland argues, "the old and new, the local and global, are kept together and everything is passed 'through the prism of Christology.'"[10]

On the other hand, Nigerian theologian Victor Ezigbo criticizes Bediako's Christology, and particularly his affinity for the scholarship of mid-twentieth-century British Anglican missionary and bishop J.V. Taylor. Bediako found Taylor's scholarship compelling; and both in his lectures and his writing, made extensive use of Taylor's book *The Primal Vision*, which explores Christian engagement with African religions. Ezigbo, however, finds Taylor's theological queries and premises out-dated, and therefore a weak aspect of Bediako's Christology. As he concludes, "Surprisingly, Bediako who predicted the new shift in christological discourse has continued to write and wrestle with the deep cultural issues that stem from the Western derogatory estimation of the African pre-Christian traditions. Thus, his Christology and theology have largely remained heavily influenced by the Taylorian christological presupposition."[11] Not dissimilarly, Beninese theologian Valentin Dedj calls Bediako's achievements "impressive, consistent and groundbreaking in many respects," yet questions whether he is in fact "at risk of being too 'traditional'" and not pushing African theology in more current directions.[12]

Conversely, Bediako has come under criticism from a number of evangelical scholars who find his theology too *non*-traditional. One such example is Keith Ferdinando, a British theologian who, among other roles, served as lecturer in mission studies at Bediako's *alma mater*, the London School of Theology, three decades after Bediako's time there. In a lengthy analysis of *Theology and Identity*, Ferdinando argues that while it is admittedly a work in "comparative historical theology rather than in biblical theology," he finds that Bediako's lack of an explicitly stated biblical basis for the book leaves it on shaky ground.

He sharply challenges Bediako's argument for continuity between primal religion and Christianity, and concludes by saying, "[I]t is questionable whether [Bediako's] approach—accomplished and scholarly as it undoubtedly is—has a sufficient biblical foundation, and whether its theological response to the issue of identity concedes more than it should to the validity

---

9. Fotland, "The Christology of Kwame Bediako," 45.
10. Ibid.
11. Ezigbo, *Re-Imagining African Christologies*, 19–20.
12. Dedji, *Reconstruction and Renewal*, 209.

and worth of pre-Christian African religions . . . The resulting danger, albeit unintentional, is that the matchless and utterly revolutionary character of the gospel of Jesus Christ, which must lie at the heart of any authentically Christian theology, may not be grasped in its fullness, with inevitable consequences for mission within Africa and beyond."[13]

In a 2013 article, American missionary Kevin Howard raises similar concerns and employs the neo-colonial "Africa as exotic and dangerous" motif, saying, "Randomly running into a forest in Africa without knowing what is there could be ill-advised . . . It is always better to have a guide, someone who knows the trails and the terrain. Perhaps Bediako could be our guide in African Christian theology."[14] He goes on to challenge Bediako's view of the role of culture in biblical interpretation; his support for African Catholic theologians; his argument for continuity between African primal religion and Christianity; and the role of ancestors within African Christian scholarship. He ultimately pronounces judgment on Bediako—quite literally—saying, "One of the most damning things we can accurately say about Bediako's theology and methodology is that they diminish the importance of Christ's first coming, namely his death and resurrection . . . While much good may be gained by walking into the bushes with Bediako, some danger may lurk in the shadows, and perhaps something deadly."[15]

More recently, Ghanaian theologian Yaw Attah Edu-Bekoe has offered a sharp reply to Howard and challenged this derogatory approach to African scholarship in an article aptly titled, "Describing an African Dancing Without Hearing His Music: Kevin Howard has Generally Misunderstood Kwame Bediako."[16] As Edu-Bekoe rightly argues, "Africa and African Christians are not, as Howard posited, all jungle . . . Africa and African Christians are not associated with myriad spirits . . . Africa and African Christians do not engage in ancestral worship . . ." And responding to Howard's "damning" criticism of Bediako, Edu-Bekoe calls it a statement "made out of the usual Euro-American negative attitude towards African cultures."[17]

Dutch scholar and former missionary Benno van den Toren accurately identifies Bediako as a unique combination of "a positively open and appreciative attitude towards the traditional African religious context and at the same time a solid Christocentric stance."[18] He supports Bediako's scholarly

13. Ferdinando, "Christian Identity," 142, 143.
14. Howard, "Kwame Bediako," 1.
15. Ibid., 23–24.
16. Edu-Bekoe, "Describing an African Dancing."
17. Ibid., paras. 1, 3.
18. Van den Toren, "Kwame Bediako's Christology," 226.

trajectory and argues that for those who seek to represent Jesus in new and diverse contexts, "a Christocentric theology should be the starting point and an openness to the context is essential; but in many theological positions both poles are more rivals than allies."[19] He anticipates critics such as Ferdinando and Howard when he says that such views "can be expected from more conservative streams within the wider evangelical movement, for example from the North American type of evangelicalism . . ."[20]

Offering a contrasting perspective, South African theologian Tinyiko Maluleke describes Bediako's scholarship with terms such as "brave," "innovative," and "far-reaching." However, while he to some degree supports Bediako's intellectual agenda, he ultimately rejects his argument for continuity between Christianity and primal religion as a diminishment of the uniqueness of African indigenous religions.[21] For some, Bediako goes too far; for Maluleke, not far enough. He engages a wide range of Bediako's scholarship, and commends him for his "appeal to early 'Christian history' to justify and clarify the African Christian Theology project . . ."[22] As if in response to Ferdinando's suggestion that Bediako's work may not be perceived as "authentically Christian theology," Maluleke argues that "the era of African Christian theology having to search for 'proper,' 'historical,' 'doctrinal,' or 'biblical' foundations—*in order* that it may be acceptable as true Christian theology—is past."[23]

In a departure from these theological assessments, British academic James Cox offers yet another perspective when he engages Bediako on a methodological basis from within the field of religious studies. He discounts Bediako's argument for continuity between Christianity and primal religion as an incorrect globalization of a local religious phenomenon, and contends that Bediako's approach is more Western in orientation, arguments we will consider more fully in the following chapter.[24]

This is not by any means an exhaustive discussion of all who interact with Bediako; we will continue to examine other responses in due course. Nevertheless, we begin to see the range of often contradictory viewpoints of those who engage him: he gives too much credence to primal religion versus not giving enough; being biblically unfounded in his scholarship versus

19. Ibid.
20. Ibid., 226–27.
21. See Maluleke, "Black and African Theologies," 3–19.
22. Maluleke, "In Search of 'The True Character of African Christian Identity," 211.
23. Ibid.
24. See Cox, "The Globalization of Localized African Religions," 56–65.

being unusual as an academic in regularly referencing the Bible; his work is brave and innovative versus dangerous.

Walls observes that one of Bediako's key lines of investigation into the small first generation of African theologians lay in questioning why "the efforts of pioneers such as Bolaji Idowu and John Mbiti cause[d] equal disturbance in the evangelical stables in which they were nourished and among African intellectuals such as Okot p'Bitek, who had rejected Christianity."[25] Ironically, as this brief *mise en scène* reminds us, through the course of his life, Bediako joined their ranks as one causing similar discomfort in these circles. Bediako himself is fully aware of this, and offers this response:

> Conceivably, it may be objected that the approach I propose is too open-ended, and, perhaps, even risky, for I leave many questions unresolved from the start, and I hold many Christian theological propositions and creedal formulations in abeyance. My response would be that such an approach, precisely, through openness and vulnerability, is what Christian witness to the divine incognito in Christ requires.[26]

Bediako's reach and impact as an African Christian scholar cannot be underestimated. Indeed, the diversity of those interacting with him, together with their widely diverging responses, bears witness to the significance of his contribution and points to the fact that much work remains to be done to more fully understand this theologian. For this reason, he remains an important figure for further consideration within African Christian scholarship, as well as within the wider study of religion in Africa.

As a study in intellectual history, this book locates Bediako historically as a leading African Christian scholar within an important and emerging African religious discourse from within his context of twentieth-century post-colonial Ghana. This is important for three reasons. Firstly, it uncovers some of the key influences on Bediako's thinking, several of which, as we will discover, are traced back to his decade of Négritude scholarship. While this does not resolve the theological debates (which is not, in any case, our aim), it helps to clarify Bediako's intellectual itinerary, which in turn reveals constructive approaches for future scholarly engagement with his work.

Secondly, viewing Bediako from within his historical context sheds light on the broader development of an important and emerging discourse: the African study of African religions, and more specifically, the African Christian voices within this discourse. Thirdly, Bediako himself clearly advocates for the use of historical-biographical approaches to engaging

---

25. Walls, "Kwame Bediako and Christian Scholarship in Africa," 189.
26. Bediako, "How is Jesus Christ Lord?," 44.

African Christians. Yet, to date, scholars have failed to apply such an approach to Bediako. This book therefore addresses that oversight and offers a fresh approach to reading this African Christian scholar.

In the following quotation, Bediako outlines his research comparing second-century Christian writers with the concerns of twentieth-century African theologians. He offers a cogent argument, which serves as a helpful explanation for the framework adopted here:

> Traditionally, the early Christian writers . . . have been studied largely for their contribution or otherwise to the development of Christian doctrine. Accordingly, their careers have tended to be assessed in terms of their relation to orthodoxy or heresy. However, looked at from the standpoint of the Christian identity problem and how it was faced in relation to the issues raised for the Christian consciousness by the Graeco-Roman [sic] culture in which they all shared to varying degrees, these writers become more interesting in themselves as persons. Their careers gain a significance beyond questions of dogma alone; they become important witnesses to a more enduring problem: the Christian's response to the religious past as well as to the cultural tradition generally in which one stands, and the significance of that response for the development of theological answers to the culturally-rooted questions of the context.[27]

This statement is significant for several reasons. It serves as a challenge to what may be understood as traditional theological scholarship—or perhaps Western theological scholarship—in that Bediako pushes us to read the text not apart from, but alongside of, the context and life of the scholar. As he points out, to do otherwise produces research that may overlook significant pieces of the puzzle. Here we see Bediako's historical-biographical approach emerging.

He articulates this more clearly when he argues that African Christian scholars are best understood when we "place them in continuum with the historical movement that has produced and is likely to produce in the future, people like them."[28] To do so, he says, elucidates both the scholars and the historical contexts which have shaped them. And he is right: such holistic engagement provides a window into how African Christian scholarship reflects and responds to cultural, historical, and geographical forces. It also offers tools for anticipating and analyzing new paths in the study of religion in Africa. Furthermore, it may help us to avoid some of the interpretational

---

27. Bediako, *Theology and Identity*, 7.
28. Ibid., 6.

pitfalls that can arise from reading African Christian scholars from overly narrow theological perspectives.

In getting to know Bediako personally, I began to perceive the truth of his argument. To understand him as an African Christian scholar, I needed to move beyond his text to his context, engaging him within his academic community at ACI and the surrounding town of Akropong, reading his scholarship from within the broader historical, religiously plural Ghanaian setting from which he emerged. In the case of Bediako, such an approach, just as he says, casts the scholar and his scholarship in a new light. This changes the discourse from questions of "orthodoxy" and "heresy" to a much broader, and in Bediako's case, highly interdisciplinary, dialogue. In turn, this approach reveals that the concerns of African Christian scholarship differ to varying extents from those of Western theology. This challenges us to be mindful and attentive to our approaches to interdisciplinary scholarship, and reveals areas where African Christian scholarship may helpfully inform both Western theology and the non-confessional study of religion in Africa.

While we no longer have the privilege of interacting with Bediako, a significant body of his unpublished writing remains to be examined. This is in addition to the curriculum and community that he designed at ACI, as well as broader Ghanaian and European mission history which informed his thinking. Taken together with his published work, using this material offers an important and more comprehensive approach to engaging with this academician.

There is always a place for engaging with theological concepts on their own merit. However, the practice of reading only select works of Bediako's and making sweeping judgments with scant consideration for, or understanding of, his historical and cultural context, or his wider body of scholarship, while similarly failing to interrogate his scholarly itinerary, is problematic. It runs the risk of misunderstanding him, and missing the significance of his wider contribution to the African Christian study of African religions. Furthermore, in reading Bediako apart from his Ghanaian context, with all of the complexity of twentieth-century political, cultural, and religious developments, we overlook his pioneering role as an African Christian scholar within this emerging religious discourse.

Therefore, in this book I will assess a number of his unpublished works, including "reading" ACI as text, as well as providing an in-depth analysis of his twentieth-century postcolonial Ghanaian context. This includes drawing upon his unpublished first masters and doctoral dissertations on Négritude literature, his unpublished account of the vision and history of ACI (entitled "Ebenezer"), and the community and curriculum that he designed at ACI, focusing on the MTh in African Christianity, a program in which I participated at intervals over the course of a decade and completed in 2017. In this way, this book departs significantly from current theological readings of Bediako, presenting him within a broader scholarly context as a leading African Christian scholar of African religions.

A Story to Be Told

It has been said that for knowledge to be meaningful, it is best put into the context of a story. Intellectual history is no different. Elias Bongmba argues, "the historical method privileges data collection from all sources, calls for questioning of those sources and presenting the results or findings in a coherent narrative."[29] As Bediako once remarked to me, "narrative just means story, and our story as African Christians is an important one that needs to be told."

Bediako's life parallels the wider story of Ghana's birth and development as an independent African nation, and the emergence of an important African religious discourse. Bediako's story, like that of Ghana, is simultaneously familiar and yet quite remarkable.[30] He was born into a working-class, religiously plural family in 1945, towards the end of Ghana's colonial era. His mother was a committed Presbyterian, his father a practitioner of traditional religion. Like many others, Bediako received an outstanding secondary education at Mfantsipim, a Wesleyan mission school.

His is also the story of a young Ghanaian maturing into an academically brilliant and politically engaged student at the height of post-independence exuberance in the 1960s. Like the developing nation of Ghana, Bediako's story is one of a young African academic exploring questions of identity, religion, and culture, which he pursued through postgraduate studies in France and the United Kingdom in the 1970s and 1980s.

And very remarkably, his is the story of an avowed atheist experiencing an unexpected conversion to Christianity and subsequently committing himself to Christian scholarship and to the establishment of a postgraduate research institution dedicated to intellectual inquiry and the spiritual formation of future generations of African Christian scholars. He describes his

---

29. Bongmba, "Writing African Christianity," 279.

30. Details here are taken from the booklet produced for Bediako's funeral, *Call to Glory*; interviews with Gillian Bediako, Alex Glover-Quartey, and Daniel Eshun; and in consultation with the works of scholars J. Kwabena Asamoah-Gyadu, Andrew Walls, and Roar Fotland, who provide helpful and extensive accounts of Bediako's life. See Asamoah-Gyadu, "Kwame Bediako: 'Mr. African Theology,'" 11–21; Walls, "Kwame Bediako and Christian Scholarship in Africa," 188–93; and Fotland, *Ancestor Christology in Context*.

conversion experience as coming to believe that "Christ [was] the truth, the integrating principle of life as well as the key to true intellectual coherence [both] for himself and for the world."[31]

Bediako's story, and that of twentieth-century Ghana, offers much to hold our attention. From poets to presidents, there is a full cast of characters and much drama along the way. Set against the ambivalent backdrop of Ghanaian mission and colonial history, Bediako's story, with its "chapters" on Négritude poetry, Nkrumah's religio-political manoeuvring, and the emergence of the academic study of African religions alongside of rising African Christian discourse, proves to be an exciting one indeed.

Introduction to Bediako's Work

I will primarily interact with Bediako's opus, and responses to it, throughout this book where it fits in thematically and chronologically, rather than engaging with it at the start; and have elected to do so for two reasons. Firstly, as intellectual history as opposed to a narrow theological reading of Bediako, this work is equally concerned with his life, historical context, and scholarly itinerary. Therefore, it makes sense to engage these elements in turn as they emerge organically, rather than prioritizing one over the others. Secondly, in supporting Bediako's argument that African Christian scholars are best understood when placed within the historical continuum from which they have emerged, I hope to positively demonstrate this throughout this book, while seeking to avoid the very pitfall I am critiquing of reading African Christian scholars apart from their contexts. This bigger-picture analysis will help to clarify what Bediako was doing, why he was doing it, and how he fits into the broader African Christian study of African religions.

As I read more of Bediako's work and considered the array of responses to it, I became increasingly aware of three things. Firstly, as previously stated, there is currently no scholarship engaging with Bediako in the historical manner that he himself advocated. This includes a lack of scholarship evaluating the significant influence of his decade of engagement with Négritude and the poetry of Tchicaya U Tam'si. This is particularly important, given its lasting impact on his subsequent Christian thought. This struck me as a surprising oversight, given that his study of Négritude and Surrealist poetry served as the backdrop to his radical conversion to Christianity, and remained a strong influence on his later theological work. One exception here is Roar Fotland's *Ancestor Christology in Context*, in which he does provide a significant account of ancient Ghanaian history, as well as a detailed

---

31. Bediako, *Jesus in Africa*, vii.

biographical account of Bediako. However, he fails to engage twentieth-century Ghana or Bediako's Négritude scholarship in any significant depth, both of which I have found to be essential for evaluating Bediako.

Secondly, as we have briefly seen, among those who engage with Bediako's theological ideas, there are frequently strong reactions from both critics and supporters alike. The strength and disparate nature of these responses puzzled me. Having studied and interacted with Bediako at ACI, I failed to recognize him in many such views. Rather, I had encountered an academic who was neither saint nor sinner, but quite human: a scholar with a keen intellect, quick wit, and insatiable curiosity; and a man who was gentle-spirited and humble, though at times enigmatic and idiosyncratic![32]

In the lecture hall, he fostered an environment in which all were warmly received, and he prodded students to wrestle with challenging questions of religious faith and praxis, community, and culture. Controversy and disagreements were not avoided; but neither were they necessarily resolved. From my perspective as a student in his classes, it seemed to me that his goal was to encourage scholarly exploration and creative methodological experimentation in the study of religion in Africa, as opposed to necessarily arriving at concrete answers. Above all, however, I was struck by the fact that he conveyed his deep and abiding love for the person of Jesus Christ at every turn, and demonstrated an unwavering commitment to the Christian scriptures that reveal him.

This led to my third observation: within these divergent views, it became increasingly clear that Bediako, as an African Christian scholar, had a unique approach to the study of African religions. And it was an approach that did not necessarily correspond to those of his Western counterparts, whose study of religions in Africa more readily separated into the familiar categories of Theology and Religious Studies. Instead, in Bediako's lectures at ACI, and in his writing, I saw an interdisciplinary scholarly itinerary that shared concerns with, but stretched and challenged, those categories.

Maluleke correctly identifies Bediako's approach as an intellectual endeavour "concerned with responding to the charge of African intellectuals who say that Christianity can never become an adequate frame of reference for the full expression of African ideals of life."[33] As I watched Bediako, it occurred to me that within the study of African religions, African Christian scholars may be using different tools and addressing different concerns than

---

32. See Appendix A for a list of the published works and unpublished masters and doctoral dissertations on Bediako that I have consulted for this research.

33. Maluleke, "Black and African Theologies," 6.

their Western counterparts assume. I wondered whether, with regard to Bediako's pioneering contribution, we had missed the forest for the trees.

Controversy stirs intrigue and warrants inquiry. So, I set out in search of a fuller picture of Kwame Bediako as an African Christian scholar of African religions, attempting, as he advocated, to place him within his historical context and to more fully understand his intellectual itinerary. The result has been the ability to identify some of the complexities of African Christian scholarship as an emerging discourse in twentieth-century Ghana, as well as discovering unexpected influences on Bediako's Christian thought. At the start of this research, Andrew Walls offered the following caveat: "You will be aware, I am sure, that this subject is not the path for the person wanting a 'normal' academic career or a quiet untroubled life. But, it could have much reward in more important ways." His prophetic words continue to ring true.

A Historical and Biographical Approach

This book addresses two overarching questions: how did events and personages in nineteenth- and twentieth-century Ghana shape and contribute to the emerging African Christian study of African religions; and critically, in what ways can Kwame Bediako be seen as a leading figure within this discourse? These questions have implications for our reading of Bediako, of course; but they also raise important considerations within the wider field of the study of religion in Africa, and point to methodological challenges within the fields of Theology and Religious Studies.

Further questions have arisen throughout the course of this research: how did mission and colonial education contribute to Ghana's development, and to an understanding of Christian and indigenous religious traditions? How was religion used as a political tool in the establishment of a national Ghanaian identity, and how did this in turn shape the African study of religions? How did Négritude literature engage questions of religion and identity, and how did this influence Bediako's later scholarship? And how are we to "read" the institution he founded? In what ways is ACI distinct from either a university or seminary, and what contributions is it making to twenty-first-century African Christian scholarship? These are some of the questions which shaped my study, and which are addressed in turns throughout the following chapters.

With this in mind, this historical study analyzes key unpublished and published primary source materials by Bediako, strategic secondary source texts, and further draws upon select interviews and participant-observation at ACI. Among Bediako's unpublished works, my primary focus here is his master's and doctoral dissertations on Négritude literature, which analyze the work of Congolese poet Tchicaya U Tam'si, as well as his vision for ACI and the curriculum of the MTh in African Christianity as its core program.

The Négritude dissertations are important for several reasons. Firstly, and perhaps most significantly, for an African scholar of religion such who is hailed as "the outstanding African theologian of his generation,"[34] it is puzzling that while others have consulted these works, none to date have critically engaged these foundational texts. This is despite the fact that they represent the culmination of a decade of Bediako's scholarship and include his earliest study of African identity, history, primal religion, and Christianity. For a scholar whose views on these topics are frequently challenged, this would seem to be a straightforward starting point. Therefore, one key focus of this book is to critically evaluate Bediako's scholarship on U Tam'si; and in doing so demonstrate important ways in which Négritude literature shaped his later Christian thought.

Other unpublished primary sources I have used include Bediako's lecture notes for his Duff Lecture Series at the University of Edinburgh (1989–1992), course notes for the Master of Theology in African Christianity program that he designed and taught at ACI, and a document entitled "Ebenezer." The latter, written by Kwame and Gillian Bediako, traces their vision for, and establishment of, the Institute. As Kwame later recalled of this document, "as the vision poured out from my soul, Gillian wrote down the ideas."[35]

Like Bediako's unpublished dissertations, these texts have not yet been properly analyzed. Yet, the MTh program in African Christianity, which Bediako designed and taught over the course of more than two decades, and which continues as a core program at ACI today, may easily be considered his magnum opus. Within this curriculum and the wider institutional community, it represents the drawing together of what he deemed the most important lines of thought for the training of African Christian scholars for the study of Christianity and African indigenous religions. Therefore, I have also chosen to "read" the Institute as text by Bediako, considering it a key primary source for this book.

Another primary source that I have used is unpublished transcripts from unused portions of filmed interviews by documentary filmmaker James Ault. In these interviews, Bediako reflects on the impact of his early Négritude scholarship and his time spent studying in France; a serendipitous

---

34. See Walls, "Kwame Bediako," para. 21.

35. Asamoah-Gyadu, "Kwame Bediako and the Eternal Christological Question," 39.

discovery, as he did not write or speak extensively about his Négritude scholarship anywhere else after moving into theological study. Additionally, these transcripts further elucidate the depth of Bediako's commitment to maintaining a geographical and philosophical connection with the pietistic Basel Mission through the location, vision, values, and community life of ACI. This is similarly highlighted in Ault's finished documentary, *African Christianity Rising*, which includes footage of interviews with Bediako at the Institute and throughout the surrounding town of Akropong.

In being anchored by these unpublished texts, this book offers a fresh and expanded view of Bediako's opus, as well as important insights into the diverse influences on his thinking. These are discoveries which, I hope, may contribute to future scholarship; both for those seeking to engage with Bediako's theological concerns more holistically, as well as for scholars analyzing methodological approaches and historical developments within the African Christian study of African religions.

This research was further supported by another six-month period of study undertaken at ACI (January–June 2010), during which time I participated as a student in the Master of Theology in African Christianity program. This offered further insight into Bediako's vision for scholarship done in the context of a Christian academic community, as well as further experience of the MTh curriculum. Being at ACI also gave me the opportunity to conduct a few select interviews with friends and colleagues of Bediako's, allowing me to confirm details and answer queries as this research progressed.

Historically, the book encompasses the 1830s to the 2000s, though it is not in strict chronological order. Chapter 2 introduces the African study of African religions as an emerging discourse and highlights the growing voices of African Christian scholars herein, as well as noting the significant methodological divisions in this discourse which emerged as a surprising but significant aspect of this research. Then we turn our attention to Ghana in chapter 3, beginning with select mission and colonial history (1830s–1930s). This includes the Basel Mission's work in Akropong, followed by an examination of aspects of British colonial contributions to educational and religious engagement, including efforts to develop the University of Ghana. In chapter 4, pivotal events in Ghana's independence period are analyzed (1940s–1960s), including interactions between politics and religion, as seen in the roles of Kwame Nkrumah and Kofi Abrefa Busia as politicians and African scholars of religion.

Chapter 5 offers an examination of Négritude as an anti-colonial movement from the 1930s–1950s. This chapter locates Bediako in France in the 1970s and analyzes his Négritude scholarship, giving attention to his conversion experience within this context. Bediako's second doctoral dissertation, later published as *Theology and Identity*, is also assessed here, seen as a continuation and extension of concerns he first encountered in Négritude poetry.

Chapter 6 moves to the 1980s–2000s and explores Bediako's establishment of ACI in Akropong-Akuapem, Ghana. Here we will see how the community and curriculum that he designed reflect a further continuation of themes and questions that he pursued within his study of Tchicaya U Tam'si and within *Theology and Identity*, as well as historically linking his academic itinerary with the work of the Basel Mission. Finally, chapter 7 considers what these findings mean for ongoing engagement with Bediako specifically; and more broadly as an evaluation of his legacy within the study of religion in Africa.

The African Christian Study of African Religions

The late-nineteenth through mid-twentieth century was a period of seismic change in Ghana as it transitioned from an era of British colonization to a politically independent African nation, a change of identity and leadership similarly reflected in shifting approaches to the study of religions in Africa. Within this period, a paradigmatic shift with lasting implications was the rise in African-led scholarship in the study of African religions. This African religious discourse—"the African study of African religions"—emerged as a distinct field of study and engaged a diverse range of voices, from poets and politicians to philosophers and theologians, with African Christian scholars playing an important role.

Scholars label this field in slightly differing ways.[36] I have chosen to use the term the "African study of African religions" as I find it the most straightforward description, broadly including Christian and non-confessional scholars. While the phrase, "the study of religions in Africa" may appear to describe the same field, it is more likely to be understood generally as the Western or European study of religions in Africa, whereas the focus here is specifically on the emerging *African* discourse, and particularly *African Christian* discourse.[37]

Ghanaian scholar Mercy Amba Oduyoye speaks incisively when she says, "writing about Africa is a hazardous enterprise." As she rightly states, "one needs to draw up many parameters and make explicit the extent of the study," a difficult task within the study of religion. "Whose experience of

---

36. For further discussion, see, for example, Adogame et al., *African Traditions*.
37. See, for example Ludwig and Adogame, *European Traditions*.

God are we dealing with?" she asks, and "What is the extent of the Africa we are talking about?"[38] These are all salient and probing questions.

To begin to draw up some parameters here, there are three key terms that need to be addressed. Firstly, as others have acknowledged, "Africa" is a contested term, and may be used for a variety of purposes. I use the term *Africa* to refer to sub-Saharan Africa; and for the research at hand, this focus is primarily on Ghana and Anglophone West Africa, although the Congo is included within discussions of Tchicaya U Tam'si.

Secondly, the term *African religion(s)* is admittedly fraught. The question as to whether to employ the singular or the plural is important, as both offer semantically different nuances. The singular— *African religion*—would likely be understood as what has variously been termed African Traditional Religion, primal religion, or African indigenous religion. Conversely, the plural *African religions* might be taken as an umbrella reference to "Africa's three religions," Islam, Christianity, and indigenous religions. Bediako, in agreement with earlier African Christian scholars such as John Mbiti and Bolaji Idowu, strongly advocated for Christianity to be understood as a thoroughly African religion alongside of African indigenous religions. Therefore, in keeping with Bediako's preference, and in acknowledgment of Africa's religious plurality, I have chosen to use the plural, *African religions*, by which I am referring equally to Christianity and to African indigenous religions. In the case of twentieth-century Ghana and within this particular study, however, Christianity and indigenous religions take a more central role; therefore, Islam is not implied here within the term "African religions."

Thirdly, the term *primal religion* merits clarification due to its position as a key concept within Bediako's thought, and because it is a contested term upon which he strongly insisted. While Bediako did not offer clarification for why he insisted upon using this term despite significant scholarly opposition, it seems safe to suggest that it speaks to the lasting influence of his decade studying Négritude literature, and particularly the Surrealist poetry of Tchicaya U Tam'si. In his first master's thesis on the subject, Bediako regularly references the "primitive" or "primal imagination" to signify universal human conceptions of the transcendent, and quickly dismisses any concerns over this terminology, arguing that it can be used "[w]ithout troubling ourselves over the pejorative connotation that the expression 'primitive imagination' could convey."[39]

---

38. Oduyoye, "The African Experience of God," 493.

39. Bediako, "Négritude et Surréalisme," 21–22. In a footnote following his first use of the term, Bediako refers to Bowra's *Chants et Poesie du Peuples Primitifs* for further discussion on the concept of "primitive imagination," suggesting this to be his source for use of the term "primal imagination."

My own sense is that his attraction to an expansive, open-ended approach to religious cosmology, first nurtured within his study of Surrealist poetry and later within African Christian thought, found its closest expression in the term *primal*, which Bediako understood as marked by anteriority and as common to humanity, though with localized expressions. For Bediako, something bigger was conveyed by the term primal than by the more scientific or theological labels of "indigenous religions" or African Traditional Religion. Similarly, Gillian Bediako describes the term *primal religion* as "universal . . . elements of human understanding of the Transcendent and the world . . ."[40] This forms an important substructure to engaging with Bediako, for whom we shall see the insistence on taking primal religion and Christianity *together* is crucial.[41] Therefore, reflective of Bediako's insistence on the term, I use *primal religion* regularly, though I also use the terms African indigenous religions and Akan religion interchangeably.

The Problematization of Gender and Ethnicity: Ongoing Challenges

Issues of gender, ethnicity, and particularly questions of "insider/outsider" status within African scholarship require continued attention. Africanist Elizabeth Isichei is a sensitive commentator in this regard, and I stand in agreement with her comments and caveats on the issue of Western scholarship on Africa: "The underlying critique is that all western analysis, however sympathetically intentioned, is, in Mudimbe's words, an 'invention' of Africa . . . This makes sober reading for the western scholar. It sheds a precious and invaluable light on the limitations of our scholarship, and reminds us that the sympathetic Africanist creates the Other, whether working from oral sources or archives, just as the Victorian missionary or colonial administrator did."[42]

Isichei is right: this is certainly a sobering prospect, and one that I have endeavoured to approach with attendant care and respect as a Canadian scholar in this field. Nigerian scholar Kehinde Olabimtan boldly argues that within the study of African Christianity, "[o]nly African scholars who feel at home with their cultural heritage or non-African investigators who have,

40. Bediako, "Primal Religion and Christian Faith," 12.

41. From personal email correspondence with Andrew Walls, March 4, 2010: Walls writes, "This is the context of Bediako: *Theology and Identity* was written, we should remember, in a Department of Religious Studies, not of Theology. And crucial to it is the insistence on taking African 'Traditional' (or, as he and I would prefer, 'primal') religion and African Christianity together, not as different entities."

42. Isichei, *A History of Christianity in Africa*, 7.

at least, been partially constituted by African experience are in a position to carry out such a project."[43]

My experiences living in Ghana and other sub-Saharan African countries, together with many years of engagement with West African Christian communities in Canada and the United Kingdom, have certainly influenced my thinking and worldview, and cultivated my interest in this field of scholarship. Nevertheless, I am not an African scholar; but I hope that as a Western scholar investigating an African discourse, I may be found sympathetic and respectful.

Nevertheless, my identity has at times been much more central and problematic than I anticipated. My assumptions at the outset of this research were informed by my interactions with Bediako and the ACI community in 2006. During that visit, I had the opportunity to participate in lectures, personal discussions, and community interactions with Bediako. Any concerns I may have harboured over whether or not I would be made welcome in this African institution were immediately allayed, and I was struck by the warm and expansive welcome that Bediako extended to all of us: men and women; Africans and non-Africans; senior faculty and junior gardeners. All members of the community were viewed as having equally valuable, though unique, contributions to make. I particularly noted that while men outnumbered women as lecturers and students, women were always accorded equal positions of respect within this academic community.

Similarly, non-Africans were invited and encouraged to enter fully into the academic life of the Institute as welcome partners in an important academic and spiritual discourse. The focus, of course, was primarily Afro-centric, but also included a world perspective; and non-Africans were encouraged to consider how African Christian history and perspectives might speak to our Western contexts. Bediako consistently emphasized the need for partnership, unity, and collaborative scholarship over and above competition or division. ACI was (and remains) a welcome example of a multicultural, ecumenical, collaborative academic community. This experience stands in stark contrast to some of my later research experiences in which my gender and ethnicity were at times viewed as problematic.

With regard to the issue of gender, it is forthrightly acknowledged that the African study of African religions remains, to its detriment, a male-dominated field. Nigerian scholar of religions Oyeronke Olademo bluntly describes the situation she observes in Nigerian universities: "The composition and implementation of religious studies . . . curriculum at tertiary institutions in Nigeria do not prioritize gender and women's issues. The

---

43. Olabimtan, "The Study of African Christianity," 297.

implications of these for religious studies as a discipline and for women who teach the subject are profound.[44] Adogame et al. echo these sentiments when they state, "the low numbers of women African scholars of religion has had a negative impact on the growth of 'African traditions' in the study of religion in Africa." And, as they rightly concede, "any discipline that does not accord space to women will not operate at optimum capacity."[45]

The situation in African churches is no better. Ghanaian feminist theologian Mercy Amba Oduyoye alerts us to the reality that while we may assume exemplary governance on the part of churches, this is "far from the case" if we listen to women's experiences therein. "A Christian appraisal," challenges Oduyoye, "cannot neglect to examine the implications of the omission of women from critical spaces of the church's life."[46]

I experienced challenges relating to my gender and ethnicity at several points in my research. On one occasion, I was informed that I was "wasting my time with academic research," since the "truly valuable" contribution I could make was at home, and that as a woman my research "would not count anyway." Olademo speaks forthrightly to this issue when she states that a significant challenge for Nigerian female scholars of religion is that "there is an unspoken but inherent assumption of society that women are best suited for marriage and childbearing rather than graduate studies and the building of a career. Some female scholars who brave the combination . . . have stories to tell."[47] Oladetmo is not alone in her observations; fellow Nigerian scholar Umar Habila Dadem Danfulani confesses that in the study of religion in Africa, "[w]omen scholars . . . are even fewer and this is a reflection of the huge gender divide to the disadvantage of women within academia in Africa."[48]

My ethnicity was also viewed as problematic on some occasions: what did *I*, as a white Westerner, think I could contribute to an *African* discourse, I was pointedly asked. On another occasion, I was told that I should urgently change my research focus away from Kwame Bediako, for two reasons. Firstly, my interlocutor argued, Bediako's arguments about primal religion as a substructure to Christianity amounted to a Western imposition on Africa, and by extension, my research was a further imposition. And secondly, this colleague argued that Bediako's arguments about identity held no further relevance for any African Christians born after independence, and

---

44. Oladetmo, "Gender and the Teaching of Religious Studies in Nigeria," 67.
45. Adogame et al., *African Traditions*, 5.
46. Oduyoye, "African Culture and African Development," 321.
47. Oladetmo, "Gender and the Teaching of Religious Studies," 73.
48. Danfulani, "African Religions in African Scholarship," 27.

therefore Bediako was to be avoided as a meaningful focus for research. "We are African and Christian, full stop, no further discussion," he informed me. "If you do proceed and try to argue that Bediako has any current relevance, be prepared for your research to be ridiculed."

While my gender and ethnicity have at times posed unexpected challenges for this research, these encounters have also bestowed unexpected gifts in the form of added insights that I would otherwise have missed. Significantly, these exchanges continually demonstrated that, far from being an out-dated or irrelevant field of study, or a "full stop" settled discussion, the African Christian study of African religions is a profoundly important, at times contentious, and as-yet emerging discussion, where issues such as gender, ethnicity, identity, and insider/outsider status urgently require open, honest dialogue.

In Bediako's 1987 Duff Lecture on African Christian scholarship and identity, he addresses some of these complexities facing scholars in this field. "The issue of identity [for African Christian scholars]," he argues, "also forced the theologian to become in himself the locus of this struggle for integration through a dialogue which, if it was to be authentic, had to be an inner dialogue, and thus became infinitely more intense and more personal."[49]

Such scholarship is indeed intense and personal; but as Bediako rightly intimates, such openness is necessary for authentic engagement. Yet, this level of discomfort is not one that we as scholars often choose for ourselves. Nevertheless, a willingness to address these issues openly and critically is imperative. As one senior African scholar remarked to me, "We all know these issues exist, but few would put it into writing." In doing so here, I acknowledge those who have already taken bold stands in speaking out on these challenging issues, and hope that others will be similarly encouraged to add their voices to this important dialogue. Whether in Africa or in diaspora, we need to carefully consider how we interact as colleagues within this field.

It is admittedly a very complex discussion requiring honesty, respect, and sensitivity all around. But for scholarship in this field to progress, such discussions must continue, with space given for a wide diversity of voices and concerns. Ultimately, these experiences added depth and nuance to my research and concretized what could otherwise have remained theoretical. Such encounters forced me to continually consider my role within this emerging discourse, a critical practice for all engaged in the study of religion in Africa. And, indirectly, these experiences further demonstrated the

---

49. Bediako, "The Genesis of African Theology," 12.

uniqueness and importance of Bediako's expansive welcome at ACI, in itself an important aspect of his legacy as an African Christian scholar.

It is to the emerging study of African religions in West Africa, with its diversity of voices and methodological concerns, that we now turn our attention.

Chapter 2

The African Christian Study of African Religions
An Emerging Discourse

One needs epistemological flexibility and openness that will allow theories and ideas from one discipline to provide insights into the object of study, in this case African Christianity.[1]

—Elias Kifon Bongmba

---

1. Bongmba, "Writing African Christianity," 291. Adinkra symbol *Mpatapo*, or "knot of pacification/reconciliation." It is a symbol of peacemaking after strife.

African Christian Scholarship:
Fresh Perspectives, New Methodologies

AN ESSENTIAL COMPONENT OF this study is the location of Bediako within a wider African Christian discourse: one that moves beyond the typical boundaries of theology, incorporating a variety of methodological approaches and assumptions more common to the Humanities and Social Sciences, while maintaining a clearly Christian perspective within the study of religion in Africa. Among others, Jan Platvoet and John Mbiti both describe a shift in the study of religions in Africa throughout the twentieth century as being a shift from "Africa as object," when the majority of research had been undertaken by non-African scholars such as missionaries and anthropologists, to "Africa as subject," when such research was increasingly undertaken by African scholars.[2] Ezra Chitando further notes the important contribution made by African Christian scholars to the study of religions in Africa.[3]

It is within this group of scholars that I wish to locate Bediako. Chitando acknowledges that African Christian scholars are often categorised as African theologians, but notes that to fail to clarify what is meant by "theological" scholarship in this context "is misleading."[4] In agreement with Chitando, I therefore prefer to use the term African Christian scholar when referring to Bediako as it avoids some of the misplaced expectations that the label "theology" might convey. While he uses the term "theologian" to describe himself, he does not provide the clarification that Chitando correctly seeks; as such, African Christian scholar is a more straightforward term.

But in what field of scholarship do we find African Christian scholars—theology, religious studies, phenomenology, or something else? The editors of this series have provided helpful clarification for defining the African Christian study of African religions in their description of the African Christian Studies Series included at the start of this book. They emphasize the interdisciplinary and emerging nature of this discourse:

> African Christian studies is defined here as any scholarship that relates to themes and issues on the history, nature, identity, character, and relevance of African Christianity and the place of African Christian mission within the wider African history, and world Christianity . . . [including] texts in the areas of religious studies, theology, mission studies, biblical studies,

---

2. See Platvoet, "From Object to Subject," 105–38; and Mbiti, "Challenges Facing Religious Education," 170–78.

3. See Chitando, "African Christian Scholars," 391–97.

4. Ibid., 392, 394.

philosophy, social justice, and other diverse issues current in African Christianity. We define these studies broadly and specifically as primarily focused on new voices, fresh perspectives, new methodologies, new approaches, historical and cultural analysis which are emerging because of the significant place of African Christianity and African religio-cultural traditions in world Christianity.[5]

The editors go on to say that the series is expected to help shift contemporary discourse "from narrow theological concerns to a broader inter-disciplinary and multi-methodological engagement with African religio-cultural history and traditions."[6] Accordingly, this book sets out to interact with Bediako as a significant African Christian scholar whose contribution is most fully seen from within the broader inter-disciplinary perspectives of the African Christian study of African religions, as a clear departure from other studies that engage "narrow theological concerns" of Bediako's.

What was once mainly the preoccupation of Christian and Muslim clergy, argues Jacob Olupona, "the study of religion in Africa now involves a multidisciplinary scholarly field. This field has produced significant thematic, conceptual, theoretical, and methodological innovations as well as a substantive focus on the socio-cultural dimensions and contexts of religion, while at the same time taking very seriously religion qua religion."[7]

However, there remains a surprising dearth of research on the complex and diverse factors influencing the historical development of this discourse within Ghana, despite the fact that Ghana plays a vital role within this discussion. There is also a lack of scholarship on the growing voice of African *Christian* scholars. In a helpful overview on their contribution to this discourse, Chitando states that unfortunately, "'religious studies' scholars have tended to minimise the contributions of African Christian scholars."[8]

Current research has typically focused on the development of secular university departments for the study of religions; or, on the other hand, narrow theological assessments of particular Ghanaian scholars, including Bediako. For the most part, however, such research fails to see important links between the two. Such scholarship overlooks Ghana's complex historical context, and does not sufficiently explore the interplay between

---

5. "African Christian Studies Series," para. 1. http://wipfandstock.com/catalog/series/view/id/1/.

6. Ibid., para. 2.

7. Olupona, foreword to *The Wiley-Blackwell Companion to African Religions*, ix.

8. Chitando, "African Christian Scholars," 393.

missionaries and colonialists, nationalistic politicians, poets, theologians, and church leaders, all of whom variously shaped this emerging African religious discourse in Ghana.[9]

Additionally, there is almost no current research evaluating Kwame Bediako in non-theological terms as a representative African Christian scholar within this field, nor is there any current scholarship analyzing how he creatively adapted some of the concerns and approaches which he encountered in his literary studies for use in his Christian scholarship. To this end, his perceived need for, and establishment of, a unique postgraduate institution for the Christian study of religion in Africa, distinct from either a university or seminary, is of particular importance. Such interdisciplinarity, or "epistemological flexibility and openness," as Bongmba rightly terms it, is precisely what is needed.

This chapter therefore addresses the following areas: firstly, it provides a historical overview of the development of African Christian scholarship, with specific attention to West Africa. This includes the early contributions of key British scholars who, beginning in the mid-twentieth century, made signal contributions to the establishment to the study of religion in Africa, as well as African scholars who increasingly took the lead in this field.

Secondly, this chapter analyzes methodological and thematic differences between Christian and non-confessional African and non-African scholars in this field, in order to better discern African Christian perspectives, while identifying alternative and dissenting voices. As we shall see, the lines between confessional and non-confessional approaches have become increasingly divisive in the literature. This discussion allows us to identify Bediako as a leading figure in this field, as seen through his efforts to, quite literally, institutionalize the African Christian study of African religions through his establishment of ACI. Furthermore, it highlights some of the unresolved tensions between African and Western approaches to the study of religion in Africa, as well as between the disciplines of Theology and Religious Studies.

African Voices, Contested Identities

As I touched on in the previous chapter, questions surrounding identity remain challenging within the scope of the study of religion in Africa. Before

---

9. For further discussion on the development of university departments of religious studies in Africa, see, for example, Westerlund, *African Religion in African Scholarship* and Walls, "Geoffrey Parrinder (*1910)." For discussion on the development of African Christian institutions, see Walls, "Of Ivory Towers and Ashrams," and "Kwame Bediako and Christian Scholarship in Africa."

proceeding with this chapter, it is important to engage these issues further. Adogame et al. highlight the role of "insiders" and "outsiders" within this field, arguing that "although 'outsiders' are helpful, they should never be a substitute for the indigenous scholar. It must be African scholars who are at the forefront of research and publication on religion in Africa."[10]

Bediako offers a broader approach to the question of "insiders" and "outsiders," arguing that inclusivity is in itself an African characteristic. In defining "African Christianity," he offers the following explanation:

> I include not only Africans on the continent, but also those in Diaspora who have been shaped by the African experience. This is not a matter of ethnicity or race. Indeed, there is only one race—the human race—and most African languages articulate this, for they have no terms for racial distinctions, only for human beings. African indigenous knowledge systems may have something to contribute here in their holistic, integrating and reconciling nature, and their profound tolerance of diversity.[11]

South African Christian scholar Anthony Balcomb offers a more concrete approach to defining these categories; though like Bediako he is similarly generous in his approach and begins by acknowledging that "the question of what defines an African is a vexed and controversial one."[12] He states that while he was born and raised in Africa, his (European) ancestors were not. In deference to the sensitivity of this discussion, he prefers to allow Africans "who were born and brought up in Africa, whose languages are African and whose ancestors are African, [to] decide whether I am African or not." However, he states that what he takes as the defining characteristic for being considered "African" is ideological rather than racial or necessarily geographical, though he freely admits that his is a controversial perspective:

> I would like to believe, however, that Africans are those who have decided to make Africa their home, that is, they have decided to take their bearings from the horizon of Africa. You can be born in Africa but decide to take your bearings and orient your life according to the values and norms of another society . . . Your ancestors can be European or American but you can decide to make Africa your home and be more African than

---

10. Adogame et al., *African Traditions*, 8.

11. Bediako, "A New Era in Christian History," 4. This was precisely the open perspective that I encountered when studying with Bediako in 2006; only in hindsight have I realized how unique and important his example was.

12. Balcomb, "Theology and the Quest for the African Renaissance," 3.

those whose ancestors are African. I know that what I am saying is controversial . . . It is all a question of the horizon from which we choose to take our bearings.[13]

The issue of identity and legitimacy is one that scholars engaged in this field must continually face and consider for themselves. As Bongmba wisely states, "The scholarship on African Christianity has grown to the extent that one can only speak from a perspective."[14]

The African Study of African Religions

West Africa and the Study of Religion

Events of the late-nineteenth and early-twentieth centuries produced rapid social and cultural shifts in Anglophone West Africa. This culminated in the end of the British colonial period, the birth of the independent nation of Ghana, and the emergence of the African study of African religions, which, as we have begun to see, came to the fore in innovative and exciting ways. Catalyzing forces within this intense period included European Christian missionary efforts, British colonial rule, African nationalism, economic growth, and educational development. Additionally, the residual impacts of World Wars I and II in West Africa contributed to the complexity of this period.

Within this period, African religious consciousness played an important role in anti-colonial and nationalistic movements as part of the effort to recover an African past and establish independent national identities. While the study of religion in Africa was by no means a new academic endeavour in the mid-twentieth century—with its modern history rooted predominantly in the missionary and anthropological itineraries of non-Africans, and primarily focused on African indigenous religions—this period represented something new, energizing, and creative. It was an emerging religious discourse, with African scholars taking the lead. In Ghana and throughout West Africa, this change was experienced in university departments, seminaries, churches, and political parties, and represented changes both to theology and to religious studies, which itself first came into existence as a field of study in West Africa as part of this development.

Adogame, Chitando, and Bateye point to this emerging discourse within the context of academic institutions in Sierra Leone, Ghana, and

---

13. Ibid.
14. Bongmba, "Writing African Christianity," 276.

Nigeria in the 1950s and 1960s, locating it within the complex matrix of decolonization and the task of identity formation:

> In line with the spirit of decolonization that gripped the continent in the 1960s, most departments of religious studies devoted themselves to the task of addressing African issues. Whereas Christianity had originally enjoyed pride of place in departments/faculties of theology, there was now emphasis on adopting a pluralist approach. In particular, the study of African Traditional Religions . . . was promoted, as it was felt that these religions offered hope in the project of recovering the lost African identity. African scholars of religion therefore positioned themselves as relevant actors in the struggle for growth and vitality.[15]

Indeed, following the largely British and European participation in the establishment of Christianity and Western educational structures in West Africa, Africans increasingly took the lead as scholars of African religions, variously building upon, rejecting, and reshaping inherited views and academic approaches.[16] At times, this emerging discourse was indirect, as in the case of Négritude poet Tchicaya U Tam'si, or nationalistic politician Kwame Nkrumah, both of whom grappled with issues of African history, identity, and religious affiliation using the unexpected platforms of poetry and political propaganda as a means to achieving quite non-religious ends.

In other cases, African theologians and philosophers explicitly examined African indigenous religions and Christianity in order to expand scholarship and understanding of the African religious past and present.[17] As Olupona observes, "Ever since John Mbiti's classic work *African Religion and Philosophy* [1969] broke down the boundaries constricting the study of African religion, this discipline has expanded in exciting new directions."[18]

The emergence of African scholars, and particularly Christian scholars, within the study of African religions is increasingly evident from the mid- to late-twentieth century: "[f]rom the writings of John S. Mbiti and E.B. Idowu in the 1960s and 1970s to the contemporary period, one can indeed uphold the verdict that there has been a decisive move towards

---

15. Adogame et al., *African Traditions*, 2.

16. For a helpful account of the African contribution to the establishment of Christianity, see, for example, Hanciles, "Missionaries and Revolutionaries."

17. Here we might take as examples (among others) the Ghanaian philosopher Kwasi Wiredu or Ghanaian theologians such as John S. Pobee or Kwame Bediako.

18. Olupona, foreword to *The Wiley-Blackwell Companion*, xx.

Africanization in the study of religion in Africa."[19] Similarly, the 1960s was a period of Africanization for African historians, as they uncovered critical insights from an African perspective. Their painstaking efforts in historical studies "opened a new chapter in African scholarship that provided rich resources for theological education."[20]

Canadian scholar Diane Stinton subsequently elucidates aspects of this "new chapter" when she traces the emergence of Christian scholarship within this African context: "On the socio-political scene, African theology as an intellectual discipline arose during the 1950s, when the struggle against colonialism led to several newly independent states."[21]

There is a growing body of work broadly analyzing the African study of religions, including African Christian voices, which addresses historical, methodological, and thematic concerns. Larger works such as the *Wiley-Blackwell Companion to African Religions* and *African Traditions in the Study of Religion in Africa: Emerging Trends, Indigenous Spirituality and the Interface with other World Religions* are important sources here, as is a more recent article by Elias Bongmba entitled, "Writing African Christianity: Perspectives from the History of the Historiography of African Christianity."[22] However, there remains a lack of country and scholar-specific research; but, we may assume this will continue to grow.

European Pioneers

Moving back in time slightly, it is also important to consider some of the non-African scholars who contributed to the development of this field in West Africa. Texts such as Frieder Ludwig and Afe Adogame's edited volume, *European Traditions in the Study of Religion in Africa*,[23] point to the fact that there are acknowledged European approaches to such study. A clear understanding of these "European traditions," Adogame argues, provides a framework not only for examining the historiography of the European "mental maps" of Africa, "but also for situating current scholarly traditions of the study of African religions within the purview of fruitful academic interactions and interdisciplinary exchanges between Africa and Europe."[24]

19. Adogame et al, *African Traditions*, 7.
20. Hanciles, "Missionaries and Revolutionaries," 146.
21. Stinton, *Jesus of Africa*, 7.
22. See Bongmba, *Wiley-Blackwell Companion to African Religions*; Adogame et al., *African Traditions*; and Bongmba, "Writing African Christianity."
23. Ludwig and Adogame, *European Traditions*.
24. Ibid., 2.

Ludwig and Adogame further outline the historical background to this field of study and contend that descriptions and theories of Africa's religious history have been a critical part of the cultural interactions between Europe and Africa, starting from the earliest Euro-African encounters, continuing right through to the present.[25] Their argument underscores the multidisciplinary, multicultural, and historically complex nature of the African study of African religions, such that one quickly perceives the need for a wide-angle as well as a zoom lens to engage this emerging discourse.

Within the European (i.e., Western) camp of pioneering twentieth-century scholars of African religions, James Cox, a British scholar of religions, cites the foundational contribution of British scholars Geoffrey Parrinder and Andrew F. Walls to the academic study of Africa's religions.[26] In Cox's estimation, the key to this new academic development lay, to a large extent, in the view that an understanding of God could be found within pre-Christian indigenous peoples. This was a view voiced most explicitly by early "missionary academics" working in Africa, such as Parrinder and Walls, who, Cox argues, "drew a line of continuity between the basic beliefs of African indigenous peoples and fully developed monotheism."[27] However, this argument has many critics, Cox among them.

But it was this early scholarship which critically led to the inclusion of "African Traditional Religion" as a separate religious category within the "entirely new field called 'Religious Studies' at the University College Ibadan in Nigeria" under Parrinder.[28] Notably, this West African academic development came almost two decades before the establishment of the first similar department in the United Kingdom, at Lancaster. Walls describes Parrinder as being "part of that Ibadan ideal staff . . . set to do a new thing." This was important, because in pluralist Nigeria, a Department of Divinity, such as was found in Fourah Bay or the Gold Coast, was problematic: "a Department of Religious Studies was established instead, with Geoffrey Parrinder as its first lecturer."[29]

Parrinder's first book, *West African Religion* (1949, 1961), became the textbook for this fledgling department and field. As Walls acknowledges, there was "no conceivable alternative" then in existence which

25. Ibid.

26. Cox, "The Significance of Approaches," 255–64. Cox also cites Edwin W. Smith as a significant European pioneer in this field; and we may also mention Adrian Hastings, Harold Turner, and J. V. Taylor as European scholars who similarly made important contributions to this emerging discourse.

27. Cox, *From Primitive to Indigenous*, 17.

28. Ibid., 17.

29. Walls, "A Bag of Needments," 144.

could be used to effectively engage with African primal religion.³⁰ The book is based on Parrinder's research and observation of the religious systems of those among who he had been living, including the Ewe and Akan of Ghana and the Yoruba of Nigeria; and in a later edition, he also included Igbo perspectives.³¹

Parrinder's text admittedly follows in the missionary-anthropological tradition of scholarship, though this is not necessarily a criticism of the work as such. As Walls rightly argues, "it is hard to see this tradition of missionary writing as a discourse of domination, as current fashion declares it to be; on the contrary, it is tentative; conscious of puzzlement and sometimes of defeat."³² Ultimately, Parrinder's work contributed to the development of a new academic tradition in writing about African religion.³³ He explains the basis and motivation for his work in the following way:

> My understanding of African Traditional Religion (a term I may claim to have invented and that others have used) was partly shaped by study of the historical and literary religions. It seemed important to consider African religion in the manner of the study of World Religions . . . There are problems with this approach but also advantages in that African religion is not taken as isolated from the rest of the world or scorned as mere fetishism, and with its social and personal characteristics.³⁴

Parrinder taught the first Religious Studies course at Ibadan in 1948. In addition to coining the term *African Traditional Religion*, Parrinder was the first to include it as a subject in a course syllabus alongside of Old and New Testament Studies.³⁵ Cox and Walls are in agreement as to the significance of this development for the emerging African study of African religions. As Walls unequivocally states, "the Ibadan experiment had made African Traditional Religion an academic subject."³⁶

Cox observes that up until Parrinder's developments, traditional theology programs would have included church history or possibly philosophy or religion alongside of Old and New Testament courses. However, by introducing these West African religions as an integral part of the Religious Studies program, Parrinder broke new ground by insisting that the study of

---

30. Walls, "Geoffrey Parrinder," 211.
31. Ibid., 208, and Walls, "The Discovery of 'African Traditional Religion,'" 12.
32. Walls, "Geoffrey Parrinder," 208.
33. Ibid., 209.
34. Parrinder, *In the Belly of the Snake*, 5.
35. Walls, "Geoffrey Parrinder," 211.
36. Walls, "The Discovery of 'African Traditional Religion,'" 13.

African indigenous religions, transmitted orally from one generation to the next, should be accorded "the same academic status and credibility as the study of Christianity and its written scripture."[37]

This view was expanded upon by African Christian scholars such as E.B. Idowu and John S. Mbiti, who contended that African primal religions "deserve[d] to be treated with respect and to be studied as religions in their own right alongside the other religious traditions around the world."[38] Through his efforts at Ibadan, Cox observes, Parrinder "instilled a positive regard amongst his African students for their own indigenous cultures"[39]; important for emerging African approaches to the study of African religions.

Mbiti addresses this shift in scholarship and particularly the value placed upon the study of African primal religion with the following statement, made in 1969: "The world is just beginning to take African traditional religions and philosophy seriously. It is only around the middle of the twentieth century that these subjects have begun to be studied properly and respectfully as an academic discipline in their own right."[40]

Walls was also highly instrumental in helping to establish the academic foundations for the African study of African religions. He did this first through his time lecturing at Fourah Bay (Sierra Leone) and subsequently at Nsukka (Nigeria). Another of his early contributions, which has proved of significant and lasting value, was his establishment of journals and professional societies for the study of religion in Africa. As has been rightly observed, "Already at Fourah Bay Walls began to identify the new *instrumenta* that would be needed to support the kind of research program that was emerging: professional societies, journals, bibliographies, archives, and new university departments and research centers that would encourage wide-ranging scholarly investigation of religious history and movements."[41]

Returning to the U.K., Walls' later contribution to the African study of African religions may be seen in the research centres he developed, first at the University of Aberdeen and subsequently Edinburgh, and quite recently, Liverpool Hope. These centers focus(ed), broadly speaking, on aspects of

---

37. Cox, *From Primitive to Indigenous*, 18.
38. Ibid., 18.
39. Cox, "From Africa to Africa," 257.
40. Mbiti, *African Religions and Philosophy*, 6.
41. Shenk, "Challenging the Academy," 39. Shenk enumerates the journals and bulletins founded by Walls, which include: the *Sierra Leone Bulletin of Religion* (1959); *Bulletin of the Society for African Church History* (1962); *Journal of Religion in Africa* (1967); *Bulletin of the Scottish Institute of Missionary Studies* (1967). See Shenk, "Challenging the Academy," 39–43.

African indigenous religion and non-Western Christianity and include important library and archival collections. One significant outcome of his work in Aberdeen in the 1980s was that "African students flooded into the Aberdeen programme [sic] during this period, many of whom became leading scholars in their own right and assumed positions of leadership . . . throughout Africa."[42] This included Bediako. In this sense, what Parrinder started at Ibadan, Walls continued in the U.K., continuing to support the training and equipping of African and Africanist scholars for the study of African religions.

Emerging African Christian Scholars

After Parrinder's introduction of African Traditional Religion to the academy, African scholars began to take leadership in these new departments and the study of African religion began to grow and develop in interesting areas. Among the most influential of these scholars were the late Bolaji Idowu and John S. Mbiti, whom we have just encountered.[43] As van Rinsum similarly observes, "in the late sixties and early seventies, there was a critical period when both the discourse itself and the opposition to it, became entangled in the decolonization process."[44] Within this period, "Africans, who had specialized in religious studies and theology began to further the discourse on 'African Traditional Religion.'" Significantly, while Mbiti and Idowu wrote within the borders of this discourse, "they made every effort to Africanize the concept of 'African Traditional Religion.'"[45]

The "discourse" to which Rinsum refers, of course, is the study of African religions; and here we begin to see the shift: African scholars were moving away from their study of Western Christian theology, but they were not pursuing the study of African religions in the same manner as many of their secular Western counterparts. They were forging a new path.[46]

Further elucidating the aims of these African scholars, Rinsum argues that they were seeking to offer a Pan-African alternative to Western Christianity. In this way, "'African Traditional Religion' was transformed into 'African religion,' a symbiosis of Christian and African religious elements. In the sixties and seventies, this discourse was actively institutionalized

---

42. Cox, "From Africa to Africa," 259.
43. See Walls, "The Discovery of "African Traditional Religion,'" 14.
44. Rinsum, "'They became slaves of their definitions,'" 24.
45. Ibid.
46. For African non-confessional scholars of religion who take a different approach, we will shortly consider the voices of Okot p'Bitek and Kwasi Wiredu.

in the intellectual practices of the new African universities and thus came to play a decisive role for later generations of anthropologists as well as theologians and specialists in religious studies."[47] While Rinsum offers this as a criticism, other scholars seek to highlight the importance of African Christian contributions. Chitando speaks forcefully when he says that within the study of religion in Africa, "there is the need for the discipline to accord greater respect to the contributions of the African Christian scholars. To dismiss their writings on the grounds that they are 'theological' is not convincing. The assumption is that anything 'theological' is not scholarly. The inspiration behind most of the attacks has come from Western secularisation. The superiority of seculardom to theology has to be argued for and cannot be assumed."[48]

These African Christian scholars were indeed charting new paths and bringing scholarship together in new and creative ways. For many, this was a departure not only from Western theology but also from some of the non-confessional, social science-based approaches to the study of religions in Africa. As Walls reflects, "Idowu and Mbiti were Christians and active churchmen, trained in Christian theology, and they saw more of that theology within African religion than most European writers, whether missionaries or anthropologists, had done. African Christians were now studying the pre-Christian religion of Africa, not simply denouncing it, but seeing God there."[49]

Bediako further clarifies the important scholarly role of African Christians when he argues that they should be "understood as drawing on their sense of belonging within Christian tradition and using categories which to them describe their understanding of *their* pre-Christian heritage when related to *their* Christian commitment."[50] As Chitando responds, "Bediako insists that African theologians have a right to contribute to an understanding of their own religious heritage."[51]

Methodology: The Great Divide

Within this emerging discourse, methodology remains a problematic area. One key reason for this is that Western approaches are not particularly suitable for this African field of study; yet African scholars are still developing

---

47. Rinsum, "'They became slaves of their definitions,'" 25.
48. Chitando, "African Christian Scholars," 394.
49. Walls, "The Discovery of 'African Traditional Religion,'" 14.
50. Bediako, "Understanding African Theology" [*Bulletin for Contextual Theology*], 4.
51. Chitando, "African Christian Scholars," 394.

salient methodologies. The book *African Traditions in the Study of Religion in Africa* explores this challenge and specifically emphasizes the pitfalls of imposing European methodologies and theories onto an African field.[52] As the editors note, "the post-colonial period requires that African scholars challenge their total dependence on methods and theories developed elsewhere. African scholars of religion must demonstrate innovation and confidence to leave their imprint on the discipline in Africa."[53] Indeed, creative methodological approaches are one important area where Bediako makes a unique contribution to this field, as seen within the community and curriculum of ACI.

The issue of methodology in this context therefore merits careful attention. In fact, methodology is a key area in which the contributions of African scholars can be seen to offer fresh and important insights more widely to scholars in Theology and Religious Studies, challenging scholars in both fields to expand their methodological mind-sets and hermeneutical horizons. As Adogame et al. explain,

> Despite the challenges that characterize efforts to develop and strengthen "African traditions" in the study of religion in Africa, there have been some notable gains in this direction. African scholars in various fields have sought to reflect on methodological issues and to provide fresh data on religious phenomena. In fact, this has been a significant difference between religious studies in Africa and religious studies in Europe: whereas the study of religion in Europe has tended to be caught up in recondite methodological debates, the study of religion in Africa has been keen to describe religious vitality on the continent.[54]

The differing approaches of Western and African scholars are clearly elucidated. And, what is more, it becomes evident that attempts to superimpose European "recondite methodological debates" on emerging African descriptions of "religious vitality" will likely prove ill-fitting: new wine requires new wineskins.

Fresh approaches are indeed necessary; and within these African traditions, the creative contribution of African Christian scholars must be highlighted: "[Africans studying] African Christianity/Christianity in Africa have . . . demonstrated a lot of confidence and willingness to initiate 'African traditions' within the discipline. Whereas the historiography of African Christianity had been dominated by 'outsiders,' there has been

---

52. See Adogame et al., *African Traditions*.
53. Ibid., 2.
54. Ibid., 6.

a growing interest and critique by African church historians . . . [This is observed in] the trend where African scholars have begun to feel confident to narrate the history of African Christianity."[55] Bediako is certainly a figure who brought confidence and a willingness to initiate new traditions to the study of Africa's religions; perhaps demonstrating this most strikingly in his establishment of a unique postgraduate institution for such study.

Here we need to consider the significance of Walls' methodological impact on the field. He established the Department of Religious Studies at the University of Aberdeen on the phenomenological principle that religion as a subject in its own right is best approached from an empathetic position "that includes the perspectives of believers in any eventual interpretation of its meaning."[56] Harold Turner similarly argued that the nature of the field of study dictates the methodological approach, such that the study of religion might legitimately require religious approaches.[57]

This principle was clearly seen in action in Aberdeen, evidenced by the fact that a majority of African scholars who studied there were Christians who tended to view their indigenous religious traditions positively.[58] As Bediako rightly observes, "it is precisely on the question of the validity of applying Christian theological categories to the elucidation of African religious experience, that the debate over 'African Theology' has been most intense."[59]

On this point, Cox singles out Kwame Bediako and Lamin Sanneh as two notable African Christian scholars associated with Walls and the Aberdeen program who viewed their indigenous religious heritage positively. Cox interprets Bediako as arguing that primal religion finds universal expression in Christianity, with the universality of the Christian message finding its roots in the primal. Cox, a critic of this perspective, calls this practice "globalizing the local," or "glocalization."[60] Furthermore, he sees Bediako's emphasis at ACI on studying the Bible in vernacular languages, and Sanneh's argument for synonymy between language and culture, "a variation of this theme."[61]

---

55. Ibid., 7. Here they specifically point to Ogbu Kalu's *African Christianity* as indicative of this trend.

56. Cox, "From Africa to Africa," 257.

57. See Turner, "The Way Forward," 1–15.

58. See Cox, "From Africa to Africa," 259.

59. Bediako, *Theology and Identity*, 4.

60. Cox, "Globalization," 56–65.

61. Cox, "From Africa to Africa," 260.

This, argues Cox, is the legacy of Parrinder and Walls: "African postgraduate students developed . . . analytical skills, honed in the phenomenological and historical methods, that enabled them to affirm their deep-seated religious feelings, usually expressed in Christian language, while at the same time interpreting their ancestral traditions as consistent with African forms of Christianity."[62]

A significant trend within this emerging African discourse was that most African graduates from Aberdeen returned to Africa, where they introduced into university departments and theological colleges "that which, through Geoffrey Parrinder and the African connection in Aberdeen, had originally begun on African soil. African scholars of religion thereby responded positively and enthusiastically, yet thoughtfully and analytically, to Walls' form of 'global religionism.'"[63] In both of these areas—i.e., a value for a religiously empathetic (in this case Christian) approach to the African study of religions and a positive view of African indigenous religions—the foundational contributions of Parrinder and Walls are clearly evident in this emerging African religious discourse.

African Methodological Approaches

Further discussion shows that methodological approaches are not at all clear-cut, particularly with regard to African Christian scholars. Firstly, Cox strongly disagrees with the practice of what he terms "globalizing the local." In his view, scholars such as Bediako pursued religious and theological studies in the West and subsequently evaluated local African primal religions along more global lines. In this way, Cox argues, Western academic disciplines have "globalized" what would typically be localized African cultures both by "extracting African scholars out of Africa into Western institutions," and by training them to "apply the methods used in the social sciences and humanities to the study of Africa."[64]

For Cox, the problem lies in the fact that these African scholars often returned to Africa and re-interpreted their own cultures through their globalized perspectives; troubling, in his view, primarily because African cultures are "primarily localized, kinship-based systems." Cox sees this particularly among African Christian scholars of religion, who, he argues, under the influence of both theological and religious studies approaches imparted by the Western academy, applied globalized religious interpretations

---

62. Cox, "From Africa to Africa," 261.
63. Ibid.
64. Cox, "Globalization," 57.

to localized African religions. He singles out Bediako for criticism in this regard: "Nowhere can this be seen better than in the writings of Kwame Bediako, who studied in Aberdeen . . . and who returned to Ghana to establish a Center aimed at reaching deeply into the local Ghanaian culture by training theologians and church leaders through a globalized understanding of African indigenous religions."[65]

For Cox, the crux of the problem lies in the fact that he finds this globalization incongruent with African indigenous religions. In his words,

> Bediako was not just another participant in an academic discipline situated among the humanities, the value of whose contribution depends on the strength of his argument. His 'Africanness' is not irrelevant to the deliberate and calculated role he took in recreating local contexts in Africa. Nor is his Western education irrelevant to his impact on the culture he influenced. Quite clearly, he chose to remain close to the Akan culture by working among indigenous peoples in Ghana, where local, kinship-based religion still thrives. It is equally clear that he sought to globalize the local by elevating vernacular language and thought forms into contexts with universal applicability, something that would never have occurred in traditional thought forms.[66]

Cox deems this approach to African indigenous religions disingenuous to the Akan worldview; but on this point, he and Bediako would appear to be at a stalemate, with Bediako as a Christian Akan scholar finding it a meaningful approach for creatively engaging with his religiously plural context. But, rather than entrenching ourselves further in seemingly irreconcilable differences—or, alternatively, ignoring them—such differences should instead prompt us to listen to one another more openly and attentively, acknowledging the value of each one's perspective. Such division here is also a reminder that in many cases, African Christian scholars like Bediako are doing something quite different, and are motivated by different concerns than their Western academic counterparts, making straightforward critiques difficult.

On the other hand, with regard to differing approaches between African and Western scholars, there is the argument that some African scholars of religions have continued to employ European religious studies models in their studies of African religions, to the detriment of the growth of African

---

65. Ibid., 57–58.
66. Ibid., 63.

traditions in this field.[67] Indeed, it has been argued that not only are such scholars failing to contribute to the development of African traditions, they are in fact "perpetuating the hegemony of European traditions in the study of religion in Africa."[68] As will be discussed further, the encouragement to explore and experiment with African approaches to the study of African religions is a unique methodological approach supported at ACI.

Nigerian scholar Kehinde Olabimtan, who studied under Bediako at ACI, demonstrates such methodological experimentation in several articles he has written explicitly dealing with methodological approaches to the African study of religions. One notable example is the series of essays and responses that went back and forth between Olabimtan and co-authors Jan Platvoet and Henk van Rinsum. In the first article, Olabimtan argues that while European methodological traditions within secular history and the social sciences may serve to elucidate aspects of the social and political implications of the Christian message, "they are not inclined to take seriously the religious dimension of that situation on its own terms . . . leading to biased interpretation of texts and misrepresentation of intentions."[69]

Platvoet and van Rinsum, both European scholars of religions, disagreed, arguing instead for the use of "methodological agnosticism" in the study of religions in Africa. They contend that such an approach is compatible with essentially any viewpoint, but is incompatible with the perspective of "the radically orthodox believer who takes his or her religion for the one and only truth and as the exclusive way to 'salvation' . . . Historical analysis shows that this 'theological reductionism' is incompatible with academic scholarship in religions and has not contributed to its growth but for a few, highly polemical exceptions."[70]

Their description would include many African Christian scholars, and certainly Bediako. But the claim that such a perspective—what Cox terms "religionism"[71]—is incompatible with the academic study of religions remains at odds with Bediako's scholarship on African religions, and that emanating from other scholars at his Institute. Nevertheless, Platvoet and van Rinsum contend that a "methodologically agnostic" approach does take the religious dimension seriously; but for Olabimtan this is insufficient.[72] He

---

67. See Adogame et al., *African Traditions*, 4.

68. Ibid., 8.

69. Olabimtan, "The Study of African Christianity," 290.

70. Platvoet and van Rinsum, "Is Africa Incurably Religious?," 162.

71. For further discussion on "religionism" and on the interaction between African and Western institutions in the formation of the African study of African religions, see Cox, "From Africa to Africa," 257–58.

72. For the extended exchange between Platvoet, van Rinsum, and Olabimtan

instead argues for two methodological options for African (and I will assume, Africanist) scholars of African religions that he perceives will produce research "germane to the African intellectual environment" while avoiding "pandering to the hegemony of Western intellectual method."[73]

The first, Olabimtan argues, is the acceptance of subjectivity in partnership with the social scientific method. He argues that subjectivity, or what he terms a *"laissez faire* experimentation with information," has become accepted within a Western post-modern intellectual tradition and that as such, African scholars need make no apology for adopting a similar approach.[74] He argues that both the post-modern West and an essentialist African approach are engaging with a subjective experience of reality, "the former launching out from the belief that reality is illusory and the latter ... from the presupposition that reality has essence."[75]

While Olabimtan's African–Western dichotomy is overly simplistic, he nevertheless points to the underlying polemical nature of the tensions between European and African methodological approaches to the study of African religions, and makes the important argument that African Christian scholars need not follow Western academic dictates nor apologize for creative engagement and experimentation. Bongmba offers a similar argument in "Writing African Christianity":

> In my view, postmodernism has opened up a critical space for historians, and in our case scholars of African Christianity, to move away from the illusion that we had the whole story, or a comprehensive narrative. One does not need to be a committed postmodernist to recognise what Jean François Lyotard described as 'that which in the modern invokes the unpresentable in presentation itself, that which refuses the consolidation of correct forms, refuses the consensus of taste permitting a common experience of nostalgia for the impossible, and inquiries into new presentations – not to take pleasure in them, but to better produce the feeling that there is something unpresentable.'[76]

---

on the issue of methodology, see Platvoet and van Rinsum, "Is Africa Incurably Religious?" *Exchange* 32/2 (2003) 123–53; Olabimtan, "Is Africa Incurably Religious? II: A Response to Platvoet & Henk van Rinsum," *Exchange* 32/4 (2003) 322–39; and Platvoet and van Rinsum, "Is Africa Incurably Religious? III: A Reply to a Rhetorical Response" *Exchange* 37 (2008) 156–73.

73. Olabimtan, "The Study of African Christianity," 295.

74. Ibid.

75. Ibid.

76. Bongmba, "Writing African Christianity," 281. He references Jean François Lyotard, *The Postmodern Explained: Correspondence 1982–1985*.

The second approach that Olabimtan deems useful for African scholars of African religions is the biographical method. As he argues, "in many African societies, the human person is a historical being in correspondence with both natural and transcendent environments." While scholarship that fails to recognize this reality "may succeed in courting acclaim in scholarly circles of the global North," he contends, "it is questionable whether the African subjects of such studies would recognize themselves in the research."[77] He sees this as a particularly important element of Bediako's writing, and of some of the research being produced at ACI.

Furthermore, with regard to ACI itself, Olabimtan observes Bediako's "appreciation of the value of human identity for institutional identity and of the value of 'ancestors' for building a tradition" through the naming of the Institute after C. A. Akrofi and J. G. Christaller.[78] However, ultimately Olabimtan, van Rinsum, and Platvoet never resolve their disagreement. Instead, their exchanges reveal some of the enduring differences between African Christian scholarship and non-confessional scholarship of African religions, and further suggests that to some degree, this may be a division between African and Western academic approaches.

Ultimately, the methodological divide between these perspectives appears insurmountable. However, here we must side with Adogame et al. who, as we have noted, call, not quite for a moratorium on Western scholastic involvement, but for clear African leadership within the study of religions in Africa. Writing nearly twenty years before Cox, Bediako anticipates the division between Western and African theological scholarship when he makes the following argument:

> [T]he departure of modern African theological interest from modern Western theology could not be more pronounced. It is not hard to see what had happened; the very religious tradition which was generally deemed unworthy of serious theological consideration in missionary times, now occupied a central place on the African theological agenda. Consequently, even though Africa's theologians would make use of categories of description inherited from the Western Christian theological tradition, they were obviously setting themselves to give to the African pre-Christian religious heritage an interpretation which the European missionary understanding of Africa was, on the whole, unable to achieve. The real significance of modern African

---

77. Olabimtan, "The Study of African Christianity," 296.

78. Here Olabimtan points to Bediako's *Theology and Identity* (1992) and *Christianity in Africa* (1995) as key works which draw upon a biographical perspective. See Olabimtan, "The Study of African Christianity," 296.

theological writing lies in the attitude that is taken towards the African religious past."[79]

This "attitude to the African religious past" may be summed up in Bediako's description of African theology as being "neither 'from below', nor strictly 'from above'; rather [it is] indicative of the way the primal imagination grasps the reality of Christ in terms in which all life is essentially conceived—as spiritual."[80] Bediako further underscores these methodological divisions when he says that among both Christians and non-Christians, there is a widespread tendency to think of religious plurality "in terms of distinct and autonomous religious systems, as belief-systems or creeds, in relation to which Christianity also functions as a belief-system," with some Christians subsequently identifying their faith as the true belief-system.[81]

Here we may recall the "orthodox believer" whose views Rinsum and Platvoet deemed "incompatible with academic scholarship." Bediako offers a response to such a position when he says, "the secularised environment that followed the Enlightenment has tended to suggest that specifically religious claims are no longer decisive."[82] He does not mince words as he cogently analyzes the consequence of such a perspective:

> As a result of this Western handicap, the encounter with religious pluralism may lead to either religious fundamentalism, or else the diminishing of religious conviction . . . It also means that the tradition of biblical exegesis established in the West may be limited in its capacity to unearth the dynamics of religious engagement implicit in the biblical records.
>
> For it is doubtful whether the Scriptures lend support to a view of religious plurality as a plurality of separate religious belief-systems. The religious plurality that emerges from the Scriptures themselves is the plurality of persons, seen in the quality of response—not to be confused with individualism—to the intimations of the divine impact upon human life and on the plane of human history.[83]

With such diverse views, we may conclude that these methodological and ideological divides are indeed insurmountable. But, perhaps surmounting them is not the goal. Bediako's emphasis on spirituality brings us back to the point that African Christian scholars may in fact be pursuing quite

79. Bediako, *Theology and Identity*, 2.
80. Bediako, *Christianity in Africa*, 176.
81. Bediako, "Biblical Exegesis in the African Context," 19.
82. Ibid.
83. Ibid.

different ends. He is equally clear that a Western secular approach that treats religions as belief-systems is likely incompatible with an African approach to Christian scholarship; indeed, he argues that it is incompatible with a *biblical* approach to religious plurality.

In this sense, Bediako and other African Christian scholars would not offer a particular rebuttal to scholars such as Cox, van Rinsum, and Platvoet, because, ultimately, they are discussing very different concerns in what may increasingly be seen as a different field of study. In fact, as Bediako suggests, "looked at from the perspective of an organic view of Christian history, therefore, the encounter of the Christian faith with the African religious heritage ceases to be the meeting of *Western* culture and *African* values. Rather . . . it becomes important to insist that some of the criteria for understanding the nature of that encounter can be discovered in the history of the people of God and His Christ."[84] Developing new methodological approaches remains an important feature of African Christian scholarship; and, as we will continue to see, is an important component of scholarship at ACI.

African Christian Approaches

Within this growing discourse on African religions, another significant development became evident, which we have previously noted within the Aberdeen tradition: African Christian scholarship began to emerge as a particular strand, with Christian scholars taking an important lead. As Rosino Gibellini states, "The dawn of black awareness and the African personality had already occurred, say authors, historians, and students of culture, in the colonial period . . . with the development, in Anglophone Africa, of the African personality . . . and in Francophone Africa, of the concept of negritude [sic] . . . It is against this backdrop of an African cultural rebirth that the problem of an 'African theology' arose in the 1950s and 1960s."[85]

For Bediako, this African Christian methodological approach was centered on the issue of identity. In his words, "at the heart of the new methodological method would be the issue of identity, which would itself be perceived as a theological category, and which therefore entailed confronting constantly the question as to how, and how far, the 'old' and 'new' in African religious consciousness could be integrated into a unified vision of what it meant to be African and Christian."[86] In putting this approach into

---

84. Bediako, *Theology and Identity*, 6–7; italics his.
85. Gibellini, *Paths of African Theology*, 5–6.
86. Bediako, "Understanding African Theology" [*Jesus in Africa*], 53.

action, Kalu notes that Bediako was "'hands-on,' intentional, and dedicated to nurturing African Christians."[87]

Going back a little bit, the concept of African Personality, championed by Nkrumah, was an ideology attempting to promote the concept of distinct African values, foundations, and identity, and was in keeping with Nkrumah's vision for Pan-Africanism. However, the concept remained ill-defined, with most proponents of the African Personality having their own image and definition of it.[88] Négritude, as we shall see, was a similarly ephemeral and fluid concept. As Gibellini correctly observes, it was against this background of ideological and cultural reflection and renaissance that the need for African Christian approaches to studying African religion emerged.[89]

John Parratt makes a similar statement when he argues that a number of factors contributed to the call for a Christian theology "with an African face." Newly independent African states, and indeed the pre-independence political movements themselves, certainly played a significant role.[90] Further elucidating the motivations behind the emergence of this African Christian discourse, Asamoah-Gyadu states that "[g]enerally, early African theologians of the 1950s onwards took serious exception to the disdain with which western missionary activity treated African religious cultures. This is what gave birth to African theology as an academic discipline."[91]

Another key factor promoting the emergence of this discourse relates to the circumstances in which these scholars found themselves in mid-twentieth-century West Africa. To this end, it has rightly been argued that "African Christian theology . . . must not be seen to exist in a vacuum but must be seen as an expression of a much wider phenomenon, namely, Africa's rediscovery of identity and selfhood against the background of colonial rule and imperialist domination . . . This process had implications for African politics, economics and religion."[92]

For this very reason, this book engages with Bediako and this emerging discourse from a historical perspective, taking seriously the significant impact of the complex developments within this period of Ghana's history on the emerging African study of African religions. As the following chapter

---

87. Kalu, preface, *African Christianity*, xii.

88. See Mbiti, *African Religion and Philosophy*, 268.

89. For further discussion on this period as an "African Renaissance," see Leonard Barnes, *African Renaissance*.

90. See Parratt, *Reinventing Christianity*, 12.

91. Asamoah-Gyadu, "Kwame Bediako and the Eternal Christological Question," 47.

92. Clarke, *Pentecostal Theology in Africa*, 31.

deals with at length, the twentieth century was a complex post-missionary, post-colonial, post-independence era. To agree with Justin Ukpong, the emergence of this African discourse involves a long and complex process, which is determined not only by scholarly ingenuity, but also by particular circumstances and factors, which, he argues, "must be taken not separately but together." These circumstances include "the cultural factor, the historical factor, the socio-political factor, contribution of social sciences, and the theological factor."[93]

To engage with African theological concepts qua theological concepts therefore leaves scholars vulnerable to misinterpreting African Christian scholars. It is clear that in engaging African Christian scholarship, a wider consideration of the African cultural, historical, and socio-political factors, within frameworks which give appropriate consideration to both social scientific and theological methodological approaches, are needed—and "not separately but together."

To elaborate on the term "African theology/theologies," we might note that from the 1960s–1980s there were three major currents in African theological thought. The first, inculturation theology, is simply referred to as "African Theology." The second current is Black theology, and third, African liberation theology, both of which were much more closely associated with South African theological discourse.[94] In comparison, Parratt condenses this slightly: "It has become customary to divide Christian theology in Africa into two main areas, 'African' and 'black' theology. The former is usually taken to mean Christian thought that concerns itself fundamentally with the relationship of Christian theology to African culture, and that evinces a particular concern to relate this to the Bible and Christian tradition."[95]

The cultural factor, Ukpong argues, is a function of the interaction between African indigenous religions and culture with Europeanised Christianity, which produced both a careful consideration and integration of elements on both sides, as well as cultural tensions. This points us to the significant role of history in this emerging discourse. This degree of interdisciplinary interaction is one reason why a failure to engage African Christian scholars within their broader historical context provides an incomplete and potentially inaccurate reading of their work. To this end, African history remains an important source for the African study of African religions.

Hanciles further underscores the connection between the significant contributions of African historians to providing a foundation for subsequent

---

93. Ukpong, "Current Theology," 502.
94. See ibid.
95. Parratt, *Reinventing Christianity*, 25.

African Christian scholarship when he argues that their efforts provided important resources for theological education.[96] Similarly, Olabimtan points to the efforts of Nigerian historians Jacob Ade Ajayi and Emmanuel Ayandele as examples of mid-twentieth-century scholars seeking authentically African avenues for engagement with African history. Though dealing primarily with history, Olabimtan makes the case that these "intellectual attempts at renewed self-understanding and at recovering the past" were not limited in their impact to the field of African history but gave rise "to a vigorous interest in the study of African religions and to a spirited Africanization of the academic study of Christianity."[97]

Hastings makes a similar argument when he observes that Ajayi and Ayandele were not simply engaging with mission history, but with African Christian history.[98] Ghanaian theologian Charles Sarpong Aye-Addo adds that "since the turn of the second half of the twentieth century, which also marked the beginning of the end of colonialism, determination of who Jesus is by Africans for African Christians, using indigenous categories, has become imperative for theological enterprise."[99]

Here Bongmba provides an important overview of the trajectory of African Christian historiography.[100] He outlines five distinct phases of scholarship, with the earliest histories of African Christianity articulating outcomes of the missionary enterprise, and the most recent engaging major movements and themes significant to the history of the church.[101] However, the salient question for those engaged with the study of African Christianity, he rightly points out, is what future scholarship will entail.

"First," Bongmba begins, "studies of African Christianity must be grounded in research methods and rules of historiography. This calls for research that will bring together quantitative and qualitative research skills. Scholars must continue to gather data from interviews, direct observation, from archival materials and use the best tools available to ethnographers and archeologists. Ethnographic and archeological studies will strengthen research and analysis of data and offer a broader spectrum for interpretation

---

96. Hanciles, "Missionaries and Revolutionaries," 146–52.

97. Olabimtan echoes Hanciles' earlier argument that African historians of the 1960s, such as Ajayi, Ayandele, and Tasie elucidated the African perspective in their historical accounts, including accounts of Christian missions, which resulted in the provision of "rich resources for theological education." See Hanciles, "Missionaries and Revolutionaries," 146.

98. Hastings, "African Christian Studies," 265.

99. Aye-Addo, *Akan Christology*, xvi.

100. Bongmba, "Writing African Christianity," 275–312.

101. Ibid., 278.

and theological analysis that will significantly change historical writing."[102] Here again we are reminded of the importance of interdisciplinary scholarship within this emerging African Christian discourse.

Voices of Opposition: Non-Confessional Scholars of Religion

Andrew Walls argues that "religion can best understand religion . . . [because] it at least presupposes the reality of the subject matter."[103] But there is strong opposition to this approach from both African and non-African scholars who are predominantly non-confessional in their approach to the study of African religions, some of whom we have already encountered. Robin Horton is a notable example. Writing in 1984, he acknowledges the shift towards Christian scholarship within this comment:

> For much of the past fifty years, the study of the indigenous religious heritage of Africa has been dominated by social or cultural anthropologists of Western origin and agnostic or atheistic religious views. In recent years, however, the dominance of this set has been challenged by a new wave of scholars, some Western and others African, who repudiate the established approach to the field and advocate a radically different one. Some of these scholars . . . have been anthropologists . . . Others . . . have been affiliated to such disciplines as theology and comparative religion. Yet others . . . have been philosophers. They are united, however, by a methodological and theological framework which has been strongly influenced, first and foremost by their own Christian faith . . .[104]

Horton raises several important points. He corroborates the claim that the study of African religions shifted within the course of the twentieth century to being more African-led, with a notable Christian cohort rising. He further acknowledges that such research is not necessarily theological in nature, although it can be. Rather, he argues, it includes scholars in fields such as anthropology, theology, comparative religious studies, and philosophy. Throughout this book, we will continue to see examples of African scholars of religions within these diverse areas, and, I would add, sociology and literary studies. This points to the fact that on the one hand, the study of African religions has been undertaken by scholars in many fields, and

---

102. Ibid., 278–79.
103. Walls, "A Bag of Needments," 143.
104. Horton, "Judaeo-Christian Spectacles," 391.

on the other, that African Christian scholars should not be read solely from the narrow confines of theology.

However, Horton argues strongly against this Christian approach, which he terms the "Devout Opposition." He finds fault with this approach in three key areas. Firstly, he argues against an emphasis on the centrality of a supreme being, based on the fact that conceptions of a supreme being vary and are not always present within African indigenous cosmologies, in contradiction to the arguments of scholars such as Mbiti. Secondly, Horton disagrees with the approach to a supreme being that emphasizes "the 'mysterious,' the 'inscrutable,' the 'uncanny,' or the 'praeternatural [sic].'"[105] He rather harshly labels this "Christianity's own most cherished defensive tactic," and argues that in the face of challenges to the rationality of their faith, Christian scholars prefer to hide behind these intangible concepts instead of providing a rational counter-argument.[106] And thirdly, he disagrees with what he views as an emphasis on communion as the leading motive of the religious life, as opposed to explanation, prediction, or control.[107]

Further opposition may be found among scholars of religion such as Cox, Platvoet, and Westerlund, among others, who argue for the clear separation between the "religionist" and social scientific approaches to the study of African religions. Cox, following Horton's line of thinking, defines the term "religionism" as an approach to the study of religions which is not solely for the purpose of social scientific research, but also—and perhaps primarily, in his view—"to corroborate the scholar's religious view of the world."[108]

He argues strongly against this ideology, stating that there is the need to guard against "the incursion of theology into the science of religion . . ."[109] Otherwise, he argues, there is the risk that the contributions made by the phenomenology and history of religions to this academic discipline will be overtaken by "reductionist tendencies" emanating from theology.[110]

Furthermore, Cox argues strongly against the use of the term "primal" by African Christian scholars. He argues that the term is a "non-empirical theological construct" which, while introduced as an attempt at providing a neutral alternative to the more pejorative term "primitive," is unsuitable due to what he and others argue are its "non-empirical scientific status" as

105. Ibid., 422.
106. Ibid., 422, 423.
107. Ibid, 423.
108. Cox, "From Africa to Africa," 257.
109. Cox, "The Classification 'Primal Religion,'" 57.
110. Ibid., 74

an invention of Western scholarship. Moreover, he is opposed to the use of this term because of what he identifies as a theological agenda implicit within the category.

In Cox's view, the term primal "appears to be used not only as a scientific classification but also as a construct employed in Christian theologies of contextualization. If this use means that it is actually a theological category rather than a scientific one, the term should be removed from the academic study of religion and placed within theology or, at least, acknowledged as an empirically questionable classification which is valuable for theology."[111]

Herein lies a critical separation between the African Christian study of African religions and the more Western-oriented social scientific approach: according to Cox, the inclusion of a category or concept which he deems "theological" renders this approach unscientific and incompatible with academic study of religion. However, for most African Christian scholars, primal religion plays an important role in their study of religions, and is a term used where none more appropriate have yet been coined. Cox argues that the term should be restricted to Theology and removed from Religious Studies ("the academic study of religion"); yet he fails to address the reality that within the African Christian study of African religions, boundary lines here are often blurred, as with a scholar such as Bediako.

Australian scholar David Pym offers a carefully delineated rebuttal to Cox's argument. He firstly provides an overview of the emergence of the term and seeks to defend it as "an appropriate way of referring to Africa's so-called tribal and traditional religions." He admits that those are similarly unsatisfactory ways of referring to African indigenous religions, but uses the terms with the acknowledgement that more acceptable terminology has not been agreed upon.[112] In response to Cox's charge that the term is an invention of Western academics, Pym offers the rejoinder that the majority of present designations in this field have their origins, at least to some degree, in the West. And as Bongmba wryly notes, "it is perhaps the irony of history that some of the best terms used to describe local religions came from [Western] social scientists..."[113]

Echoing Adogame et al. on the need for further methodological input from African scholars, Pym argues that "[u]ntil such time as an alternative arises from within the African context and receives wide acceptance, it

---

111. Ibid., 56.
112. Pym, "'Primal Religions,'" 60.
113. Bongmba, "Writing African Christianity," 287.

would appear that any designation . . . runs the risk of both appearing and being an imposition from outside."[114]

Pym identifies Cox's position as being based upon a methodology that is grounded in a scientific approach to religion. This, argues Pym, means that for Cox, "academic research on religious phenomena [must] pass through the prism of the scientific method . . . [which] inevitably leads him to require that 'primal religions' be shown to be an empirically verifiable designation before it can be accepted as legitimate within the science of religion."[115] But such an approach, counters Pym, is very different from that of many African Christian scholars of African religions, again underscoring the divisions within this wider field of study.

African Non-Confessional Scholars of Religion: An Intellectual Critique

While much opposition to African Christian methodologies has come from Western scholars, there has also been strong opposition from African scholars of religion. Some of the most vocal opposition has come from Ugandan scholar Okot p'Bitek, who has been called "the preeminent African critic of Western scholarship on African indigenous religions."[116] P'Bitek was later joined by scholars such as Ghanaian philosopher Kwasi Wiredu. Amongst these non-confessional African scholars, there is a pervasive view that this drawing together of Christianity and African primal religion is little more than continued Western colonization of African thought and religion, or "Hellenization," as p'Bitek calls it.

In his best-known work, *African Religions in Western Scholarship*, p'Bitek argues against African scholarship that stands on the premise that Africans had a conception of God that was almost identical to the Christian concept of God prior to the arrival of the missionaries. Wiredu argues that for many African scholars of religion, including Idowu and Mbiti, and certainly Bediako in the following generation, it seemed an important achievement to demonstrate that Africans had arrived "at the belief in a God who created the world out of nothing."[117] P'Bitek, however, "had no

---

114. Pym, "'Primal Religions,'" 62.

115. Ibid., 64.

116. Rinsum, "They became slaves of their definitions," 11.

117. Wiredu, "Decolonizing African Philosophy and Religion," xxxvi. This text is a revised and updated printing of p'Bitek's 1971 *African Religion in Western Scholarship*.

such assumption. He was a sceptic, and found nothing necessarily creditable in such a belief," a view firmly shared by Wiredu.[118]

Within the study of African religions, p'Bitek identifies three categories of scholars: African and Western Christian apologists; African nationalists; and twentieth-century missionaries who wanted to engage with African indigenous religion. His main argument, and a view he held firmly, was the perception that these efforts were attempts to "Hellenize" African deities rather than interpreting them as entirely distinct and discontinuous with Christianity.

Expanding on this, he argues that these scholars were "dressing up" African deities in "Hellenic robes" in order to make them acceptable to the Western world, and to proclaim that earlier generations of anthropologists had "erred grievously when they reported that African peoples were mere 'pagan savages' and assert that Africans are, as they have always been, highly religious and moral peoples."[119] While p'Bitek agreed that Africans were highly religious, he maintains the argument that interpreting African primal religion through Christian, or Hellenic terms, is a complete misunderstanding of African religion and a clear manifestation of the Western colonization of African thought.[120]

Wiredu agrees with p'Bitek on this point, though he explains it slightly differently. Like p'Bitek, Wiredu views Christianity as a Western religion and argues that any African who espouses Christianity without acknowledgement of the cultural and philosophical differences between Western and African thought "must incur the label of being an intellectually colonized African."[121]

It is not impossible, Wiredu concedes, for an African to become a Christian in a "non-colonized manner," but only if he or she readily acknowledges that there are "definite incompatibilities between Christianity and various African religions."[122] There is nothing wrong, he continues, with evaluating both religions and choosing Christianity. But what *is* wrong, he challenges, "is the apparent attempt on the part of some African Christians to have it both ways."[123] Here p'Bitek points to African Christian scholars

---

118. Ibid.
119. p'Bitek, *Decolonizing African Religions*, 19.
120. Ibid., 23.
121. Wiredu, "Decolonizing African Philosophy and Religion," xiv.
122. Ibid., xiv–xv.
123. Ibid., xv.

like Mbiti, whom he charges with being "more Christian than African."[124] Certainly he would paint Bediako with the same brush.

Chitando strongly criticizes p'Bitek's argument, describing it as a "hankering after pristine, unadulterated 'traditional' religions, unsullied by Christian scholars like Mbiti." But, he contends, such an approach amounts to an "essentialist concept of what it means to be 'African.' . . . To deny that Mbiti is African because he is Christian is to participate in the myth of a reified and static African identity."[125]

This is in stark contrast to Bediako's persistent argument that his identity is firmly African *and* Christian. His argument that Christianity is *not* a Western religion is evidenced in part by his book entitled, *Christianity in Africa: The Renewal of a Non-Western Religion*. He expresses his own sense of identity as an African Christian more fully in this following statement, recorded in an interview with James Ault:

> "I wish to define myself as a Christian—as an *African* Christian—not because a European has told me so; indeed, my exposure to Europe made me atheist. In becoming Christian, thirty-three years ago, in France, on my own, under the shower, in the summer break, on the campus of the University of Bordeaux, I discovered I was becoming *African* again. I was recovering my sense of the spiritual of life. I was recovering my sense of the nearness of the living God. I was recovering my African sense of the *wholeness* of life. I find in becoming Christian, I'm becoming more African than I think I was. I'm being more . . . who I *am*."[126]

Parratt takes a more balanced approach, acknowledging both the veracity of some of p'Bitek's claims while supporting the position of African Christian scholars. He does this with the "adaptationist" approach in mind. This approach endeavours to draw out the essential features of African religious systems and relate them to the Christian gospel.[127] In this sense, Parratt sees p'Bitek's major argument as being that much systematic analysis of primal religions has been undertaken by African Christian scholars, who have interpreted indigenous religious practices "in Christian terminology and categories."[128]

---

124. p'Bitek, *African Religions in Western Scholarship*, 108.

125. Chitando, "African Christian Scholars," 394.

126. Ault, "Kwame Bediako," in Educational Extras, *African Christianity Rising*. 0:01–0:55 seconds.

127. Parratt, *Reinventing Christianity*, 199.

128. Ibid.

Parratt disagrees with p'Bitek's classification of this as Hellenization, acknowledging that if African scholars view primal religion through the prism of Christian theology, it is unsurprising that they should draw parallels between the two. However, Parratt is more critical in his assessment of adaptationism for failing to address what he calls "discontinuous" elements of African primal religion, or "those aspects of traditional religion that cannot by any leap of faith be reconciled to Christian teaching."[129]

In response to these various critics, Bediako observes that there are African intellectuals who "have retained a suspicion of the Christian religion in Africa," as well as "secular-minded Westerners who are distrustful of any claim that a religious conviction can form the basis for developing a viable social and intellectual tradition for new and young nations seeking paths to modernisation."[130] He concedes, however, that in the initial emergence of African Theology, the focus may have been so significantly on challenging derogatory European estimations of African traditions that methodological challenges may have been insufficiently addressed, in the sense that "the blemishes of the religious past have not so far been adequately clarified and set in perspective."[131] However, that time is passed, he argues.[132]

Bediako recognizes p'Bitek as the foremost African critic of African Christian scholarship, and interestingly offers this concession to p'Bitek, along with a challenge to African Christian scholarship: "[T]he fact that African Theology has yet to produce a full-scale response to Okot p'Bitek and other African non-Christian critics . . . may be an indication of the strength of his criticism that by seeking to 'christianise'[sic] the African religious past, African Theology is merely 'continuing the missionary misrepresentation of the past.' But the absence of a major theological response to Okot p'Bitek may also reveal a more fundamental lack which needs to be addressed in the agenda of the future."[133]

Bediako wrote this more than twenty years ago; yet to date, there remains very little response from African Christian scholars to p'Bitek and other non-confessional scholars of African religions on these points. Olabimtan is a notable exception, engaging as he does with some of these methodological concerns. However, this extended lack of discussion may point to the depth of the divide, with African Christian scholars pursuing

---

129. Ibid., 200.

130. Bediako, *Christianity in Africa*, 178.

131. Bediako, *Theology and Identity*, 437.

132. Ibid., 439.

133. Ibid., 438. He cites p'Bitek, *African Religions in Western Scholarship* and p'Bitek, *Song of Lawino*.

a different academic itinerary and remaining unconcerned to interact, respond, or challenge the accusations levied against them.

And for their part, there is certainly a strand within non-confessional scholarship that is quite dismissive of the African Christian scholarly enterprise, deeming it unfit for the academy. Such avoidance is a weakness on both sides. Robust scholarship calls, not for universal agreement or a singular perspective, but continued engagement with one's interlocutors as a way to address blind spots, correct errors, and sharpen arguments.

Apart from p'Bitek and Wiredu, however, a significant portion of the opposition to the African Christian itinerary has come from Western scholars. This suggests that the division may reflect some cultural and academic differences, with the Western academy drawing a sharp boundary between theology and religious studies, with the former viewed as unscientific and unwelcome in the academy and the latter, the appropriate way forward in the study of religions. It remains important to attend to these divergent voices. They help to clarify the unique perspective of African Christian scholars, and they also have contributions to make within this emerging discourse.

Bediako himself is well aware of the complexity of this discourse, both among Christian and non-Christian scholars, and in response offers the following challenge: "[I]s it mostly in social science studies of religion in relation to Christianity that the significance of the new Christian reality is recognized. Here, however, reactions range from puzzlement and near incomprehension to a sense of apprehension and even threat, on the understanding that such a transformation of the Christian world is introducing a disturbance in the geopolitical balance of power between the West and the rest, the North and the South."[134] Greater dialogue and scholarly engagement is needed if there is hope of moving from apprehension and threat to confidence and collegiality.

This chapter has demonstrated the clear emergence of what may rightly be called the African study of African religions, as seen in West Africa throughout the course of the twentieth century, and has highlighted the voices of African Christian scholars within this discourse. This has included the early work of key British scholars in contributing to laying an academic foundation for this field; a variety of African voices; and also more recent non-African responses. Through tracing the historical development of this discourse, we have seen that African Christians in particular represent a strong voice within this emerging field, finding value and validation for both an African and a Christian identity in pursuing the study of African religions from a Christian perspective.

134. Bediako, "'Why has the summer ended?,'" 5.

However, we have also noted the critical voices of scholars who fundamentally disagree with privileging a Christian perspective within this discourse, with some like p'Bitek arguing that it "Hellenizes" African religions, and others like Cox contending that it globalises what are essentially local religions. This has elucidated some abiding methodological and ideological divisions which persist between African, non-African, Christian, and non-confessional scholars. Furthermore, as Chitando has suggested, this may point to deeper fissures between African and Western scholarship, with a more secularised Western perspective tending to dismiss the scholarly contributions of African Christians to the study of religion in Africa.

"If the pioneering work by African Christian scholars is acknowledged," argues Chitando, "there is no need to pretend that the study of [African indigenous religions] is starting from nowhere . . . Although they may have relied on the Christian template, Mbiti and Idowu's formulations have given shape to the discipline. The aversion to the tag 'theological,' while understandable, needs to be revisited. It is hoped that . . . scholars will pause and reflect on developments that gave shape to the discipline within African Christian theological formulations."[135]

In Bongmba's article "Writing African Christianity," he helpfully outlines "considerations for future accounts of African Christianity."[136] His article, and the above discussion in particular, warrant careful attention; however, a brief summary of the six key considerations for African Christian scholarship that he delineates must suffice here for drawing this chapter to a conclusion. Firstly, he argues that scholars will need to maintain a critical balance between time periods and geographic locations in their study of African Christianity. Secondly, he calls for critical engagement with the colonial period, including creative approaches to mission histories, while preferencing the African story. Thirdly, scholars should "carry out a critical analysis of local and global developments which began with the Africanization of African Christianity."[137] Fourthly, he calls for the "religious factor" to continue to animate the study of African Christianity. Fifthly, "an account of African Christian scholarship must continue to interrogate the claims and challenges of culture."[138] Sixth, future scholarship must engage the challenge of language, with serious attention given to engaging the variety of literature available in many African languages. As we will continue to see, Bediako leads the way with several of these key considerations, most notably in the

---

135. Chitando, "African Christian Scholars," 395.
136. See Bongmba, "Writing African Christianity," 282–89.
137. Ibid., 285.
138. Ibid., 288.

latter three. Bongmba's argument that these are areas for future research should alert us to the fact that Bediako is an African Christian scholar with contemporary and future relevance in this field, whose work will require continued scholarly attention.

Having gained a broad historical and ontological understanding of the complexities of this emerging discourse, we can now begin to trace the African study of African religions more specifically in twentieth-century Ghana. We will see how African Christian voices gave shape to this discourse, using such diverse platforms as poetry, education, sociology, and politics, in addition to explicitly theological scholarship; and we will begin to see how Bediako, through his writing and through ACI, emerges as a leading figure in the African Christian study of African religions. It is to this historical trajectory that we now turn our attention.

Chapter 3

Reading, Writing, 'Rithmetic, and Religion

Nineteenth- and Twentieth-Century Mission and Colonial Contributions to the African Christian Study of Religions in Ghana

[Christian] missionary education in the majority of African countries helped provide the first wave of modern African nationalists. What can all too easily be overlooked is the concurrent influences of missionary education in the direction of global awareness and the beginnings of pax humana.[1]

—Ali Mazrui

---

1. Mazrui, *Political Values*, 168. Adinkra symbol *Mmere dane*, meaning "time changes," signifying life's dynamics and times of change.

As we have just noted, one aspect of ongoing research in African Christianity is a critical assessment of the colonial era, as it "significantly altered the map and complicated the account with the proliferation of missions and agencies that significantly influenced the development and growth of the church. While the story that should be told must be an African story, the nature of the dialogue between Africa and the rest of the world needs to be mapped out carefully." Such an endeavour "calls for creative approaches to mission histories, which tell more than the story of the missionaries and their work."[2] This chapter endeavours to do just that: tracing key historical developments as well as interrogating the motivations of relevant missionaries and colonial officials within nineteenth and twentieth-century Ghana and highlighting African and European dialectics within these accounts, in order for the African story to come to the forefront.

Nineteenth-Century Missions: Sowing The Dragon's Teeth of Education

Parrinder correctly observed in 1960 that "[o]ne of the most effective fields of activity for the churches [in West Africa] has always been that of education, and it is well known that most of the schools have been run by the missions, and that the universities would be impossible without their work." Parrinder further emphasizes the critical role of education when he declares that anyone who imagined that Africa could be permanently kept in tutelage was forgetting the fact that Christianity had been there before them "and had sown the dragon's teeth of education."[3] The interconnectivity between Christian missions, colonial education, and mid-twentieth-century nationalistic politics, and the contributions made by each one in shaping emerging African religious discourse in twentieth-century Ghana, cannot be underestimated.

Teasing out the distinct threads of this period reveals a cacophony of competing voices. This includes those of European missionaries, British colonialists, and Ghanaian politicians and scholars, who variously laid a foundation for this emerging discourse and in some cases entered into this discussion as African scholars of religion. This chapter therefore firstly explores the role of the Basel Mission's engagement with African culture,

---

2. Bongmba, "Writing African Christianity," 284.

3. Parrinder, "The Religious Situation in West Africa," 41. He notes that his comment about "sowing the dragon's teeth of education" is a reference he recalls from a statement made by Roland Oliver, Professor Emeritus of African History at SOAS, in a public lecture.

education, and translation in late-nineteenth and early-twentieth-century Ghana, with a specific focus on the roles of German and Ghanaian Mission translators J.G. Christaller and C. A. Akrofi. The contribution of the Basel Mission is important to this discussion because through its foundational contribution to Pietistic Christianity, vernacular education, and Bible translation it is historically, geographically, and theologically linked to Bediako and ACI, as we will continue to see.

Secondly, this chapter considers the role of the British colonial government and the forward-thinking efforts of Sir Gordon Guggisberg, demonstrating how British and European efforts impacted the study of religion in Ghana in surprisingly positive ways. After considering these missionary and colonial endeavours, we shall turn our attention to the post-colonial Ghanaian politicians and church leaders who took up the educational mantle and wrestled with questions of religion and culture. This includes a focus on "bridging figures" such as Ephraim Amu, whose roles overlapped between missions, colonial, and post-colonial institutions, as well as an in-depth consideration of politicians Kwame Nkrumah and K.A. Busia, each of whom creatively engaged Christianity and Akan religion and made foundational contributions to the study of religion in Ghana.

Parrinder wrote with great acumen and foresight: the dragon's teeth of education had indeed been sown, and education contributed to cultivating the environment and leaders that forged the path to Ghana's political independence. Furthermore, it was the "educated elite"—i.e., those having completed their secondary education in mission and later government schools and universities—who were equipped and positioned to become nationalist leaders.

As a result, understanding the development of education in Ghana is essential to any study on the rise of nationalism. Such a study is also necessary for exploring the emergence of the African study of African religions. The educated elite did indeed become the nationalist leaders of independent Ghana. But they also became the academicians, sociologists, poets, theologians, and citizens; and in these myriad capacities, began to develop the study of African religions within the Ghanaian context.

The Basel Mission in the Gold Coast: 1828–1917[4]

In its earliest formations, the Basel Mission was linked with a group called the German Society for Christianity, which brought Swiss and German

---

4. The designation "Basel" and "Presbyterian" are used interchangeably in quoted references, as Presbyterian missionaries continued the work of the mission when Basel

pietistic clergy and laity together for Bible study and discussion, and later formed a seminary in Basel in 1815 for the training of overseas missionaries.[5] Jenkins paints a clear picture of the rural farming communities from which these Swiss-German missionaries emerged when he describes them as being dedicated to "a Christian critique of life" in the towns and villages near Wurttemberg. These pietistic Christians were rooted in a communitarian ideology, invested in building up the kingdom of God in visible ways. For this reason, they were deeply committed to working towards establishing stable populations of Christian farming families.[6]

At the heart of this vision for Christian communities was the father, modelled on "the master-craftsman farmer of the Wurtemberg [sic] countryside."[7] This father-farmer had at hand his extended family, servants, hired workers, and apprentices, all of whom would join him in daily family prayer and reading of the Bible. This figure played a significant role in community discipline and order, understanding it as his duty to "dominate and correct" in this circle.[8] In an effort to replicate these communities overseas, these pietistic missionaries often cast themselves in this leading patriarchal and punitive role. For many of us today, Miller admits, their strict practices may appear racist, dysfunctional, or at the least, paternalistic. However, he enjoins us to recall that these missionaries "took with them the authority patterns they already knew in their homeland, which were regarded in Pietism as one of the means by which the Christian communities were to be built up" and through which the Christian faith could be spread.[9]

The first group of Basel missionaries arrived in the Gold Coast in 1828; all died within a short period of time and a second group arrived in 1832. Of this envoy, only one missionary couple survived: Andreas Riis (1804–1854) and his wife Anna, who took up residence along the coast. This was a period of almost unmitigated disaster for the Basel Mission, as Riis himself became very ill in 1833. In a noteworthy turn of events, it was a local fetish priest who saved Riis' life.[10]

Riis was eager to move the Mission away from the coastal community, and was eventually given permission to move inland. He relocated the

---

missionaries were deported during the First World War and thus date their work in Ghana back to the start of the Basel Mission. However, earlier Basel records of course only refer to their mission as the Basel Mission.

5. Miller, *Missionary Zeal*, 14.
6. Ibid., 15.
7. Ibid., 16.
8. Ibid.
9. Ibid.
10. See Agbeti, *West African Church History*, 63.

Mission to the town of Akropong in the Akuapem hills, a royal town and seat of Asante power. There are diverse reasons posited for the Basel missionaries' preference for rural areas in general and for Akropong in particular. It is possible that they believed they could be more successful both as missionaries and educationists in rural areas, which, unlike the urban centres, were not tied to an exchange economy or to the disreputable merchant classes.[11]

However, Sanneh hints at less pious motives for this move when he observes that "the Basel Mission decided to penetrate inland from the coast in order both to avoid excessive dependence on European agency and to reach populations relatively unspoilt by European contact."[12] Ghanaian scholar Seth Quartey echoes Sanneh's view when he notes that, in addition to experiencing continual health problems, Riis struggled to make any evangelistic headway within the various merchant and indigenous populations on the coast and therefore sought to establish mission work "in regions less likely to resist his religious messages and where the climate favored his survival." Furthermore, argues Quartey, in Riis' thinking, "[t]he best locations to convert were the least Europeanized."[13]

With perhaps a combination of these motivations at play, Riis moved the mission inland, and the Asante king ordered a house to be built for him and selected a few young boys to be set apart as students for Riis' school.[14] Evangelism in Akropong did not begin easily. With no baptized converts after eight years, there were thoughts of abandoning the mission entirely. But, as Reindorf writes, "[t]he Lord, however, had already chosen new ways; it was not his will to leave this stronghold of Satan [Akropong] in the peace of death."[15] As it turned out, these "new ways" were in fact new missionaries: black African missionaries. As the story goes, in a meeting between Riis and the King of Akuapem, the King commented that "[w]hen God created the world, he made the Book for the Whiteman and Juju for the Blackman. If you can show us some Blackman who can read the Whiteman's Book, then we would surely follow you."[16]

After a period of home assignment, this was the impetus for the Basel Mission's decision to send Riis back to Akropong accompanied by a small nucleus of black Moravian Christians from Jamaica. These Moravians completely revitalized the Mission and provided a living example

---

11. Graham, *The History of Education in Ghana*, 55.
12. Sanneh, *West African Christianity*, 113.
13. Quartey, *Missionary Practices on the Gold Coast*, 48.
14. Reindorf, *History of the Gold Coast and Asante*, 315.
15. Ibid., 226.
16. Schweitzer, *Survivors on the Gold Coast*, 50–52.

to the Akropong community that they could indeed be both African and Christian. Without a doubt, in the history of the successful establishment of Christianity in West Africa, "the constant element in all of this was the African factor which, more than any other consideration, sustained the Christian and humanitarian initiative in the development of the continent."[17]

Despite achieving greater credibility in the community through the Jamaican Christians, the Basel Mission's practice of creating separate Christian communities ("salems") was problematic in several ways. In Akropong, the Christians occupied a part of the town with buildings and houses built for Riis, some of which are still in existence today. These salems were a deliberate attempt at removing Ghanaian Christians from what the missionaries saw as "immoral and 'heathen' townspeople."[18] This in part fostered the troubling belief that to become Christian meant a clear separation, and in many instances rejection, of one's culture, religion, and non-Christian community. Furthermore, it inculcated the view that Christianity was a foreign religion, one that required adherents to leave their communities and adapt their lifestyles to the pietistic ideal of Christian communal living.

Another challenge was that for both Ghanaians and the European missionaries, salems contributed to friction between Christians and non-Christians, with conflict typically focused around issues of power and authority. The missionaries taught that Christianity required allegiance to a higher authority, with the result that Ghanaian and European Christians did not necessarily abide by the local authority patterns. This undermined the authority of the chief, who functioned as both a religious and political leader. Adding to this conflict, the missionaries claimed that converts were morally free of obligations to the chief specifically where "fetish" practices were required, which further fuelled tension and undermined the chief's power.[19]

One final contentious issue was that the Christians accepted slaves as equals, a practice that upset community power and social structures. Such practices sowed seeds of discord between followers of Christ and indigenous religious practitioners, as well as between the chiefs and the Christian missionaries. This resulted in a fractured community and disjointed religious and cultural identities.

Bediako, however, argues for viewing the salems in a more positive light. He sees them as an effort on the part of the Basel missionaries to replicate a living situation with which they were already familiar, and as an effort

---

17. Sanneh, *West African Christianity*, 106.
18. Middleton, "One Hundred and Fifty Years of Christianity," 5.
19. Kimble, *A Political History of Ghana*, 155–56.

to provide a positive example of Christian community to Ghanaians. In his words,

> Some textbooks suggest that the Salems divided our society and argue that we have suffered from that. I hold a different opinion ... The Basel missionaries ... came from something similar to Salems. They were on the fringe of society, despised villagers, ordinary people with little education ... What was the Salem for? It was not a way of demarcating the town. The missionaries realised [sic] quite early that it was impossible to achieve results overnight ... The idea was to build a model community beside the traditional community ... The idea was to show how one could be a Christian in a context that people could observe.[20]

Herein lie some of the complex roots of engagement between Akan culture, primal religion, and this newly introduced brand of pietistic Christianity. The propagation of the views that African culture, authority structures, and religious values were to be, at best, disregarded, and at worst, viewed as evil, would have lasting and unforeseen consequences for both Christian thought and Ghanaian culture. Such views were, to a large extent, diffused through the educational institutions established by the missions, and in this way they began to shape African Christian scholarship, promoting the view that to be Christian meant a rejection of African culture and worldview.

However, not all mission efforts were so controversial. During this same time, missionaries and mission schools were making indelible contributions to the field of translation, which, as we will see, has been an important component of the African Christian study of African religions.

Translation and the Use of Vernacular Languages

Translation remains one of the most significant contributions of the Basel Mission to Ghana, and indeed to the African Christian study of African religions. In colonial interactions of the late-eighteenth and early-nineteenth centuries, specifically among the European-based communities concentrated at the forts and castles along the coast, English was the *lingua franca* for Europeans and Ghanaians. It was used for trade and education, functioning as a gateway to opportunity and the primary mode of communication between educated Africans of different tribes.[21]

---

20. Bediako offered these remarks in response to questions raised following a paper that he gave during a series of Gospel and Culture workshops held at ACI in 1998 and 1999. See Bediako, "Gospel and Culture: Some Insights for our Time," 17.

21. See Kimble, *A Political History of Ghana*, 510.

However, this began to change with the arrival of the Basel missionaries, who were truly the linguistic pioneers of the Gold Coast.[22] While the communities at the coast could comfortably communicate in English, this was not the case for the community in Akropong. The Basel missionaries spoke German, and the Ghanaians, Akuapem Twi.[23] Therefore, language learning and translation were immediate necessities for the missionaries.

In a discussion on translation, the figures of J.G. Christaller and C.A. Akrofi loom large. Johannes Gottlieb Christaller (1827–1895) was a gifted linguist who paved the way for the Basel Mission's work in Twi. He began his career with the Mission in 1853 and made the signal contribution of writing a Twi dictionary and grammar. In addition, he is recognized for his signal contribution of translating the Bible into Twi, together with David Asante and Jonathan Bekoe, Ghanaian students of the Mission.[24] Christaller also wrote various devotional materials, hymns, and prayers, and compiled an extensive collection of Twi proverbs.[25]

This earned him the designation "the most distinguished ... of the German missionary-scholars,"[26] whose efforts contributed to making Twi the most important African literary language in Ghana.[27] As Bediako observes, "[t]he whole monumental achievement of Johannes Christaller in Twi ... all went to ensure that the formation of 'Christian nations' out of the peoples of the Gold Coast would have the necessary tools to be carried forward."[28]

The fullness of his linguistic efforts came to fruition in the person of Clement Anderson Akrofi (1901–1967), a Ghanaian born almost a century after Christaller and educated by the Basel Mission. There is a Twi proverb

---

22. Ibid.

23. Twi is the dominant language of the Akropong-Akuapem region, and is the primary language of the Akan, and is also Kwame Bediako's mother tongue.

24. Kimble, *A Political History of Ghana*, 511.

25. See, for example, J. G. Christaller, with David Asante and Theophilus Opoku, *Anyamesem anase Kyerew Kronkron Apam-dedaw ne Apam-foforo nsem wo Twi kasa mu = The Holy Bible translated from the Original Languages into the Twi Language* (Basel: Basel Evangelical Missionary Society, 1871); Christaller, *A Grammar of the Asante and Fante Language called Tshi (Chwee, Twi)* (Basel: Evangelical Missionary Society, 1875); Christaller, *Twi Mmebusɱm mpensæ-ahansúa mmoaano = A Collection of 3,600 Tshi [sic] Proverbs in Use Among the Negroes of the Gold Coast Speaking the Language* (Basel: Basel Evangelical Missionary Society, 1879); Christaller, *A Dictionary of the Asante and Fante Language called Tshi (Chwee, Tŵi): With a Grammatical Introduction and Appendices on the Geography of the Gold Coast and Other Subjects (1881)* (Basel: Basel Evangelical Missionary Society, 1881).

26. McWilliam, *The Development of Education in Ghana*, 24.

27. See Ofosu-Appiah, "Christaller, Johann Gottlieb 1827–1895," para. 1

28. Bediako, *Christianity in Africa*, 51.

that says, "A son sees further because his father carries him on his shoulders." As Bediako claims, Akrofi may rightly be seen as Christaller's intellectual heir.[29] With a similar affinity for language, Akrofi was the foremost authority on Twi during his lifetime and was heavily engaged with teaching, examining, and translating. Like Christaller's Twi dictionary, Akrofi's book on Twi grammar, *Twi Kasa Mmara*, proved indispensable to further translation efforts, though his largest undertaking was his 1965 complete revision and update of Christaller's Twi translation of the Bible.[30]

In Akrofi, we see the Mission's value and respect for the study of Twi grammar and orthography being carried forward in a new generation of Akan scholars. Akrofi, however, did not just expand upon Christaller's earlier work; he far surpassed it. Indeed, his *Twi Kasa Mmara* was what Christaller's work could never be: "an African language interpreted by an African scholar writing in his own language."[31] In this way, Akrofi is a pioneering example of a Ghanaian scholar of Ghanaian language and religion, which, as we will see, is one of the key reasons why Bediako chose him as a namesake for ACI.

The Basel Mission undertook these translation enterprises for their own evangelistic purposes and could not have envisioned the long term consequences of their efforts for African Christian scholarship. While the Mission failed for the most part to integrate Christianity with Ghanaian culture and indigenous religious practices—often working against such ends, in fact—they inadvertently provided essential tools for the African study of African religions.

Education

Bediako draws our attention to this repeated phenomenon of the "dragon's teeth" of Christian education being sown and providing a significant scholarly foundation for future generations:

> Of course, parallels to the Twi story are found in many other parts of the world, where Christianity has come into contact with other previously pre-literary cultures . . . But whether it is in Anglo-Saxon England . . . or in the Gold Coast through South

---

29. Ibid., 53.

30. Darkwo, "Akrofi, Clement Anderson," paras. 3, 5. He references C. A. Akrofi, *Twi Kasa Mmara: A Twi Grammar in Twi* (London: Longmans; Accra: Scottish Mission Book Depot, 1937).

31. See Bediako, *Christianity in Africa*, 53. Bediako cites Westermann, Foreword, *Twi Kasa Mmara* (Accra: Presbyterian Book Depot; 1937), vii.

German, Swiss and Scottish missionaries, the basic process is identical: a vision of Christian education, centred [sic] on the Bible, which, though intended for mission and congregation, in actual fact begets a tradition of Christian scholarship which comes to serve the community far beyond the church.[32]

This theme runs through the remainder of twentieth-century Ghana. True to Bediako's words, the efforts of the Basel missionaries, as well as those of other mission organizations, had repercussions far beyond the Church, with significant implications for the African study of religion.[33]

To return to the story of Riis' nineteenth-century work in Akropong, his methods in developing an educational structure incorporated the following three essential—and at the time, novel—components. First, having a good supply of well-trained teachers; second, providing education for girls as well as boys; and third, offering training beyond strictly academic subjects. While such principles would now seem patently obvious, for over half a century, "the Basel Mission was the only educational body in [Ghana] that both recognized them and succeeded in putting them into practice."[34]

Subjects covered included literacy in the two dominant indigenous languages, Twi and Ga; English; arithmetic; natural history; geometry; world geography; and world history. In terms of their contribution to girls' education, by 1918, the schools in the Akuapem area had close to as many female as male students, and the overall ratio from all of the Basel Mission's schools in the Gold Coast was 2.7 boys for every girl. By way of comparison, in government and Wesleyan schools this ratio was markedly lower, at 6:1 and 7:1 respectively.[35] In the Seminary, the training was modelled on the *Missionhaus* at Basel where the missionaries undertook their theological training, and included Greek, Hebrew, Bible History, and biblical translation between English and vernacular languages, as well as other traditional theological subjects.[36]

However, such education came at a high cost socially and culturally. Reindorf is a useful informant here, speaking from his perspective as a Ghanaian Basel minister and reflecting the co-existing constructive and destructive forces: "Our schools," he records, "received every attention, because we

---

32. Bediako, *Christianity in Africa*, 53–54.

33. For discussion of the history of Wesleyan missions in Ghana, see Agbeti, *West African Church History* or Bartels, *Roots of Ghana Methodism*, 3–19. For specific discussion on the Wesleyan contribution to education in Ghana, see Graham, *The History of Education in Ghana* and McWilliam, *The Development of Education in Ghana*.

34. McWilliam, *The Development of Education in Ghana*, 19.

35. Ibid., 20.

36. Bediako, *Christianity in Africa*, 49.

must have a staff of well educated native assistants, before we reach our aim, the future independence of a native church. Boarding-schools were therefore opened in all our districts for boys and girls."[37] As with the salems, the rationale for having boarding schools was in part to separate children from their "heathenish families." As Reindorf continues, "the good influence of the school is often weakened by the venomous influence of paganism. This is less the case with our boarding-scholars, who live entirely with the missionaries under strict discipline."[38]

We see only a hint of the culturally and personally disruptive consequences of these boarding schools when Reindorf acknowledges the difficulty in persuading families to relinquish their children to the Mission. He concedes that it was especially challenging to persuade families to send their daughters to school. This was primarily because the Mission firmly rejected the traditional initiation rites for girls, deeming them incompatible with Christianity due to the public exposure of their bare breasts. However, girls who did not participate in these rites and ceremonies became social outcasts and were left essentially unmarriageable. Families, of course, did not want to jeopardize their daughters' futures or community economic or social stability, and hesitated over whether to embrace Christianity and education at such a high cost. This clash served to emphasize the growing divide between Ghanaian Christians and non-Christians, and presented a painful dilemma for families.[39]

Within this context, the strong links between education and religion in Ghana's history become clear, manifesting their variously conflicting and competing agendas. Despite the complexity of this period and these challenging realities, the impact of the Basel Mission's educational efforts on later African Christian scholarship cannot be underestimated. Bediako asserts that "[i]t is possible then to see the outcome in the twentieth century of the Basel Mission's educational policy during the nineteenth century as having surpassed by far its original narrowly-conceived intentions. It has resulted in a tradition of genuine scholarship..."[40]

In addition to translation and educational efforts, another key contribution of the Basel Mission was its establishment of "practical industry" and new farming practices, underscoring the pietistic emphasis on the importance of vocation alongside of education for the development of Christian society. This had important long-term consequences for economic growth

---

37. Reindorf, *History of the Gold Coast and Asante*, 228–29.
38. Ibid.
39. Ibid., 229.
40. Bediako, *Christianity in Africa*, 53.

and stability in the Gold Coast, contributing, albeit inadvertently, to future university development and to Ghana's independence.[41]

Transformation into the Presbyterian Church of Ghana

With the advent of the First World War, hostilities between Britain and Germany resulted in the expulsion in 1917 of German personnel, including the Basel missionaries. Sir Gordon Guggisberg, governor of the Gold Coast, lamented that it was "the greatest blow which education in this country has ever suffered."[42]

The history of the Basel Mission is remarkable in that, while it ended in one sense with the deportation of these missionaries, it continued and evolved under the auspices of missionaries from the Free Church of Scotland, who arrived in 1919. From 1926 onwards, the Mission was identified as the "Presbyterian Church of the Gold Coast." Because of the Basel Mission's heritage in the Reformed Church and its continued links with the Lutheran Church, "its affinity with the Presbyterian Church was self-evident."[43]

This new missionary body is perspicaciously described as "'Presbyterian' in structure while remaining thoroughly a 'Basel' Church in ethos and outlook."[44] Bediako describes its structure as "*Presbyterian* in constitution, *Reformed* and mildly *Lutheran* in spirit."[45] He further breaks down the various contributions of the pietistic Basel missionaries and the Scottish Presbyterians, attributing educational developments primarily to the Presbyterians, while seeing pietistic spirituality as the main contribution of the more rural, less educated, Basel missionaries.

The Scottish, he observes, "carried the importance of education in the life of the Church and for the Church." However, there is a significant third element to consider: the Ghanaian sense of religion and religiosity. Taken together, the Presbyterian Church is therefore shaped by "an intense piety . . . [taking] faith seriously . . . an earnestness about education . . . And the Ghanaian's own sense of the religiosity of all life . . ."[46]

41. See Miller, *Missionary Zeal*, 27–28 for more detailed discussion of industrial and farming practices. For further discussion of the role of Basel missionaries in developing Ghana's successful cocoa industry, see, for example, Middleton, "One Hundred and Fifty Years of Christianity," 6, and Cooksey and McLeish, *Religion and Civilization in West Africa*, 123.

42. McWilliam, *The Development of Education in Ghana*, 45.

43. Sanneh, *West African Christianity*, 115.

44. Williamson, *Akan Religion and the Christian Faith*, 5–6.

45. Ibid., 6; italics are Williamson's.

46. Bediako, filmed interview by James Ault, 1998, DigiBeta Reel GB 108: 37–38.

While the Scottish missionaries continued the work of the Basel Mission, their arrival closely coincided with the arrival of Sir Gordon Guggisberg (1869–1930), a forward-thinking British colonial administrator whose changes to educational policies marked the shift from missionary to colonial educational oversight in Ghana. Addressing this early twentieth-century shift, Kimble remarks that "missionary education continued to expand, providing more clerks and teachers, and a good many restless young men who did not quite know to what use to put their newly acquired reading and writing."[47]

The dragon's teeth of education had indeed been sown, and signs of the resulting crops of nationalism, cultural renaissance, anti-colonialism, and self-government were beginning to spring up, which we will continue to see more fully in the following chapter. As the missionary era drew to a close, the perhaps unlikely figure of this British colonial administrator made a surprisingly positive and lasting contribution to education and to the African study of African religions in Ghana.

Colonial Education: 1919–1950

Sir Gordon Guggisberg and Educational Reforms

The end of World War I marked a critical turning point: the colonial enterprise was well underway and the sun was setting on the missionary era. But while much has been made of the negative aspects of colonialism, especially with regard to its alleged destruction of culture, the situation in Ghana offers a surprisingly different picture under Guggisberg's visionary leadership.

By the end of the First World War, the British colonial government was responsible for more than half the schools in the country; but poor conditions of service and pay for teachers led to a high number of resignations even while student enrolment was rising, resulting in poor standards of student achievement. These were "the gloomy facts" facing Guggisberg on his appointment as Governor of the Gold Coast Colony in 1919.[48]

However, with his strategic approach to education this situation changed dramatically. "Education," remarks Sanneh, "became, not the wayward mistress of *déraciné* Africans but the legitimate handmaid of those wishing to transform a state of subservience into one of freedom. The seeds

---

For further discussion on the Scottish contribution, see Walls, "The Scottish Missionary Diaspora," 259. This essay offers important historical details and useful insight into the Scottish missionary enterprise and their educational itineraries in the Gold Coast.

47. Kimble, *A Political History of Ghana*, 71.
48. McWilliam, *The Development of Education in Ghana*, 47.

of the nationalist awakening were sown in the grounds of mission schools, as colonial authorities were not slow to appreciate."[49]

After the war, the economic situation improved greatly and Guggisberg determined that education was to be made the top priority in Ghana, such that it would later be identified as "the keystone of what would now be called Guggisberg's Africanization policy."[50] It is helpful to recall that it was only by the wartime expulsion of the Basel missionaries that the colonial government suddenly became responsible for 60 percent of the schools, compared with just 8 percent at the start of World War I.[51] Guggisberg's own words provide important insight into his vision for the Africanization of education. I quote him here in full:

> We want to give to all Africans the opportunity of both moral and material progress by opening for them the benefits and delights that come from literature, and by equipping them with the knowledge necessary to success in their occupations, no matter how humble. We want to give to those who wish it an opportunity of becoming leaders of their own countrymen in thought, industries and the professions. Throughout all this, our aim must not be to denationalize them, but to graft skilfully on to their national characteristics the best attributes of modern civilization. For without preserving his national characteristics and his sympathy and touch with the great illiterate masses of his own people, no man can ever become a leader in progress, whatever other sort of leader he may become.[52]

There is no avoiding the Eurocentric tone of his words. However, the revolutionary nature of Guggisberg's approach in seeking to equip Ghanaians for leadership and to avoid stripping away an African identity is remarkable. This is especially so when contrasted against the often negative missionary view of African culture and religion that we have just seen.

The argument may justifiably be levied that Guggisberg's mind-set remains paternalistic, with his assumption that Ghanaians wanted British "modern civilization." And, moreover, that it was in the hands of British politicians to extend the offer of self-government to a country (region) which had governed itself for millennia prior to being claimed as a British colony

---

49. Sanneh, *West African Christianity*, 147.

50. See McWilliam, *The Development of Education in Ghana*, 48 and Kimble, *A Political History of Ghana*, 109–10.

51. Kimble, *A Political History of Ghana*, 109–110.

52. McWilliam, *The Development of Education in Ghana*, 48, quoting from Guggisberg's Educational Policy Outline, paragraph 199.

only about half a century earlier. Nevertheless, for someone of his generation and political position, Guggisberg's vision was remarkably forward-thinking and contributed directly to preparing Ghanaians for independence, and indirectly to developing the African study of African religions.

Following Guggisberg's caution against denationalization, it was determined that in the primary schools, "English should be introduced as early as possible as a *subject* of instruction, but that the vernacular should be the *medium* of instruction." In this way, the earlier emphasis of the Basel Mission on providing education in vernacular languages was now applied to the school system throughout the whole of Ghana.[53]

Another critical contribution from Guggisberg was the establishment of Achimota, a secondary boarding school still regarded as one of Ghana's premier educational institutions. He drafted "Sixteen Principles of Education," which he presented to the Gold Coast Legislative Council in 1925. Some of the particularly notable points include the provision of equal educational opportunities for girls and boys; secondary education to appropriately prepare students for university, as well as the provision of a university; the importance of religious training and character development in schools; and cooperation between Missions and Government, with the Government having ultimate control.[54]

In the shadow of the Second World War, the Colonial Office in Britain established a committee to consider educational developments in West Africa, especially within higher education.[55] Guggisberg's reforms were well received by the Commission, and they responded by saying that "[i]t should be our aim to maintain whatever is good in African custom, institution or thought. One inestimable good is the close relation in African thought between religion and the common things of life."[56]

It is significant to recall the earlier missionary views of the "evil pagan practices" in African culture and religion and to take note of this paradigmatic shift within just a few decades to viewing primal religion and Ghanaian culture as something positive and worthy of study. While the missionaries laboured to keep Ghanaian Christians separate from their culture, this new colonial administration recognized value in Ghanaian culture and religion, and implemented this vision within both secondary and university education.

53. Ibid., 49.
54. See ibid., 49–52.
55. Walls, "Geoffrey Parrinder," 209.
56. McWilliam, *The Development of Education in Ghana*, 112. McWilliam records in a footnote that the Committee's quote is taken from Sessional Paper No. IV of 1919–1920.

Achimota

When Guggisberg took up his post, the two strongest schools in the country were the Methodist and Anglican schools, Mfantsipim and Adisadel College, both situated in Cape Coast. With his proposed reforms he wanted to exceed all previous educational exploits, maintaining some of the positive aspects of mission schools—vernacular education and moral and religious training—while raising academic standards, maintaining a high value for African culture, and preparing the Gold Coast for democratic leadership. He brought these visions together in the formation of Achimota School through a unique Scottish-Ghanaian partnership co-led by the Rev. Alexander Fraser and Dr. James Emman Kwegyir Aggrey.

Alexander Fraser (1873–1962) had a successful career in mission education both in Uganda and Sri Lanka, and coincidentally had been instrumental in leading Guggisberg to Christian commitment at an earlier period.[57] Fraser was offered the principalship of this new school and accepted only on the condition that Aggrey would accompany him as Assistant Vice Principal of the school. Ghanaian scholar Philip Laryea contends that "Fraser's strong evangelical background prepared him to serve as a missionary educator " and that his approach to education was "radical," being marked both by high academic standards and the aim of culturally relevant curriculum based on Christian principles.[58] One of these Christian principles was that of racial equality, as shown through Fraser's insistence on only working in partnership with a Ghanaian.

James Aggrey (1875–1927), a Ghanaian and the third figure in the Guggisberg-Fraser-Aggrey triad, pursued doctoral studies at Columbia University in New York City and met Guggisberg and Fraser during subsequent visits to Ghana and England. At Fraser's insistence, Aggrey became the first Assistant Vice Principal of the school when it opened in 1927, forming a positive Euro-African partnership that set the bi-cultural tone for the school.

In addition to Fraser and Aggrey, Ephraim Amu is another Achimota figure whose considerable and unique contribution to the African study of African religions merits our attention. Amu (1899–1995) is an important example of a bridging figure between the differing mission and colonial approaches to education, Christianity, and African culture. Amu himself was a product of the Basel Mission, having studied in the Seminary and the Presbyterian Training College. He made a deep impact through his

---

57. Walls, "Alexander Gordon Fraser," para. 1.
58. Laryea, *Ephraim Amu*, 184.

teaching and preaching, and is especially known for the composition of many songs and musical arrangements in the Akan praise-song format. Amu was a great proponent of the use of vernacular languages, writing many of his songs and also sermons in Ewe (his mother tongue), Twi and Ga, and he was a great advocate for incorporating aspects of traditional culture into Christian worship.

While he was deeply appreciated by many, he was dismissed from the College under the pretext of having disobeyed ministerial dress regulations after delivering a sermon dressed in traditional cloth.[59] Immediately following his dismissal from the Presbyterian Church, however, Amu was invited by Fraser to take up a teaching post at Achimota in 1934. Amu's vision for promoting both Christianity and Ghanaian culture through traditional Akan praise-songs dovetailed perfectly with Achimota's mandate to include and promote indigenous culture. Amu subsequently lectured at the University of Ghana from 1962–1971 in the Institute of African Studies.[60]

As a theologian, poet, and musician, Amu honoured the positive contributions to translation and education by men like Fraser, Aggrey, Akrofi, and Christaller, writing songs celebrating them. In his song "*Adikanfo, Mo!*" ("Pioneers, Congratulations!"), Amu, whom Bediako calls a "Christian cultural patriot,"[61] commemorates their achievements and celebrates such men as pioneers "who laid the foundations for what would become Achimota School, one of the leading schools in Ghana."[62] The song hails them as "men of valour and pioneers of our struggle" who have "fought and won victory for us . . . fought the good fight . . . run the good race . . . held unto the faith . . . [and] wrought victory."[63]

Laryea remarks that "[i]n Amu's mind, all pioneers like Fraser are men of valour who fight to bring to fruition their cherished dreams, hopes and ambitions."[64] Notably, in Amu's case, it was British colonial officials—and not Christian missionaries—who recognized the importance of his contribution to Christianity and culture in Ghana. In Amu's experience, we see clear evidence of the legacy of mission efforts in promoting the use of in-

---

59. Ibid., 10–12, 19–26. Intriguingly, Laryea suggests that Amu's reason for choosing to continue wearing traditional cloth despite ecclesial warnings was not out of a sense of protest or defiance, but because he needed to wear the more comfortable traditional sandals due to a painful foot ailment, and they would not have been deemed appropriate with a European suit.

60. See ibid., 26–27.

61. Bediako, filmed interview by James Ault, 1998, DigiBeta Reel GB 109: 57.

62. Laryea, *Ephraim Amu*, 182.

63. Ibid.

64. Ibid., 183.

digenous languages on the one hand, and the positive colonial approaches to the study of African culture and religion on the other. And, through his songs, we see the fruits of both.[65]

As an institution, Achimota was an innovative feather in the cap of Guggisberg's colonial administration, improving upon the educational and cultural legacies inherited from the Missions. Ultimately, Achimota bequeathed a strong legacy of its own to the future of education in Ghana: the Kwame Nkrumah University of Science and Technology developed out of its Engineering School, and the University College of the Gold Coast (now the University of Ghana) from Achimota College. Achimota's unique position may be summarized as having been "publicly funded, but independent of government, with a council involving the African community; it was marked by high academic standards, broad curriculum, public service, cultural relevance, and Christian ethos, and aimed toward ultimate university standards and status."[66]

University College of the Gold Coast

From Guggisberg's bold goal of establishing a university, it was approximately fifteen years before this aspiration came to fruition. As Walls has argued, "It is not necessary to narrate the somewhat tortuous story of the Commission's recommendations and their implementation, together with those of the parallel Asquith commission, with a brief covering the whole colonial empire." What is important to note is that the eventual outcome in 1948 was the founding of two new university colleges in West Africa: one at Legon, in the Gold Coast, and the other at Ibadan in Nigeria.[67]

It is significant to highlight that as decisions were being made regarding the establishment of these universities, one critical reason for the development of a separate University College in the Gold Coast was that it was financially viable, in part through the Basel Mission's successful establishment of the cocoa industry.[68] While the missionaries introduced the

---

65. For further discussion of Amu, see also Agyemang, *Amu the African*.

66. Walls, "Alexander Gordon Fraser," para. 1.

67. See Walls, "Geoffrey Parrinder," 209

68. Bourret, *Ghana*, 215. Bourret provides details of the exact figures provided for the establishment of the University College, shared between the Government, Cocoa Board, and Colonial Welfare Fund. In discussions on missionary and colonial involvement in Ghana, these unexpected connections are important to note: not only did this financial stability lead to the successful establishment of the University, but in turn also contributed to Ghana being the first West African country to achieve political independence.

crop, "its success story was mainly authored by the Ghanaian . . . cocoa farmer who quickly emerged as a wealthy entrepreneurial elite. Cocoa supported Achimota and explained the achievements of Governor Guggisberg. It accounted for the establishment of the first university, the University of Ghana."[69] It is interesting to observe this link between the Mission's pietistic value for labour and economic independence and the lasting and unexpected benefits this had for Ghana, for education, and later, for the African study of religions in a variety of tertiary institutions.

These universities were modelled after British institutions, with teaching staff recruited predominantly from British universities.[70] Their academic standards were equal to those of London University, with which they were initially linked.[71] From the start, it was of paramount importance as a new African institution that the new University College of the Gold Coast gain international recognition through setting and maintaining the highest standards.[72] Because of Ghana's elite schools, together with "an education policy recognized as unusual among the colonies," this University College was quickly viewed as the Oxbridge in Africa.[73]

In this post-World-War II period, the university's focus was on producing appropriately trained Africans to meet the needs of these developing nations; i.e., technicians, engineers, doctors, lawyers, and administrators. However, this was a shortsighted approach, as it could only satisfy temporary needs and did not adequately address the needs of African society. To this end, Busia makes the following argument: "The present institutions of higher education have been largely influenced by European institutions, and syllabuses [sic] and courses are closely related to those of chosen European models. On the one hand, the desire to develop and maintain good standards justifies close conformity to the curricula of well-established universities such as Paris or London. On the other hand, in certain cases, profound modifications require to be made [sic] in order to meet the special needs of African society."[74]

One area where this was especially apparent was in the study of religions. In the United Kingdom during this period, the Oxbridge and Redbrick approaches to studying Christianity were the two that most strongly

---

69. Quist, "Secondary Education and Nation-Building," 76.

70. Bourret, *Ghana*, 215.

71. For further discussion see Nicol, Introduction to *The West African Intellectual Community*, 1, 3.

72. See McWilliam, *The Development of Education in Ghana*, 78.

73. Walls "Geoffrey Parrinder," 210.

74. Busia, "The Functions of West African Universities," 79.

impacted the development of theological study in West Africa. In brief, the Oxbridge model followed Anglican theological patterns, which emphasized study of the Scriptures, Church history, and doctrines of the creeds. Free churchmen in the newer Redbrick universities instead focused more on Biblical languages, history and literature; philosophy; and Church history and comparative religion. Important to remember here too is that this is during the same period in which Parrinder first included African Traditional Religion in the syllabus alongside of Old and New Testament studies in the Department of Religious Studies at Ibadan.[75]

Ghana's University College, as the "Oxbridge of West Africa," therefore first established a Department of Divinity. This Department dealt with subjects such as Church history, biblical study, and issues of Christian doctrine. However, Busia was correct in stating that "profound modifications" were needed to meet the needs of Ghanaian society; developments that contributed to the emerging African study of African religions. As we have seen, Parrinder's successful efforts in bringing African Traditional Religion into the academy alongside of Christian history and doctrine represent exactly the type of changes that were needed to make the study of African religions increasingly relevant in an African context.

Missionaries and Colonialists: Motivations

Clearly, missions and colonial officials approached Christianity and the provision of education in different ways and with quite different goals. While there is the well-worn argument that missionaries were nothing more than colonialists in Christian garb, Sanneh challenges this view. He contends that this position, while commonly held and widely propagated in both scholarly and popular arenas, does not accurately reflect the complexity of the situation. In his view, this flawed perspective unhelpfully portrays missions as "essentially the religious version of Western political and economic imperialism, offering Africans a pious formula of otherworldly distraction while foreign conquest proceeded unchallenged."[76]

The problem with this, Sanneh argues, is that it is inaccurate to see missionaries solely as "perennial historical villains" or, conversely, to continually perceive Africans "as a victimized projection of Western ill will ... because both perspectives, ironically, keep Western missionaries as the central focus."[77] Intrinsic to such views is the perspective that Church and Acad-

---

75. See Walls, "Geoffrey Parrinder," 210–11.
76. Sanneh, "The Yogi and the Commissar," 2.
77. Ibid., 2. It is worth further noting that in this same article, Sanneh acknowledges

emy were the main vehicles for the West's exploitation of Africa. According to this argument, "[t]hrough educated converts . . . the West came within striking range of societies stripped of their ability to resist. Consequently, the missionary and the colonialist were the yogi and the commissar who complemented each other: the one supplied pacified natives for the other's aggressive strategy."[78]

A counter-argument to this view is offered by South African theologian T.S Maluleke, who critiques both Sanneh and Bediako for an overly positive assessment of the missionaries. Firstly, he argues, the relationship between African theologians and intellectuals, on the one hand, and missionaries and colonialists on the other, is not one that has necessarily preoccupied Africans, who have been more concerned to make the church indigenous.[79]

But secondly, and more seriously, Maluleke charges that Sanneh's position overlooks or even upholds the oppressive and harmful aspects of Western Christian engagement and reduces the whole effort to "vernacularization," as a positive outcome separate from the whole enterprise. In his words, "In like manner we are being told that despite the shortcomings of the missionaries, despite their racism, their ethnocentrism, despite the genocide of the imperialists, the rape of people and environment, despite all these ambiguities and temporary lapses as they are now called, '. . . the gospel was still proclaimed.' . . . And Africans are supposed to say amen to such proclamation and such a gospel?"[80] If Sanneh's approach is at times overly optimistic, Maluleke's is equally pessimistic.

In contrast to these "villains" and "victims" stereotypes, Miller offers a helpful picture of the carefully balanced position that the Basel Mission negotiated within the local colonial framework. He notes the high value placed on identity and autonomy by the Mission: "Lest it lose its identity and autonomy, themselves values of considerable religious importance for Pietists, the Mission could not allow itself to become too dependent or permit its program to be reduced to an adjunct of colonial political and commercial interest. Reflecting this delicate balance, it at times relied on colonial authorities to protect and advance its interests, and at other times found itself in open opposition to those authorities. Most of the

---

that we must "admit missionaries committed many sins of omission and commission, and that their presence initiated wide-ranging changes in the societies affected. However, saying that leaves us still considerably short of the full range of the impact of missions" (2).

78. Ibid.
79. Maluleke, "Black and African Theologies," 7.
80. Ibid., 9.

time, however, it worked in the middle region between those extremes of dependency and opposition."[81]

While the Basel missionaries did at times argue against what they perceived as exploitative colonialism, they more often held a high view of the colonial government, describing officials as "bringers of peace and as creators of the opportunity for groups like us to build up Christian social work in security."[82] Colonial officials, like missionaries, had varying motivations attached to their provision of education. In the late-eighteenth century, the colonial administration was more concerned with producing a skilled indigenous workforce to serve within the administration and to function as helpful intermediaries between local chiefs and government officials.[83] Over time, however, these motivations also shifted.

We have observed the tensions between the Christians (foreign missionaries and Ghanaians) and the chiefs. There were similarly some early tensions between this growing class of "educated elites" and the chiefs, as the British administration sought to engage and control both groups. However, fundamentally "there was never any real antagonism between the two groups, for they both belonged to the same upper class, and both were interested in winning from the British the right to eventual autonomy."[84]

Guggisberg clearly took a different approach from many colonialists in seeking to equip Ghanaians, not for colonial service, but for leadership and independence. From his lament over the loss to educational institutions with the expulsion of the German Basel missionaries, it is clear he respected the Mission's work, though his own vision differed significantly from theirs. What is particularly noteworthy in Guggisberg's approach is that he advocated for the importance of studying and maintaining indigenous religious and cultural practices when the missionaries did not. They were preoccupied with fostering a "Christian" over a "cultural" identity, little realizing that the former required the latter to authentically take root.

While the contribution of Christian missions to translation was essential, the missionaries were near-sighted in their approach; Guggisberg, in comparison, was far-sighted. He grasped the necessity of reclaiming Ghanaian history and culture, and of promoting an African identity in order to equip young men and women to be successful citizens and capable leaders. While missionaries came seeking souls, this colonial leader envisioned citizens.

81. Miller, *Missionary Zeal*, 19.
82. Ibid., 15.
83. See Kimble, *A Political History of Ghana*, 53–55.
84. Bourret, *Ghana*, 54. Also, see Kimble, *A Political History of Ghana*, 57–58.

Though their motivations differed, both the mission and colonial education systems played a pivotal role in planting the intellectual seeds of the nationalist movement and the emerging scholarly study of African religions. The Christian missionaries came with clear evangelistic intentions and used translation, education, and industry to establish Christianity and distinct Christian communities. However, their approach to Ghanaian culture was often divisive and at times destructive.

The establishment of boarding schools, and the emphasis on keeping schoolchildren separate from the "negative influences" of the community, meant that "the traditional forms of training for citizenship . . . were regarded as 'bulwarks of Satan,' and schoolchildren were trained to be citizens of minority Christian communities rather than of the community as a whole."[85] This latter task was instead taken up by the colonial government. Nevertheless, the Mission's early translation efforts made a positive and profound impact on the emerging African study of religions as it put the Twi Bible into the hands of Ghanaians almost from the start of the Mission's work, the significance of which cannot be overemphasized.

With regard to British colonial involvement in Ghana, there were some important and unexpected positive outcomes through the efforts of visionary leaders who championed the importance of African culture and the need to prepare Ghanaians for leadership. Guggisberg took education to a new level in promoting the importance of a Ghanaian cultural identity through bringing African history and culture into secondary school curriculum. This equipped students to successfully engage with both their Ghanaian culture and British-style educational systems. To this end, the establishment of Achimota School was not only a success as a secondary school but also provided the basis for the future University of Ghana.

The unique partnership between Guggisberg, Fraser, and Aggrey was a powerful example of a positive Euro-African relationship, and was critical in setting the tone for future educational development in Ghana. Furthermore, it served as a noteworthy example of the place, firstly, of Christian faith in education, and secondly, the combination of Christian faith and scholarship in setting the pace for race relations, political independence, and the study of African languages, culture, and religions. Throughout this pre-independence period there were competing and conflicting missionary and colonial intentions. There were also emerging challenges between the educated Ghanaians and traditional leaders when the latter perceived a loss of power and control, though ultimately both were united in their desire for independence.

---

85. McWilliam, *The Development of Education in Ghana*, 25.

As we turn our attention towards nationalism and independence, Pobee and Kimble remind us that traditional African society was communalistic, leaving the individual unable to (in good faith) make decisions independent from, or in opposition to, the rest of the community. However, as Christian teaching upheld "the biblical idea of the worth and dignity of the individual in the sight of God," the provision of Christian education began a process of questioning that ultimately undermined the colonial system itself.[86]

In Kimble's words, "the preaching of the moral autonomy of the person, of his right—and duty—to act according to his Christian conscience, was one of the factors that led to the questioning of the authority of the Chief under the old order. It was only a matter of time before this in turn led to a questioning of European authority and of its moral basis."[87]

Elaborating on this point, Bediako opines, "the expansion of the intellectual horizons of Africans, eased by Christianity, enhanced a new African self-understanding and self-appreciation beyond the immediate traditional circles of kinship . . . and so paved the way for the modern expressions of African nationalism which finally challenged and overturned Western rule."[88] Indeed, the dragon's teeth of education had been sown.

---

86. Pobee, "Bible and Human Translation," 8.
87. Kimble, *A Political History of Ghana*, 166.
88. Bediako, *Christianity in Africa*, 234.

Chapter 4

Seeking First the Political Kingdom
Politics and the Study of Religion in Ghana

*The revolt of Black Africa as a sudden and improvised event?
No; for more than thirty years black writers were prophesying
this. But the West did not want to hear anything!*[1]

—Lilyan Kesteloot

---

1. Kesteloot, *Négritude et situation colonial*, 6. Adinkra symbol *Funtunfunefu denkyemfunefu*, or "Siamese Crocodiles." The Siamese crocodiles share one stomach, yet they fight over food. This symbol is a reminder that infighting and tribalism are harmful to all who engage in it.

Independence and the Study of Religion in Ghana

THE BIRTH OF GHANA in 1957 under the leadership of Kwame Nkrumah as the first politically independent African nation appeared to transpire quickly. However, the roots of independence extended back several decades, touching on the missionary and colonial history that we have just seen. As Négritude scholar Lilyan Kesteloot sharply reminds us in her quotation above, this was no sudden development. In fact, Ghanaian historian A. Adu Boahen argues that it was actually colonialism, as opposed to African independence, which emerged suddenly: "The most surprising aspects of the imposition of colonialism on Africa were its suddenness and its unpredictability."[2]

In the following chapter, we will turn our attention more fully to the role of Négritude literature and philosophy as an anti-colonial force. However, for now we should simply keep in mind that while these mission and colonial endeavours were at play in the early decades of the twentieth century, Négritude writers in diaspora from the 1930s onwards were already prophesying independence and leading the way through literary engagement with African religions and culture.

The remainder of this chapter is concerned with the following developments in Ghana. Even as missions and colonial efforts helped to pave the way for political independence through education and economic endeavours, so too did that context shape the religious outlook of nationalistic politicians, and, indeed, Bediako. Within the emerging African study of African religions in this early post-independence period, the following three developments were occurring almost simultaneously.

Firstly, Kwame Nkrumah sacralized the office of president while secularizing the academic study of religions in Ghana. Ebenezer Addo describes him as a "phenomenon"; and, pertinent to our focus here, argues that any assessment of his political career must include an examination of "his ability to use existing socio-cultural forms, particularly religion, for political ends."[3]

Secondly, during this same time, opposition leader Kofi Abrefa Busia manifested the fruits of the "old guard" of British missions and education through extensive sociological research on Akan religion and leadership, culminating in his work on Akan chieftaincy. We will consider him here as a foil to Nkrumah and another interesting African scholar of African

---

2. Boahen, *African Perspectives on Colonialism*, 1.
3. Addo, *Kwame Nkrumah*, 1.

religions. And thirdly, the Christian Council of Ghana (C.C.G.) worked to maintain a strong Christian identity in the midst of competing interests. Here we will specifically assess the conflict over the pouring of libation in Ghana's handing-over ceremony as a key example of the questions of identity and conflict between Christianity and indigenous religion as well as between Church and State.

In sum, in the emerging African approaches to African religions in this period, we might say that Nkrumah *acts* it out; Busia *writes* it out; and the C.C.G. *fights* it out. This, we should remember, is Bediako's context as a young student.

Kofi Abrefa Busia: The Position of the Chief in Ashanti Society

Bediako argues that African religions provide important insight into African politics, and specifically that African Christianity has a role to play in shaping new political models and ideals.[4] He elucidates his argument in the following words, which I quote in full:

> Issues affecting church and state tend to be seen as relating essentially to the church and the political institutions that have come into place following decolonization. Such an approach ignores the fact that in many parts of Africa, the church had a previous history of relating to the pre-colonial traditional state. Furthermore, in contemporary independent Africa, the coming of central government has not totally eclipsed the traditional state, and there are many Africans who are thoroughly 'modern' in the sense of being at home with the new centralized organization who also maintain a significant degree of loyalty to traditional rule associated with kinship and its attendant obligations.[5]

As we have already seen, there was a degree of discord between the early missionaries and the Akan chiefs, with conflict rooted in the perceived undermining of the chief's authority, and particularly his religious authority. On these points, Busia is "always a sure guide into the character of African indigenous political systems."[6] As a Ghanaian statesman, committed Methodist, and outstanding scholar, Busia represents a more conservative, academic approach to both Christianity and Akan religion. He engages most effectively as a sociologist, and remains a valuable source

---

4. Bediako, *Christianity in Africa*, 180.
5. Ibid., 180–81.
6. Ibid., 239.

on Ghanaian history, culture, religion, and politics, reminding us again of the diverse approaches to African religions operating within this same complex period.[7]

Busia's published doctoral research, *The Position of the Chief in the Modern Political System of Ashanti,* remains a seminal reference in the study of Ghanaian traditional political institutions and is also a critical source for understanding the sacralization of politics. It is therefore an important starting point for further discussion on politics and religion in Ghana. As Busia delineates, Ashanti chieftaincy is a sacralised office with chiefs holding both religious and political power in the community. Therefore, any religious changes not instituted by the chief constitute a possible threat to his position.

In Akan culture, the chief traditionally functions as the successor to the ancestors, performing various rites for the welfare of his people in capacities that may be described as administrative, executive, judicial, and military.[8] The chief is also regarded as an intermediary between the community and the ancestors, a role that is key to community stability.[9] The chief's connection to the ancestors enhances his authority, such that traditionally, he "was respected as the one who linked not only with political institutions but with all social institutions."[10] Taken as a whole, traditional chieftaincy may be seen as the central religious symbol in Ghanaian culture.[11]

Accordingly, ritual functions of the chief are connected with ceremonies in which the community expresses reverence for the ancestors and the gods, acknowledging their dependence on them. This in turn promotes solidarity and a sense of continuity within the community. As we shall see, the pouring of libation is an example of this category of ceremony and was a symbol invoked by Nkrumah to demonstrate his link with the ancestors as well as to communicate his claim to religious as well as political authority.

Busia summarizes the religious aspects of traditional chieftaincy in the following way: "Chiefship [sic] in Ashanti is a sacred office. This has been shown by the rites of the chief's enstoolment and by his part in ceremonies . . . From the moment that the chief is enstooled, his person becomes sacred. This is emphasized by taboos . . . All these taboos remind the chief and everybody else that he occupies a sacred position. He is the

---

7. Ibid.
8. Busia, *The Position of the Chief,* 36.
9. See ibid., 102.
10. Busia, *Africa in Search of Democracy,* 9.
11. Addo, *Kwame Nkrumah,* 39.

occupant to the stool of the ancestors ... For this reason, he is treated with the greatest veneration."[12]

Busia's voice carries particular weight in this field, as one who had a unique perspective standing between Ashanti and British governmental systems and as a member of a royal family himself. His work is significant to consider within Ghana's independence process, as leaders sought to construct a coherent national identity and often looked to the past for guidance. For issues such as nation building, modernization, African unity, democracy, and race relations, Busia argues, "[w]e cannot fully appreciate the import of these issues, or understand how they appear to Africans without reference to their past, in an effort to appreciate the sentiments and mental dispositions with which [Africans] approach their own problems."[13]

With specific reference to Ghana's past, we must further consider the foundational role of religion. Indeed, any who consider religion to be "irrelevant" or "out of place" in modern political discourse lack "a proper appraisal of the problems of Africa as Africans see them."[14] Busia further argues that behind Ghana's search for new political and social institutions, together with efforts at modernization, "lie[s] an interpretation of the universe which is intensely and pervasively religious. It influences the decisions and choices Africa is making."[15]

Applying this to twentieth-century Ghanaian politics, the argument can clearly be made that this perspective on traditional leadership may be seen to account for "the persistence of the ritual ceremonies in the face of revolutionary changes in the political system. The chief's position is bound up with strong religious sentiments."[16] This is made exceptionally clear in the political career of Nkrumah and in the history of Ghana's independence. As such, it has ongoing implications for scholarship on Bediako and the African study of African religions.

---

12. Busia, *The Position of the Chief*, 26, 36. For further discussion on the significance of the Golden Stool, and the "enstoolment" of chiefs, see Addo, *Kwame Nkrumah*, 36–39.

13. Busia, *Africa in Search of Democracy*, 1.

14. Ibid.

15. Ibid., 16.

16. Busia, *The Position of the Chief*, 39. For further discussion on the relationship between government officials and chiefs under British colonial rule, Busia is a rich resource.

Kwame Nkrumah: The Non-Denominational Christian and Marxist Socialist

In 1957, Nkrumah declared, "To-day I am a non-denominational Christian and a Marxist socialist and I have not found any contradiction between the two."[17] In any study on twentieth-century Ghana, the figure of Kwame Nkrumah looms large, whether he is regarded as valiant leader or paranoid despot. While it is more common to examine him within a political framework, he is also a significant figure within this exploration of the emerging African study of African religions.

Nkrumah himself was a particularly creative, if ambiguous, student and practitioner of African religions, whose interpretation and use of both Akan primal religion and Christianity is truly fascinating. Beyond this, however, is the question of his lasting impact on this field of study, and particularly his impact on Bediako as an African scholar of religions.

Nkrumah was particularly adept at impression management, borrowing liberally from whatever religious tradition suited his purposes. As Addo notes, "[Nkrumah] made no commitment to any particular religion and thus was able to control how religion operated in his life and career."[18] Fittingly, he is referred to as a "political entrepreneur" who was able to skilfully manipulate the culturally shared symbols of Christianity and primal religion, alongside of Marxism and socialism, in ways that created cohesion for his own political platform and proved an important medium for communicating with his followers.[19]

He did this in a variety of ways, including casting himself as a Christlike figure—the suffering servant of Ghanaian independence—while simultaneously appropriating titles and the outward vestiges associated with traditional chieftaincy and traditional priesthood. These were clearly strategic moves for a man trying to establish a unified, post-colonial, national identity and demonstrate his keen apprehension of the sacral role of chief.

Nkrumah's Religious Foundations

Nkrumah's description of his own religious outlook is ambiguous and fluid. His autobiography provides rich insight into his religious outlook and demonstrates his ambivalent and shifting views on Christianity, indigenous religious practices, and his own personal blend of spirituality. When we recall

---

17. Nkrumah, *Autobiography*, 11–12.
18. Addo, *Kwame Nkrumah*, 3.
19. Ibid., 17.

the ethos of the period with Governor Guggisberg in power and Fraser and Aggrey emphasizing a bi-cultural educational experience, including the best of British academics alongside of African history and culture at Achimota, it is not surprising to see these tensions at play in Nkrumah's life: he was experiencing them first-hand.[20]

Here Nkrumah describes how he began to distance himself from his Catholic faith, once an important part of his life and education: "As I grew older . . . the strict discipline of Roman Catholicism stifled me. It was not that I became any less religious but rather that I sought freedom in the worship of and communion with my God, for my God is a very personal God and can only be reached direct [sic]. I do not find the need of, in fact I resent the intervention of, a third party in such a personal matter."[21]

However, in 1930 he surprisingly took up a position at a newly established Roman Catholic Seminary, calling it "an honour to be the first teacher of the Gold Coast appointed to train these young men in their preliminary studies for this great vocation."[22] Notably, Nkrumah reflects that during this period he regained his previous religious fervour to the extent that he seriously, albeit briefly, considered entering the priesthood himself.[23] To say that Nkrumah's religious inclinations were changeable is an understatement. Ultimately, however, the priestly vocation was not for him: in 1935, he had the opportunity to pursue further studies in the U.S.A.; at this point, he left both the seminary and Catholicism.

This was an academically intense period for Nkrumah. He completed a Bachelor of Arts (1939) in Economics and Sociology from Lincoln University in Pennsylvania and was then offered a lecturing position in their Theology department. While it was not his first choice, he writes that financial need and visa requirements compelled him to accept the offer. While lecturing there, he completed a Bachelor of Sacred Theology (1942) and simultaneously, a Master of Science in Education (1942) and a Master of Arts in Philosophy (1943) at the University of Pennsylvania.[24]

---

20. For further discussion on significant influences on Nkrumah's thinking, Rooney writes that C. L. R. James "encouraged Nkrumah in the study of political organization" but that Marcus Garvey was "the most important influence of all" (Rooney, *Kwame Nkrumah*, 16). Nkrumah confirms this in his autobiography and adds, "Hegel, Karl Marx, Engels, Lenin and Mazzini . . . did much to influence me in my revolutionary ideas and activities" (Nkrumah, *Autobiography*, 45).

21. Nkrumah, *Autobiography*, 18.

22. Ibid., 21.

23. Ibid.

24. Ibid., 40.

It is difficult to get a concrete sense of Nkrumah's religious beliefs during this American period, as he depicts his experience in convoluted and contradictory terms. For example, he credits "[p]overty and need . . . [and the] want of something better to do" with his participation in "various Negro religious gatherings and revivalist meetings." He concedes that, in addition to a pleasant evening's entertainment, a significant draw for him was the provision of free meals, a welcome support in the midst of his dire financial circumstances.[25] However, he also spent a significant amount of time preaching at these churches and remarks, "I really enjoyed doing it. I had made many friends, for the Negro churches play the part of community centres more than most places of worship."[26]

Nkrumah's engagement with indigenous religion is similarly ambiguous. Alongside of the above accounts of his church involvement, he reveals his perceived tension between indigenous religious views, African culture, and his personal outlook in the following dream that he had during this period. His description and inconclusive interpretation of the dream reveal his own uncertainty: "A big black umbrella seemed to be descending upon me like a huge tent until it completely smothered me . . . during which time I was fighting for breath. Then it lifted and I woke up lying staring as it seemed to disappear into the distance. According to the African, such a dream would be interpreted as a narrow escape from death or extreme danger."[27] Is he including himself within this "African interpretation," or distancing himself from it? His elusive meaning further reinforces his ambivalent relationship with religion and the link between African religions and identity.

Nkrumah's participation with African American churches and his ambiguous discussion of this dream represent a recurring theme throughout his career: correctly identifying the power and social currency inherent in Christianity and African indigenous religions and using them strategically, while keeping them at arms' length.

Nkrumah as "Saviour"

The following decade (1947–1957) was politically complex and very full. We will not engage with all of its political intricacies except to note that Ghana's independence in 1957 has been described as "the most untroubled and completely successful moment in the brilliant, dramatic and tragic life of Kwame

---

25. Ibid.
26. Ibid., 41.
27. Ibid., 121.

Nkrumah."[28] Instead, we will focus on how Nkrumah used Christian and primal religious symbols and messages to begin establishing himself as a leader with politically, culturally, and spiritually legitimate claims to such a position. This is important because it signals ways in which Christianity and African indigenous religions were being overtly used and interpreted in the context of Ghanaian identity-formation in the mid-twentieth century.

Nkrumah's brilliant apprehension of the sacralization of traditional leadership and his implementation of this role cannot be underestimated. To gain the trust of Ghanaians, he needed to operate in familiar ways, demonstrating his insider perspective and trustworthiness. In a pluralistic context, he had the challenge of solidifying his identity as a man of the people; and to achieve his purposes, he selected key religious symbols and practices from both indigenous religion and Christianity in order to create a new Ghanaian identity.

He appropriated the familiar role of chief as leader and unifying figure within the community, while attempting to transition into a new form of independent democratic leadership. He began by appropriating all of the "rites, pomp, ceremony, and splendor" pursuant to traditional chieftaincy, including having himself enstooled as a chief in 1962, though his connection to the royal family was tenuous at best. With the founding of the Convention People's Party (C.P.P.) Nkrumah astutely demonstrated his solidarity with Ghanaian culture in choosing colours and symbols for the C.P.P. flag that had religio-cultural meanings connected with traditional rituals and proverbs, which would immediately conjure up symbols of victory, danger, sacrifice, and fecundity in the minds of Ghanaians.[29]

Furthermore, and significant for projecting the image of traditional ruler, the issue of outward appearance and physical perfection had to be addressed. Traditionally, any form of physical imperfection was deemed taboo for a chief. Therefore, Nkrumah went so far as to replace his glasses with contact lenses, and had dental work done to improve his teeth.[30]

A very clear example of Nkrumah jointly appropriating the identity of a traditional leader and a Christ-like figure is found in his adoption of the title *Osagyefo*, by which he was commonly known. In Twi this translates as *saviour* or *redeemer* and is a title used for a chief, underscoring the chief's sacralized nature. With this title, Nkrumah was being publicly confirmed as a "chief" and worthy leader.

---

28. Rooney, *Kwame Nkrumah*, 6.
29. Addo, *Kwame Nkrumah*, 106.
30. Ibid., 107–8.

Bediako does not miss the significance of Nkrumah's actions here, and upholds Busia's explanation of the sacral role of the chief when he contends that Nkrumah "must have known what he was doing, for [he] was not royal, nor was he concerned to promote the interest of traditional rulers. In the religious cosmology that undergirds the traditional social organization, the traditional ruler was regarded as the channel through whom cosmic forces operate for the well-being of the community while his power was derived from his position as 'one who sits on the stool (throne) of the ancestors.'"[31]

However, there is further meaning to this title: *Osagyefo* is also the Twi word used to translate the Christian terms "saviour" and "redeemer" as applied to Christ in the Bible. When this title was bestowed upon Nkrumah, the roles of chief and messiah were merged into one; he could lay claim to no higher source of legitimacy for his authority. While there were historically "divine" characteristics attributed to the chief, these additional Christian nuances reflected Ghana's religiously plural environment and highlighted the ambiguity and overlap between politics and Ghana's religious traditions.[32] Whether in his name or appearance, it may rightly be argued that "authority and legitimacy issues were crucial for Nkrumah's quest for national integration. To achieve these he strategically sought to politicize primordial sentiments and particularly those enshrined in the institution of chieftaincy."[33]

Beyond identifying himself as chief, Nkrumah also took on external elements of traditional priesthood, further rooting himself in the Ghanaian psyche as one endowed not only with training and skills, but with supernatural power, and, critically, a divine right to rule. To this end, "[h]is hairstyle, coupled with his use of a white handkerchief, walking stick and occasionally a swish or horsetail, recalled traditional priesthood, *akomfo* in the minds of his followers."[34] Indeed, there are suggestions that even his name-change from Kofi (Friday-born) to Kwame (Saturday-born) had possible religious implications.[35] Nkrumah endeavoured to appeal to Ghanaian religious sensibilities on every possible front.

However, as an astute "political entrepreneur," Nkrumah also demonstrated his knowledge of Christianity and his awareness of the emerging Ghanaian Christian identity, though he raised eyebrows and ruffled feathers along the way. One way in which he particularly caused offense was through

---

31. Bediako, *Christianity in Africa*, 181.
32. See Addo, *Kwame Nkrumah*, 113–14, and Pobee, *Kwame Nkrumah*, 142–43.
33. Addo, *Kwame Nkrumah*, 111.
34. Ibid., 108.
35. Ibid., 51.

appropriating and parodying biblical passages, hymns, and Christian creeds to market the goals of his political party.[36]

Arguably the most famous and perhaps most controversial example is Nkrumah's adaptation of Matthew 6:33. In the King James translation, this biblical passage reads, "Seek ye first the kingdom of God, and His righteousness; and all these things shall be added unto you." In 1958, Nkrumah had a twenty-foot statue of himself erected in front of Parliament House bearing the inscription, "Seek ye first the political kingdom and all other things shall be added unto you." Pobee describes this as "part of Nkrumah's campaign of personality cult, to make Ghanaians realize that they were independent."[37]

He similarly adapted the Apostle's Creed and the Lord's Prayer for use as C.P.P slogans. The former became known as the "Verandah Boys' Creed," a subversion of the derogatory term used to describe the semi-literate and frequently unemployed youth who supported the party. They opened their creed with these words: "I believe in the Convention People's Party. / The Opportune Saviour of Ghana, / And in Kwame Nkrumah its founder and leader, / Who is endowed with the Ghana Spirit / Born a true Ghanaian for Ghana . . ."[38] With similar nationalistic fervour, the modified Lord's Prayer begins with the lines, "O Imperialism which are in Gold Coast, his grace is they name; / They Kingdom go / Our will be done in Gold Coast / As it is done to you in Britain."[39]

A further offense to the Christian community in Ghana was Nkrumah's use of the title *Asomdwehene*: literally, "prince of peace." While *Osagyefo* was a chiefly and more popularly used title, this, without a doubt, cast Nkrumah as a messianic figure, such that "[t]he ordinary Ghanaian would upon hearing it recall Messiah Jesus of the Bible."[40] This complex interplay of Christian and indigenous symbolism represents a significant aspect of Nkrumah's early success, controversial though these actions were. Such tactics show him to be not just an astute politician, but also an important Ghanaian scholar of African religions; a further reminder of the diversity of contributors to this emerging discourse.

---

36. Ibid., 40, 101–4.
37. Pobee, *Kwame Nkrumah*, 118.
38. Addo, *Kwame Nkrumah*, 102.
39. Ibid.
40. Pobee, *Kwame Nkrumah*, 143.

Nkrumah's Impact on the Academic Study of Religions

Nkrumah is also an important figure for our discussion because of the lasting changes that he effected within the academic study of African religions. This is most evident in changes he made to the Department of Divinity at Legon. The Department was first established in 1948 and, as we have previously seen, was designed according to the Oxbridge model. However, while the University Colleges were originally patterned after British universities, "[i]t was always recognized that they would develop as independent universities, and that their programmes would need to take account of West African interests and phenomena."[41] This was especially true within the field of religious studies.

Where Protestant Christianity was once the assumed religious norm and "Oxbridge theology" the standard theological model, Nkrumah saw the need to make changes to accommodate the religiously plural reality of independent Ghana. He was eager to portray the Ghanaian identity as distinct from its British colonial heritage, and was likewise concerned to avoid Christian denominational divisions that had the potential to rise up within the Divinity Department and pose a threat to his national unification efforts.[42]

Under Nkrumah's direction and with Ghanaian theologian C.G. Baëta appointed as the new Head, Legon's Department of Divinity was transformed into the Department for the Study of Religions. Baëta, a Protestant Christian, taught in the Department of Divinity from 1949–1961 before becoming the head of the new Department in 1962. His work *Prophetism in Ghana: A Study of Some "Spiritual" Churches* (London: SCM Press, 1962) is an important example of an early reflection of an African scholar on religion in Ghana. Baëta's appointment was in part so that the Department would reflect the secularity of the State, and also so that it could have a more meaningful existence in its pluralistic African context.[43]

This new Department aimed to introduce students to "the scientific and comprehensive study of religions." This included Christian theology, but also introduced serious engagement with African indigenous religions as well as other World Religions.[44] As Nkrumah and Baëta discussed the future of this new Department, Nkrumah shared the following thoughts and instructions with the new Head: "You know I do not want to interfere with the teaching of Theology or Christianity or anything, but you know this is a secular univer-

---

41. Walls, "Geoffrey Parrinder," 209.
42. See Pobee, *Kwame Nkrumah*, 62–63.
43. Ibid., 63.
44. Pobee, "Christian Goncalves Kwami Baëta," 3.

sity . . . If you are going to do this thing, then you are going to have to teach African Religion seriously and you are going to undertake also a scientific study and research into religions as a religious phenomenon."[45]

This was reflective of Nkrumah's desire to elevate the African identity (including indigenous religion) and also to curtail the influence of Christianity, perceived by some, and perhaps by him, as a continuing area of colonial control. This move also demonstrates Nkrumah's understanding of the power of religion. He had used Akan religion and Christianity very successfully to secure a position of power, and perhaps recognized the possibility of losing his authority if religion was left unchecked. In essence, he skilfully sacralised his position in an effort to secure power, and simultaneously secularised the study of religion. Furthermore, he diffused religious authority at an academic level in order to reflect the religiously plural nature of Ghanaian society as well as to minimize threats to his position from any one particular religious corner.

Overall, Nkrumah was adept and highly insightful in his intuitive use of religious idiom, appropriating powerful religious symbols and language to solidify his authority as politically, religiously, and traditionally legitimate. A religious mercenary, he successfully took on the roles of traditional priest, chief, and Christ-like messiah interchangeably. This initially secured his place in the minds of all Ghanaians as a trustworthy, competent leader with a divine right to rule, and one who had their best interests at heart.

However, Nkrumah's political career ended very differently than it began. After achieving independence for Ghana, his presidency was fraught with increasing chaos and violence (or threats thereof), coupled with limits on freedom of speech, and intolerance for any perceived opposition. After being hailed as Ghana's saviour, Nkrumah became increasingly unstable and tyrannical and was ultimately overthrown by a military coup in 1966.

The following quotation demonstrates the radical shift in Ghanaians' perception of Nkrumah, all the more drastic when we recall that it was only a decade earlier that he was joyfully hailed as *Osagyefo*: "Evidence from every possible source shows that in Accra and throughout Ghana news of the coup brought universal rejoicing. The newspapers—themselves suddenly free—came out with the headline 'Freedom at Last.' They showed pictures of excited crowds with tears of joy running down their cheeks, welcoming the first of over a thousand detainees to be released."[46]

In evaluating Nkrumah's tenure, we are left with two contradictory images: there is simultaneously the *Osagyefo*—brave leader, liberator, and

---

45. Pobee, *Kwame Nkrumah*, 63.
46. Rooney, *Kwame Nkrumah*, 254.

redeemer—whose reign was sadly synonymous with "oppression, suppression, frustration, tyranny, chicanery, roguery, cheating, nepotism, and all its attendant evils."[47] Ultimately, Nkrumah was a discerning interpreter of African religions, and made a lasting mark on the African study of religions. He did so both explicitly, through establishing the Department for the Study of Religions at Legon, and implicitly, through his religiously ambiguous actions that challenged Ghanaian scholars and religious leaders to wrestle with Ghanaian expressions of Christianity and indigenous religion.

Busia and Nkrumah in Contrast

We have already noted Busia's significance as a sociologist, particularly with regard to his work on traditional Ashanti leadership. By way of placing him in context with Nkrumah, it is helpful to consider some of their differences. Politically, Busia was the leader of the parliamentary opposition against Nkrumah from 1956–1959; and from 1969–1972 he served as the Prime Minister of the Second Republic of Ghana. While Nkrumah and Busia were peers, the latter's approach to politics differed markedly from that of the former.

Busia demonstrated concern with the more recent past and specifically his own Ashanti tribe, examining traditional systems of kinship and governance for guidance in the development of an independent democratic country. It has been said that whereas Nkrumah gave voice to many unrepresented groups in colonial society, Busia represented the "old guard and also appealed to Ashanti nationalism."[48] Here "old guard" may be interpreted as that which upheld Mission Christianity and traditional leadership structures. While Nkrumah inserted himself into the traditional royal framework, Busia was born into it; and whereas Nkrumah appropriated various religious trappings and regularly seemed to shift his allegiance, Busia was clear in his Christian convictions and commitment to the Methodist Church.

Like Nkrumah, Busia also worked as a teacher and undertook further studies overseas, teaching at Achimota (1935). While Nkrumah pursued studies in the United States, Busia went to the United Kingdom, where he completed a B.A. in Medieval History (London University), followed by a degree in Politics, Philosophy and Economics from Oxford, and by 1947

---

47. Pobee, *Kwame Nkrumah*, 24. Pobee notes that he takes this description from a document entitled *One Year of Liberty: A Review of the First Anniversary of Liberation* [n.p., n.d].

48. Schwimmer, "Ghana History Population Politics," para. 2.

had completed his doctorate in Social Anthropology, all in record time. Notably, Busia was the first black African to attend and receive a degree from University College, Oxford.⁴⁹

Glover-Quartey refers to Busia's Oxford education as "solid academic qualifications" in contrast to Nkrumah's American degrees, remarking that "at this period in Ghana, American degrees were considered inferior to those obtained in the U.K."⁵⁰ In contrast to Nkrumah, Busia therefore held legitimate membership within Ghana's elite through both his royal Ashanti and British connections.

Our particular interest in Busia here, however, is with his scholarly contribution to understanding Akan primal religion and traditional leadership structures; an achievement for which he is rightly remembered as "the doyen of Ghana's intelligentsia" and for which we may classify him as an African scholar of African religions.⁵¹ We have already noted the continued importance of Busia's research on traditional chieftaincy, which offers "a particularly good analysis of religion as a cultural subsystem that operates like glue in the Ghanaian political system."⁵²

Busia's unique position as both an ethnic and cultural insider with links to traditional chieftaincy, the Methodist Church, and Ghana's democratic political processes lend weight and credibility to his writing. As such, he is remembered as an "an astute politician, a traditionalist, a distinguished academician, and a true Christian who made the values he believed in and his personal talents reflect on the social life of the people in his country."⁵³ Furthermore, he is a significant figure to consider here because Bediako strongly supported him while an undergraduate student at Legon, as we will see.

---

49. "A Short Biography of Dr. K. A. Busia," Photo Exhibit of Dr. K.A. Busia. This online information was compiled and displayed in conjunction with a photo exhibition provided by the Busia Foundation International, displayed from April 7–11, 2008 as a courtesy of the Alexander Library in association with the April 9, 2008 documentary film screening of "The Prof: A Man Remembered, The Life, Vision, and Legacy of Dr. K. A. Busia." This event was sponsored by the Center for African Studies, Department of Africana Studies, Academic and Public Partnerships in the Arts and Humanities, Alexander Library and Busia Foundation International.

50. Glover-Quartey, "Kwame Bediako's Political Leaning," personal correspondence, dated June 25, 2013.

51. R. R. [R.S. Rattray?], Review of *Africa in Search of Democracy*, 177.

52. Addo, *Kwame Nkrumah*, 5.

53. "Symposium to Commemorate Busia's 95th Birthday Anniversary," *The Statesman* (July 14, 2008). Quote is from Ignatius Baffour-Awuah, the Brong-Ahafo Regional Minister at the time the article was written.

Church and State: Politics and Religion in Ghana

The Christian Council of Ghana

In Nkrumah and Busia, we have observed significantly different approaches to the African study and application of African religions in mid-twentieth-century Ghana, as well as very different approaches to political leadership. Nkrumah demonstrated the savvy skills of a charismatic political and religious entrepreneur using familiar religious idiom to engage his fellow Ghanaians, a tactic that was initially successful in garnering strong support. Busia instead employed his sociological training to investigate and explicate the religious aspects of Akan traditional leadership.

There remains another key angle to consider amidst these political developments: the response of the Christian Council of Ghana, which represented the "historic" or mission churches. This included, for example, the Presbyterian Church of Ghana, the Evangelical Presbyterian Church of Ghana, the Methodist Church, and the Anglican Church.[54] Tracing its origins to 1929, this organization was established under the leadership of Governor Guggisberg.

The Council understood its role as partnering with the colonial administration in the task of bringing "civilization" to Ghana. This was to be accomplished through establishing comity amongst churches, universalizing their positions on church discipline, and developing useful frameworks for engaging non-Christians. Additionally, the C.C.G. sought to develop a unified approach to addressing traditional culture and primal religious practices. Yet they did so "not as Africans, but as Euro-Christians," perceiving themselves "as the spiritual and moral guardian of the nation."[55]

In this sense, the C.C.G. may be seen as a descendent of the earlier missionary efforts. For example, we might recall how the Basel Mission established a clear divide between Christians and non-Christians in communities through the salems and boarding schools, deeming the Akan traditional worldview to be in opposition to Christianity. In adopting the mind-sets that were frequently modelled to them by these earlier missionaries, the C.C.G. missed opportunities to enter into what could have been creative dialogue on the Akan worldview.[56]

---

54. Currently the membership of the Christian Council is far more extensive. A complete list of current participating members can be found on their website at http://www.christiancouncilofghana.org/current_membership.html.

55. Addo, *Kwame Nkrumah*, 134.

56. See Williamson, *Akan Religion*, 171.

Pobee refers to this as the adoption of the missionary *tabula rasa* theory. This promoted the belief that there was nothing of religious value within traditional culture on which the missionary could build, and led to the inevitable conclusion that non-Christian culture therefore had to be swept away in order for Christianity to take root.[57] In this way, the C.C.G. weakened its ties with local custom and positioned itself to be identified as "foreign,"[58] more closely resembling European missions and British colonialism than local Ghanaian culture.

This was in opposition to Nkrumah's views on developing "cultural self-consciousness which was articulated in such terms as Négritude and African Personality . . ."[59] While the Council's shortcomings must be acknowledged, Addo is unnecessarily harsh when he says that the Christian Council acted out of "intolerance, arrogance and vindictiveness . . ."[60]

Rather, the more accurate term would be *ignorance*. Like the missionaries before them, Council members were sincere in their Christian faith and in their desire to promote Christianity in Ghana. Nevertheless, they represented an early generation of Ghanaian Christians who were still in the process of transitioning from missionary Church leadership through to partnership with British and European Church leaders, on the way to being entirely independent. They were therefore attempting to uphold an inherited European Christian perspective while wrestling with establishing a new Ghanaian Christian identity, which proved problematic and often unsuccessful.

Pouring Libation: Bediako in Dialogue with Nkrumah

One particular incident that highlights the tensions between Christianity, primal religion, and the emerging Ghanaian identity that has particular significance for Bediako, was Nkrumah's pouring of libation at the handing-over ceremony with the Duchess of Kent when Ghana received its political independence from Great Britain on March 6th, 1957.

The ensuing controversy with the C.C.G. brought to the fore the question of whether such an action could be classed as "religiously neutral" and solely a sign of "cultural identity," or whether the pouring of libation was a religiously meaningful ceremony. While this question is, itself, grounds for much wider discussion than space permits, this particular incident

57. Pobee, *Kwame Nkrumah*, 55.
58. Ibid., 55 for further discussion.
59. Ibid.
60. Addo, *Kwame Nkrumah*, 135.

succinctly highlights the various political, sociological, theological, and cultural tensions at play; and furthermore, is a topic with which Bediako remained concerned.

When the program of events was made public and included a libation pouring ceremony, the C.C.G. issued a public protest, stating that the offering of libations was a "pagan institution" and therefore not something in which Christians could conscientiously participate. In their view, pouring libations was to be interpreted in religious terms as "an attempt to thank the spirit-beings for bringing the Duchess safely to Ghana and to ask their blessing on the proceedings thereafter," which they deemed incompatible with a Christian worldview.[61]

This conflict immediately raised several urgent questions. Firstly, is the pouring of libation a cultural or religious rite, or a combination thereof? And to whom is the libation offered? In Akan history, libation would have been offered to the ancestors; was this still the case? The C.C.G. argued affirmatively on this point. Busia supports their perspective when he says, "it is the Supreme Being . . . and the ancestors that are always treated with reverence and awe, a fact which an onlooker who has seen Ashanti chiefs and elders making offerings or pouring libation to the ancestors can hardly fail to observe."[62]

A third issue was whether libation as a rite is defined by the actual pouring of liquid, or by the accompanying prayers. This question was particularly sensitive, because its answer would determine whether or not the Church could effectually participate. If the attendant prayers could be offered in the name of Christ, and if the act of pouring libation itself was deemed neutral, perhaps the Church could accommodate and integrate libation as part of a newly imagined framework for Ghanaian Christian worship.[63] However, at that point the C.C.G. was not prepared to accept such an interpretation.

At the same time, Nkrumah was working tirelessly to promote a new form of cultural and national self-consciousness, which he endeavoured to do by selectively revisiting aspects of Ghana's traditional culture in order to project what came to be known as the "African Personality."[64] We have seen how thoroughly he entered into traditional leadership categories, which, by definition, combined both the religious and political, and initially gained him favor with Ghanaians. However, from the C.C.G.'s response, it is clear

---

61. Pobee, *Kwame Nkrumah*, 120–21.
62. Busia, "The Ashanti," 205.
63. See Pobee's discussion in *Kwame Nkrumah*, 120–21.
64. Addo, *Kwame Nkrumah*, 138.

that this sentiment was not unilaterally held. On this particular occasion, the question at the heart of the controversy was whether libation represented a religious or strictly cultural act, intended to portray something that was uniquely African and distinct from a "foreigner's religion."[65]

It is perfectly understandable that at such a pivotal moment Nkrumah would be searching for visible signs that would demonstrate to all that they were no longer under British rule but had a distinct identity as Ghanaians, replete with their own history, culture, and symbolic expression. From that perspective, offering libation during the welcome for the British Duchess can be seen as a clear attempt to project "the African personality," or as Pobee states, an act of "national self-assertion."[66]

The C.C.G., on the other hand, viewed this as a religious, and not cultural, undertaking. Within this unresolved conflict, Pobee argues, Church and State were arguing at cross-purposes: "For the former the issue was one of idolatry[;] for the latter it was an issue of projecting the African personality," and doing so through the appropriation of religious symbols, essentially secularizing the symbol to push a national rather than religious identity.[67]

While Pobee is sympathetic to the Church's perceived need to speak out and raise these concerns, he is critical of the way in which it was done: "[t]he stand the Church took made it look [like] a foreign institution, indeed an imperialist institution which looked down on anything African."[68] However, Nkrumah must also be criticized for not fully appreciating the undeniably religious implications of this action, and for being deliberately provocative to the Christian community. Ultimately, however, neither side fully grasped the depth and significance of this action. Idowu refers to this as "the predicament of the Church in Africa," struggling between the views of extreme nationalists who see nothing positive in the Church's contribution to Africa, and the loyal children of the Church who feel only gratitude and who perceive any criticism as disloyalty. He instead argues for a middle ground: those who regard themselves as "true children" of the Church but who equally recognize the need for change.[69]

In scholarship written nearly four decades later, Bediako asserts that the controversy surrounding the libation event in 1957 was not an isolated,

---

65. Pobee, *Kwame Nkrumah*, 122. In this context, Christianity is the implied "foreigner's religion."

66. Ibid.

67. Ibid., 124.

68. Ibid., 180.

69. Idowu, "The Predicament of the Church in Africa."

one-time misunderstanding, or simply a politically motivated bit of showmanship. In an extended discussion on ancestors—what they are and how they function in Ashanti society—Bediako returns to the pouring of libation. He begins by noting the immediate relevance of understanding both ancestors and libation offerings for his own work: "I take particular interest in the subject, since it falls within the range of matters concerning applied theology which occupy [ACI] in the royal capital, Akropong. Of all Akan ritual acts dealing with ancestors, there is none which gives as deep an insight into how ancestors are perceived as the act of libation."[70]

For support, Bediako turns to no less an authority than the Paramount Chief of the Akuapem Traditional Area (or *Omanhene*), Nana Addo Dankwa III. Bediako finds him an interesting figure, as Dankwa identifies himself as a Christian and often attends public Christian worship in the local Presbyterian Church. However, "in view of his official duties which include regular ritual service to his royal ancestors, he is debarred from participation in the sacrament of the Lord's Supper. This is the Church's way of expressing its disapproval of ancestral rites."[71]

While we have seen the C.C.G.'s argument that offering libation is an unquestionably religious act, Dankwa disagrees: "Libation, originally, was never intended to be a completely religious act. Libation . . . consists of three separate acts, the first two being purely cultural acts, and the last one being a religious act."[72] The first is an act of invitation—not an invocation—inviting the ancestor to actively participate in the activities in which the living are engaged or are about to commence. Second, once the ancestor is presumed to have acknowledged the invitation, the person pouring the libation offers a welcoming address and explains the purpose of the invitation. "[S]ince ancestors are considered as the heads . . . of the community . . . the fatherly address of welcome and greetings as is normally made to the living head of the family, is also extended to the ancestral head."[73] This, Dankwa argues, must not be mistaken for prayer; it is strictly a cultural custom of greeting.

However, the third aspect of libation *is* a religious act: "When the roll has been called, that is, when the ancestor has been welcomed and everybody is present and all is set, prayers are made to introduce the particular act for which invitation has been issued."[74] Significantly, however, it is not

70. Bediako, *Christianity in Africa*, 219.

71. Ibid., 232 n. 43.

72. As cited by Bediako, *Christianity in Africa*, 220. In a footnote, he cites his sources for Dankwa's quotes as being both personal interviews as well as Dankwa's work, *Christianity and African Traditional Beliefs*.

73. Dankwa, *Christianity and African Traditional Beliefs*, 47.

74. Ibid.

prayers *to* the ancestors, but prayers *with* the ancestors, who are presumed to be present and participating in the activities at hand. Bediako acknowledges that while not all would agree with this assessment, "if Nana Addo Dankwa's views raise critical questions for our understanding of the African primal world-view, his opinion also opens fresh avenues for African Christian reflection in particular."[75]

Bediako makes an important point and directs us back to the importance of the emerging African scholarship of African religions. While the 1957 conflict between Nkrumah and the C.C.G. may be seen as an initial gut-level reaction, Bediako's and Dankwa's reflections some three decades later point to a much more highly developed reflexive and scholarly approach by African Christian scholars to African religions, further highlighting the development of this discourse throughout the twentieth century.

In light of Bediako's extensive interaction with religion and politics, it is surprising that some theologians criticize his contribution as being irrelevant to present-day African concerns, or as lacking political concern. Valentin Dedji, for example, dedicates a significant portion of his doctoral thesis, later published as *Reconstruction and Renewal in African Christian Theology*, to this very argument. He bases his argument primarily upon his reading of *Theology and Identity*. He criticizes Bediako for a lack of political engagement and concludes that Bediako is "too 'traditional' and therefore lacking enough commitment to the fate of millions of Africans for whom the urgent questions are not those of 'Gospel and culture,' but 'Gospel and justice.'"[76] In fact, Bediako has written quite extensively on politics and Christian responsibility in present-day Africa, though Dedji is correct that this is not a primary concern in *Theology and Identity*.[77]

---

75. Bediako, *Christianity in Africa*, 223. For further scholarship from another Ghanaian theologian engaging in part with the concept of ancestors and the role of African religion within contemporary African Christological discourse, see Aye-Addo, *Akan Christology*.

76. Dedji, *Reconstruction and Renewal*, 209.

77. For Bediako's views on politics and Christian responsibility, see the following chapters and articles: "African and Christianity on the Threshold of the Third Millennium"; "Biblical Christologies in the Context of African Traditional Religions"; "Christian Religion and African Social Norms"; "Christian Witness in the Public Sphere: Some Lessons and Residual Challenges from the Recent Political History of Ghana"; and "The Gospel and the Transformation of the Non-Western World."

Additionally, one volume of *JACT* 1/2 (December 1998) is committed to this topic. This edition is given the theme, "The Church in the African State: Ecumenical Perspectives from West Africa," and includes articles engaging with historical and biblical perspectives from both Catholic and Protestant voices, alternately focusing upon mainline and charismatic responses to the relationship between Church and State.

Clearly, when dealing with politics, if there is not yet a thorough understanding of the religious aspects of traditional leadership and of the subsequent reasons for resistance to democracy and multi-party states which Bediako labours to uncover as an African Christian scholar, the justice which Dedji envisions can never take root. On this point, we again see the risk of misinterpreting Bediako when engaging only a limited portion of his work, failing to engage with his wider context, and evaluating him along quite narrow theological lines.

Returning to Nkrumah's post-independence period, we see the complexity of religion and politics at play in newly independent Ghana. Christian scholars such as Busia were beginning to study aspects of Ghanaian primal religion and traditional structures, though for sociological rather than religious purposes: "writing it out," as it were. Such research was significant as it began to make explicit what had previously been implicit, providing important source material for further scholarship on African religions.

Nkrumah, for his part, "acted it out" by drawing upon aspects of Akan religion and Christianity as well as by implementing ideological practices with elements of Marxism and Communism. The Christian Council of Ghana, meanwhile, "fought it out," struggling to redefine its place within independent Ghana and endeavouring to uphold Christian doctrine to the best of their understanding, with the sense that they were defending Christianity against anti-Christian, secular incursions. In all of these efforts, all parties were simultaneously attempting to forge positive new religious and/or nationalistic identities while reacting to perceived threats to their efforts, thus contributing to the chaotic socio-religious atmosphere following Ghanaian independence.

Bediako in Context: Student Days

This, then, is Bediako's context as a young student, and it is imperative to consider how these events shaped his later contribution as an African Christian scholar. During this period, Bediako completed his secondary studies at Mfantsipim (1959–1963), and subsequently studied French Literature at the University of Ghana (graduating in 1968). During the first half of his undergraduate studies, the political situation became very tense due to the increasingly chaotic nature of Nkrumah's dictatorial rule.

Alexander Glover-Quartey, a close friend and classmate of Bediako's, recalls that Bediako was very passionate about politics during their time at Legon. The two were firm supporters of Busia's Progress Party (later National Progress Party), being "appalled by all the human rights abuses by the Nkrumah regime [like] the passage of the Preventive Detention Act" as well as "the corruption of Nkrumah's ministers." Glover-Quartey highlights Bediako's political fervour in his following recollection:

> "We were final years students at Legon when the ban on political activities was lifted. Kwame Nkrumah had been overthrown . . . and . . . [the] political parties' electioneering machinery went into full gear. I was quite content to argue my case but Kwame went much further. Always aware of the power of the written word, he chose that medium to put his views and convictions across. He did this in the Legon Hall [University] newspaper and . . . also printed, in a 4-page 'newspaper,' his opinions and the principles of the Progress Party, which he put out at his own expense . . ."[78]

There are no extant copies of this pamphlet; however, Glover-Quartey's recollections helpfully highlight Bediako's early political sensibilities. However, Bediako's political involvement did not end after his early university days. Glover-Quartey goes on to say that in later decades, after Bediako's conversion and ordination as a Presbyterian minister, he still remained loyal to the Busia-Danquah political cause; though for the sake of maintaining a non-partisan stance among his church members, he kept his support private. Glover-Quartey recalled that after the 1992 elections, in which J.J. Rawlings unexpectedly beat Professor Adu Boahen of the National Progress Party, Bediako asked Glover-Quartey to facilitate a meeting with the Professor. The two men went and Bediako "encouraged [Boahen] with words from Scripture."[79]

Bediako's political convictions and involvements remain under-explored, with theological scholarship failing almost entirely to consider these broader influences and thereby missing important aspects of his scholarship. However, there is a clear line of interest between politics and religion that began in his university days and continued through until the end of his life. In an essay on that topic, he argues, "Biblical reflections on the theme of Christian witness in the public sphere are important for our understanding of the Church in the African State, since biblical testimony is essential to every area of Christian witness. The Word of God must be central as we move forward in planning and engagement in the public sphere."[80]

Bediako further argues here that the purpose of "public Christian witness" is not to highlight Christian achievement, or to argue for supremacy

---

78. Glover-Quartey, "Kwame Bediako's Political Leaning."
79. Ibid.
80. Bediako, "The Church in the African State," 58.

of the Church over and against secular society, but is instead a witness to God's activity in history and in the life of nations. "The central element, the key to Christian witness in the public sphere," Bediako argues, "is always the question: how does our action as Christians relate, in motivation, mode of execution and in impact, to the Kingdom of God. Are we acting out of self-interest, or in faithfulness to the Kingdom?"[81]

While Bediako was a young man during this tumultuous period and only just becoming politically involved as a student, he was clearly impacted by these developments. His later writing in part demonstrates a continued effort to answer some of the questions raised both by Nkrumah and the Christian Council. Furthermore, as a young student, having Busia's scholarship in mind and observing Nkrumah's meteoric rise and catastrophic fall, Bediako saw first-hand the dangers of the sacralization of leadership. Within Akan chieftaincy structures, "the traditional sacral state had its own mechanism for restraining autocratic rule through the institution of royal counsellors . . ."[82]

However, in transposing sacralization onto Westernized democratic leadership structures, the checks and balances were lost and all authority was dangerously vested in one person. Bediako reflects on the political state of Ghana, from the heady days of independence in the 1960s through to the devastating economic and social decline seen through the 1980s, and finds that once again a careful exploration and understanding of African primal religion and traditional leadership is essential for understanding modern African politics.

"While such considerations have their place," concedes Bediako, "they fail to take account of forces operating within African societies themselves, chief among these forces being religion."[83] And here he brings us back to Busia and the role of religion in politics: "Curiously, however, though Busia had seen so clearly the pervasive influence of religion in traditional political life, he appeared not to have recognized that the sacralization of power in traditional society would have any significance for understanding Africa's new problems in politics, nor affect the new search for democracy."[84]

Taking the argument forward, Bediako contends that the sacralized role of a traditional leader positioned the leader as the intermediary between the community and the ancestors, with whom the community needed to maintain positive relations for the well-being of all. This effectively meant

81. Ibid., 60.
82. Bediako, *Christianity in Africa*, 182.
83. Ibid., 240.
84. Ibid.

that the leader functioned on behalf of the ancestors, a role we have seen appropriated strategically by Nkrumah. This meant that any attack on political authority essentially amounted to "an attack upon the sacral authority of the ancestors on whose goodwill and favor the community's continuance and prosperity are held to depend. Any radical political challenge, therefore . . . amounts to undermining the very foundations of the identity and continuity of the state or community itself."[85]

Bediako notes that the danger in locating the source of a leader's power in the realm of the ancestors "effectively place[s] power within the range of human capriciousness."[86] Perhaps these experiences led him to argue strongly for the Church's need to promote *desacralization* within the African political arena: "By his Cross, Jesus desacralized all worldly power, relativizing its inherent tendency, in a fallen universe, to absolutize itself. But this means also that the Cross desacralizes all the powers, institutions and structures that rule human existence and history—family, nation, social class, race, law, politics, economy, religion, culture, tradition, custom, ancestors—stripping them all of any pretensions to ultimacy."[87]

It would be difficult to perceive the depth of the significance of such an argument without some prior understanding of the Akan sacralization of chieftaincy, or of Nkrumah's abuse of such beliefs. But taken together, Bediako's view of the potential within Christianity for a radical desacralizing response to modern African politics is an important one; yet it remains almost entirely overlooked. He points out how we might move forward in this area: "What is needed is an understanding of power that secures its source beyond the reach of human manipulation, at least conceptually, and so transforms the exercise of power in human community from rule into service. African Christianity may have no greater political mission in African societies than to assist in this transformation of outlook . . ."[88]

As we saw more clearly in the previous chapter with mission and colonial contributions to education, "no single subject has attracted as much consistent attention and resources in the history of Christian penetration of Africa as education, and no subject was as effective in the revolutionary transformation of African societies."[89] As Sanneh argues, education in the hands of missionaries was utilized essentially as a tool for conversion and Christian discipleship. Then, in the hands of "conservative and some

---

85. Ibid., 243.
86. Ibid., 182.
87. Ibid., 245; italics his.
88. Ibid., 182.
89. Sanneh, *West African Christianity*, 127.

liberal philanthropists,'" education was viewed as a tool for social control, predominantly equipping Africans to make a positive contribution to Western industries; though, as we have seen, with notable exceptions in figures like Guggisberg, who arguably viewed education as a training ground for citizenship and self-governance.

"Finally, for many African populations," Sanneh argues, "education was welcomed as the gateway to a new and secure future. In all these instances modern education produced results and repercussions far greater than could be envisaged from any single standpoint."[90] As we have observed, from mission schools to politics to the Department for the Study of Religions at Legon, this has consistently rung true.

In 1969, some twenty years after African Traditional Religion was first taught at Ibadan, Mbiti made the following observation:

> Many of the tropical universities . . . have incorporated the study of religion and philosophy into their body of courses. This recognizes the great importance of religion as the backbone of African life, and the study of which is necessary for the understanding of both traditional and modern Africa. It rightly deserves a place in the university curriculum, where it may and should be scrutinized as an academic discipline . . . In this way, students of religion are learning something from each system; and each religious tradition, in its own way, is shedding new light on the understanding of one or more of the other traditions. But religion in Africa is not the monopoly of academics: it is a reality moving in the stream of current history of African peoples . . .[91]

Within the complexity of mid-twentieth-century Ghana and emerging religious discourse, Mbiti's statement is abundantly true. Furthermore, his statement foreshadows what we will discover in analyzing the combination of academic and grassroots engagement with religion at ACI. We have also seen the competing legacies of Christian missions and nationalistic politicians within postcolonial Ghana: significantly, the underlying religiosity pervading Ghanaian traditional chieftaincy structures as well as contemporary politics—i.e., the sacralization of the state—patently evident in Nkrumah's charismatic leadership style.

Hinting at the transformational role which Christianity and African Christian scholarship may yet play in the desacralization of Ghanaian politics, Bediako contends that "African religion too can give a clue to African

---

90. Ibid.
91. Mbiti, *African Religions and Philosophy*, 261.

politics, and . . . African Christianity may have an important role to play in the moulding of new political models and ideals . . ."[92] Furthermore, we have seen that within Ghana's independence and post-independence period, African approaches to Christianity and primal religion proved to be pivotal issues for a variety of figures, including politicians and Christian leaders, as well as playing an important role in shaping emerging African scholars of religion such as Bediako.

Ultimately, the issues of identity, religion, and politics, which had been brewing for the past century, came to an explosive, exciting, turbulent head in mid-twentieth-century Ghana as these various players tried to make sense of their post-colonial realities. However, this "new wine" required "new wineskins," and in the process of procuring these, some "old wineskins" clearly burst along the way.[93] With such deep-rooted changes and new identities to be forged, this was hardly avoidable but is nevertheless part of the exciting story of this emerging African religions discourse.

---

92. Bediako, *Christianity in Africa*, 180.

93. See the biblical reference in Matthew 9:17: "Neither do people pour new wine into old wineskins. If they do, the skins will burst; the wine will run out and the wineskins will be ruined. No, they pour new wine into new wineskins, and both are preserved" (New International Version).

Chapter 5

"Down From What Tree?"

The Unexpected Influence of Négritude Poetry on Bediako's Christian Thought

Négritude [is like] . . . living as a woman who is born to die and senses her own death even in the most rewarding moments of her life.[1]

—Jean-Paul Sartre

---

1. Jean-Paul Sartre, as quoted in Jules-Rosette, "Jean-Paul Sartre," 265. Adinkra symbol *Sesa wo suban*, meaning "change or transform your character." This symbol of life transformation combines two separate adinkra symbols, the "Morning Star" which can mean a new start to the day, placed inside the wheel, representing rotation or independent movement.

Négritude: Like a Woman Born to Die

JEAN-PAUL SARTRE'S ABOVE STATEMENT brilliantly captures the ephemeral, contradictory, and irreconcilable concepts that together inform this philosophical and literary tradition. Négritude refers to the work and ideology of French Black intellectual poets and politicians in France writing from the 1930s–1950s. Bediako spent more than a decade studying French literature and Négritude poetry, completing a masters and doctoral degree focusing on the work of Congolese poet Tchicaya U Tam'si. These studies began during a period of his life in which he identified unequivocally as an atheist; but towards the end of his master's study, he experienced a radical conversion to Christianity that significantly changed his subsequent doctoral analysis of this French poet, and ultimately led to his later career as a theologian.

Yet, for a scholar who has been called one of the most influential African theologians of the twentieth century, the impact of Négritude literature on Bediako's subsequent Christian scholarship remains an as-yet unexplored area. As we will see, however, careful analysis of this period of Bediako's academic life, in conjunction with U Tam'si's poetry, hold important keys for interpreting this African scholar's later writing and methodological approaches, and presents an exciting new source for analyzing Bediako in greater depth.

In this chapter, we will consider how the poetry of U Tam'si represents another early example of the African study of African religions, with a focus on how this period of study influenced Bediako and shaped his later Christian scholarship. Two key areas of affinity between U Tam'si and Bediako stand out for analysis: the quest for authentic African identity, and interactions between Christianity and primal religion. We will subsequently consider how Bediako's work *Theology and Identity* may be seen as a continuation of these concerns from his developing perspective as an African Christian.

In his *Introduction* to his master's dissertation, Bediako delineates the important ideological and historical link between poetry, politics, and religion relative to his engagement with U Tam'si and mid-twentieth-century Africa. In his words, "If we are somewhat removed from the protest poetry . . . of 1948, the passion of Tchicaya U Tam'si in 1960 is that of Africa, having achieved political independence, and searching for her spiritual equilibrium"[2]—a statement in many ways also describes Bediako's intellectual and spiritual itinerary.

---

2. Bediako, "Négritude et Surréalisme."

Chronologically, this chapter illustrates the role of the Négritude movement as a bridge between the post-World War I missionary and colonial efforts in Ghana and the independence period of the 1950s–1960s. As we have seen, an important shift was occurring in university departments in the post-independence era of the 1960s, in which African researchers "devoted themselves to the task of addressing African issues [including . . .] the project of recovering the lost African identity."[3] While we have already considered the mission, colonial, and nationalistic contributions to developing the University of Ghana, and specifically the Department for the Study of Religions, this chapter explores how the African study of African religions as an academic discourse begins to come to the fore.

An analysis of *la literature africain d'expression française* within the study of religion in Africa is therefore germane for two key reasons. Firstly, emerging in the 1930s, Négritude preceded the independence movements of the 1950s–1960s and functioned to a degree as a catalyst for those political and ideological developments. Here we may recall Kesteloot's earlier statement that independence movements did not erupt suddenly but had been brewing for decades, as demonstrated in part through the work of Négritude writers.[4]

Secondly, in evaluating the political, social, religious, and cultural shifts in Ghana in the 1960s, as well as considering the number of years which Bediako dedicated to studying French African literature, it is imperative to examine this literary movement carefully in order to assess its lasting influence on African scholars of religion. Why did Bediako throw himself into the study of Négritude poetry after experiencing the tumultuous independence and post-independence period in Ghana? Indeed, at one point he assumed he would return to Legon as a professor of French Literature.

But surprisingly, Négritude as an influence on the African study of African religions hardly appears in the literature; and as an influence on Bediako, not at all. It is regularly cited in texts on African theology as an important milestone within this period of African intellectual, political, and cultural (re)formation, but without further examination. And with regard to Bediako, typically no more than passing acknowledgment is made to the fact that he studied Négritude literature prior to his Christian conversion, with scholars moving swiftly on to his theological scholarship—seemingly assuming that his pre-Christian intellectual concerns hold no further

---

3. Adogame et al., *African Traditions*, 2.
4. See Kesteloot, *Négritude et situation coloniale*, 6.

relevance for his later Christian thought.[5] If we have learned anything from Bediako, surely it is that the very opposite is true!

History, Definitions, and Goals

In order to properly locate and assess Bediako's Négritude scholarship, some background on this movement is helpful. The Négritude movement originated in Paris in the 1930s. A literary and ideological movement, it was established by African and Afro-Caribbean francophone intellectuals, politicians, and writers in reaction to the subjugation of black Africans by various colonizing forces. The three founding fathers of the movement—*les trois pères*—came from different French colonies in Africa and the Caribbean and met while living in Paris. They included Léopold Sédar Senghor of Senegal; Aimé Césaire, from Martinique; and Léon Damas, from Guyana. All three were creatively engaged with both politics and poetry: Senghor (1906–2001) became the first president of Senegal in 1960; Césaire (1913–2008) began his political career in Martinique in 1945; and Damas (1912–1978) served in the French National Assembly from 1948–1951.

One aspect of twentieth-century Africa seen repeatedly here is that many events were unfolding at a fairly rapid pace, and involved a complex cast of competing players and motivations, with African society and culture left struggling to keep pace. African intellectuals such as the Négritude writers were simultaneously agitating against colonialism while reflecting upon changes they were still experiencing within the fading colonial framework. As Robert W. July wrote in 1964, many of these events "emerged so recently and with such swiftness that the underlying ideas which give them force and direction are still taking shape and are not always widely understood." However, supporting Keseloot's earlier statement that forces leading towards independence had been simmering for some time, he argued that these African intellectuals were "well aware that the events of the recent past did not take place suddenly and without warning."[6]

Négritude, as an ideological and literary movement, was one such "warning." It has been defined as a literary genre invented by Césaire and popularised by Senghor, and as being "the consciousness that the Black has of his status in the world and the revolt with which this consciousness

---

5. For those who include a description of the Négritude movement within discussions on African theological developments, see, for example, Dedji, *Reconstruction and Renewal*, 12–15; and Stinton, *Jesus of Africa*, 7.

6. July, "Nineteenth-Century Négritude," 73.

impregnates his artistic expression and his political aspirations."[7] For critics and Négritudinists alike, a more concrete definition of Négritude proves elusive. Acknowledging this difficulty, it has been argued that Négritude developed as a response to how black Africans saw themselves being depicted by white Europeans, with all of the attendant prejudices of slavery, colonialism, and neo-colonialism, and represented an attempt to recover and portray an authentic black identity from a black perspective.[8]

In this sense, Négritude as a literary trend can be understood as both an anti-colonial reaction and an effort at positive cultural re-appropriation. In an interview conducted in Paris in 1967, Césaire defined Négritude (both as a term and an ideology) in the following words: "It must not be forgotten that the word negritude was, at first, a riposte. The word nègre had been thrown at us as an insult, and we picked it up and turned it into a positive concept . . . We thought that it was an injustice to say that Africa had done nothing, that Africa did not count in the evolution of the world, that Africa had not invented anything of value. It was also an immense injustice, and an enormous error, to think that nothing of value could ever come out of Africa."[9]

Delineating key aspects of this black French cultural renaissance, Lilyan Kesteloot, a Congolese scholar and an early Négritude expert, argues that hallmarks of Négritude include the following three points.[10] Firstly, a criticism of rationalism, understood as a European construct. Secondly, a concern for recovering an original (African) personality while simultaneously refusing to follow European models of artistic expression. And finally, a revolt against colonial capitalism.[11] Nigerian scholar Abiola Irele, criticizing some of the more ephemeral qualities ascribed to this movement, offers his perspective: "I take *négritude* to mean not the philosophical idea of a Negro essence, which appears to me not only abstract but quite untenable . . . but rather an historical phenomenon, a social and cultural movement closely related to African nationalism. It has aroused

---

7. Beti and Tobner, *Dictionaire de la Négritude*, 6.

8. Ibid.

9. Jules-Rosette, "Jean-Paul Sartre," 267. In a footnote referencing Césaire's quote, Jules-Rosette adds, "This speech was tape-recorded at the Maison Helvetique in Paris in 1967 by Serge A. Tornay, a participant in the discussions. I am grateful to him for sharing this interview tape with me."

10. Congolese scholar Lilyan Kesteloot produced one of the first theses on Négritude, published in 1963 as *Les écrivains noirs de langue française: naissance d'une littérature* followed by a later work entitled *Négritude et Situation Coloniale* (1968).

11. Kesteloot, *Les écrivains noirs*, 26.

considerable controversy and inspired reactions ranging from enthusiastic partisanship to outright hostility."[12]

As both an important historical development as well as a literary genre, it serves as a significant link to African nationalism, and one that is particularly salient to the examination of political developments in 1960s Ghana. And, as Irele observes, we see the controversies and widely diverse opinions surrounding this literary movement becoming increasingly evident, both from literary and political perspectives.

As an anti-colonial genre attempting to reconstruct a positive Black history and identity, Négritude had a number of distinct goals. While the recovery and affirmation of African history and culture were broad aims, Négritude has been incorrectly equated with such trends as romanticism, primitivism, or even racism.[13] While Négritude may be seen to contain aspects of each of those traditions, it is much more than simply an "irrelevant agitation" or "back-to-nature" literature.

Firstly, it is primarily literature voicing "a protest, a refusal and a demand"[14]; a protest by Black writers against the oppression and racism of colonialism. Secondly, it is a refusal by the colonized community to accept the inferior identity imposed by the colonizer. And finally, it expresses a demand for the recognition that "colonized man has an important contribution to make to world civilization instead of being a passive recipient of the material and moral values of Western man."[15] On this point it further serves as a critique of the West.

When Césaire and Senghor first met in Paris in the 1930s, they shared a common enemy in the "dominant theology which insidiously claimed that 'Black' meant inferior and that the only solution for a Black person was to be or to become as white as possible."[16] This view had become so ingrained that black Africans who had been educated under the French system had to first wrestle against their own internalized sense that "their race was doomed to failure" before they could take steps to affirming a positive cultural identity. Therefore, "[f]or a whole generation of black students exiled in Paris, reclaiming their African heritage became a first positive step towards cultural liberation."[17]

---

12. Irele, "Negritude or Black Cultural Nationalism," 322.
13. See July, "Nineteenth-Century Négritude," 73–86.
14. Langley, Review of *Négritude et Situation Coloniale*, 74–75.
15. Ibid., 75.
16. Césaire, *Notebook of a Return to My Native Land*, 21.
17. Ibid.

Within the diverse aims of Négritude, a primary objective was to lead the way in restoring the dignity and sense of self-worth of colonized Africans, denouncing the racist and oppressive ideologies of European colonialism. In other words, to postulate a new, authentic African identity over and against that of the identity imposed by European missionaries and colonizers. Recalling some of the cultural tensions in Ghana illustrated in the previous chapter, the weight of these Négritudinist goals may be better appreciated. And herein we begin to see foundations of an African approach to the study of religions in this early current of writers and politicians contending for the revaluation of African history and identity.

Négritude and Politics

It has been hypothesised that since literature "may affect the way people think about politics, the way they perceive their political system, and the approach they embrace to the challenge of political change," literature may therefore be considered "an agent of political culture, and the novelist a political philosopher and teacher."[18] Négritude is a clear demonstration of this principle. Within political and liberation discourse, Négritude writers performed an important function. Theirs was the task of bringing order out of chaos: as Kesteloot argues, to "catalyze the hopes of the people, helping them to situate themselves once again in history and to deepen national sentiment . . . in short . . . [to] prepare them for liberty."[19]

Furthermore, it was the responsibility of Négritude writers to "claim political freedom and make the aspirations of the subjugated population known to the West" while also being responsible to "free the Black community mentally, helping them to understand what freedom is, and what it must be."[20] The Négritude movement therefore emerged from within this space of historical and cultural tension, creatively linking politics and literature: "The fact of political domination created areas of contact between Africans and Europeans . . . that constantly underscored racial and cultural differences. The colonial relationship thus involved the total cultural situation, and nationalist movements were in fact efforts at cultural as well as purely political autonomy."[21]

In this regard, cultural nationalism became an integral part of the liberation movement, with the Négritude movement being the main

---

18. Diamond, "Fiction as Political Thought," 435.
19. Kesteloot, *Les écrivains noirs*, 19, translation mine.
20. Kesteloot, *Négritude et Situation Coloniale*, 3–14.
21. Irele, "Negritude or Black Cultural Nationalism," 321.

expression of cultural nationalism associated with Africa.[22] Indeed, Négritude's strong organization as a literary movement and its international connections are features which pushed it beyond being a simple catchword or ideological slogan to being a philosophy. In this capacity, it reflected a number of themes and intellectual trends influential in France in the 1930s, including Marxism, existentialism, and surrealism: three currents that were particularly associated with the quest for liberation.[23] However, while the Marxist approach was predominantly an economic struggle, the Négritude movement was based on racial rather than economic lines.

Here it is helpful to remain cognizant of the chronology of events: Négritude as a literary movement was developing from the 1930s–1950s, while on the ground in Ghana this was the late colonial and early independence period. For Bediako as a young student beginning to explore this movement, it was still very new, with much of this poetry, including U Tam'si's, still being written into the 1960s and 1970s. Therefore, while Négritude as an ideology predated African independence movements, for Bediako the two were almost overlapping, with his favorite Négritude poet continuing to publish well after Ghana's independence.

Understanding the soil from which Négritude sprang is important in order to fully grasp its relationship to politics. Indeed, features of Négritude become more coherent when we consider its French colonial roots. Unlike British colonizers in West Africa, who practised indirect rule, French colonial policy was based on objectives of both assimilation and association. The goal of assimilation was for Africans to be so thoroughly "inculcated with the French language, French history, and French values that they were to be regarded as Black Frenchmen."[24] This status, once achieved, was initially intended to accord Africans full equality with the French, including full political rights.

However, assimilation was a very lengthy and cumbersome process. Furthermore, the French began to recognize the possible "threat" that this equality presented to their power by virtue of African numerical supremacy. They therefore modified their policy, and *assimilation* was replaced by *association*. As a more expedient process than assimilation, yet without the offer of total equality, Africans were encouraged to become "Black Frenchmen," and France's colonial territories in Africa were governed and viewed "as part of indivisible France."[25]

22. Ibid.
23. Le Baron, "Négritude," 272.
24. Phillips, *The African Political Dictionary*, 37, s.v. "assimilation."
25. Ibid.

Even a cursory understanding of the cultural ramifications of this colonial policy should underscore the depth and intensity of the need to reclaim a positive *African*, rather than *French*, identity. This sentiment is captured well in the following statement: "The black poet's descent into himself is an effort to disalienate his being and to re-establish a concordance with a distinct essence. For this reason, he reconstitutes this essence as much as he can from the remains in him of the African heritage. Yet this march to an original past is coloured by a historical experience to which he has been submitted, imprinted in him indelibly. So that in the effort to achieve personality, there can be no question of a return to the past in its original form."[26] This again parallels early developments within the study of African religions, and signposts the way ahead for later itineraries of African scholars of religion such as Bediako.

Négritude and Religion

There are important religious elements within the Négritude movement. Léopold Senghor, for example, was a devout Catholic, a fact that influenced both his writing and his politics. He has been described as a "cultural intellectual dedicated to finding a harmonious solution to the racial, religious, and political tensions in Africa."[27] Furthermore, it was Teillhard de Chardin "who would guide [Senghor] away from Marxism to become an intellectually strong Catholic layman," and Senghor himself indicated that his Catholic faith contributed to his optimism for the future of humanity.[28]

While religion—and frequently Catholicism, given the French missional and colonial roots— emerges as a clear theme in Négritude poetry and the lives of these poets, there is as yet surprisingly little research on Négritude and theology or on its influence within the developing African study of African religions. This suggests an area for continued scholarship that may hold interesting potential for analysing African theologians.

Challenges and Criticisms

While Négritude provides important insights into subsequent independence movements and developments within the African study of religions, there are a number of criticisms levied against it. Four stand out for consideration here. One, the self-defeating "anti-racist racism" accusation; two, the charge

26. Irele, "A Defence of Négritude," 11.
27. Melady and Melady, *Ten African Heroes*, 20.
28. Ibid., 19, 30.

of racializing identity; three, the European birthplace of this movement; and four, the reliance on a colonial framework for self-definition.

The first criticism is that Négritude represented an "anti-racist racism." In other words, exchanging the attitudes of White superiority for those of Black superiority, hypocritically defeating its own *raison d'être*.[29] This criticism, however, is not well supported. Irele, for example, contends that Négritude was a movement in which "the black poets were primarily concerned with projecting a healthier image of their race and not arbitrarily proclaiming an inherent superiority, [and that] their purpose was one of definition and affirmation and not one of aggressive confrontation."[30]

Similarly, Senghor's writing demonstrates a value for inclusivity, portraying "the attitude of one at home in a world of diversity, a world where negotiating otherness is a constant fact of human social existence."[31] The anti-racist racism challenge, therefore, may be attributed to an insufficient or unclear engagement with the aims of these writers. To argue that Négritude is nothing more than a transposition of a racist attitude is a serious underestimation of this movement.

The second criticism is the controversy surrounding Négritude's racialization of identity. It has been argued that "Négritude was the celebration of Blackness, of being Black, of specifically African culture and African values that sought to reify a precolonial African past."[32] This was exactly the criticism levied by Martinican philosopher Frantz Fanon and Nigerian writer Wole Soyinka: "Fanon's revulsion was a result of his concern that, by racializing the *problematic* of cultural oppression, the possibilities of true liberation were diminished because of the focus on the past."[33] Similarly, Soyinka argues that in the colonizer-colonized dialectic demonstrated in Négritude, the African is perpetually secondary to the European. For this reason, "[t]he celebration of Blackness for Soyinka in these terms is just as revolting as loathing the African."[34]

The argument here is that Négritude ultimately remains bound within in a perpetually defensive role within "the Eurocentric intellectual formulation of Africa's difference, thus paradoxically trapping the representation

---

29. See, for example, Irele's comments on Jean Paul Sartre in "A Defence of Négritude," 9-11.

30. Ibid., 9.

31. Williams, "Assimilation and Otherness," 253.

32. Ashcroft and Ahluwalia, *Edward Said*, 110.

33. Ibid.

34. Ibid.

of African reality in those binary terms."[35] Reasserting this perspective in *The Empire Writes Back,* Ashcroft et al. similarly note that while Négritude was, as a literary movement, "the most pronounced assertion of the distinctive qualities of Black culture and identity," this very fact caused it to adopt stereotypes reflective of European prejudice.[36] These included, for example, such stereotypes as Black culture being more emotional, stressing wholeness and integration, and having unique principles of time, rhythm, ethics, and aesthetics; with European culture on the other hand being more rational and promoting analysis and dissection.[37]

Connecting with the charge of anti-racist racism, they argue that this feature ultimately left Négritude vulnerable to being "easily... reincorporated into a European model in which it functioned only as the antithesis of the thesis of white supremacy."[38] While this is clearly not the aim of Négritude writers, there is no escaping the racial divisions and identities constantly reinforced in European-African encounter; this charge remains an unresolved structural tension within Négritude.

The third criticism of this movement is its birthplace: Paris, France, within the small but significant African community established there following the migration of Africans and West Indians immediately after World War I.[39] The paradox of an anti-colonial literary movement which endeavoured to affirm a positive, Afro-centric identity emanating not from Africa but from Europe, and in a colonial language, has certainly not gone unnoticed or unchallenged. The cry has been raised that Négritude was "a protest at a very sophisticated level" developed by African intellectuals who were "largely assimilated into European culture," writing more for a European than African audience.[40] The argument follows that many Négritude writers did not entirely reject European culture, but instead desired to establish a new Black culture drawing selectively from European and African traditions.[41]

This cultural dissonance raises questions of identity and identification. These Africans who lived in Europe, were educated in French, and exposed to European varieties of philosophy, culture and religion, were envisioning an African identity rooted within the historical black African experience,

35. Ibid.
36. Ashcroft et al., *The Empire Writes Back,* 21.
37. Ibid.
38. Ibid.
39. Jules-Rosette, "Jean-Paul Sartre," 266.
40. Le Baron, "Négritude," 268, 272.
41. Ibid., 268.

but were doing so from a European vantage point. The criticism that readily arises is that the "African past" and cultural identity that these authors were depicting was not in fact part of their own lived experience but an idealized past, imagined through Afro-European lenses.[42]

This dualism is one of the results of the colonial endeavour. The Négritude movement clearly embodies the tension experienced by these African writers living in Europe, unable to write in their mother tongues and instead using a colonial language to describe an African past that they had not personally experienced. This painful tension is an intrinsic part of Négritude and is featured heavily within the poetry of Tchicaya U Tam'si. Ultimately, the European birthplace of this movement does not lessen the significance of Négritude thought; but this paradox remains an unresolved criticism.

A related criticism is that Négritude only gave voice to the elite, serving as a mouthpiece for highly educated, French-speaking African intellectuals who were living in various parts of the world. Mbiti offers this criticism:

> The concept of Négritude with its many forms and definitions, is an ideological point of reference for the few elite . . . Nobody in the villages understands or subscribes to its philosophical expressions . . . Négritude is, then, a comfortable exercise for the elite who wants, seeks and finds it when he looks at the African [past] and hopes for an African future. It has neither dogmas nor taboos, neither feast days nor ceremonies. You only need to imagine it and you will be able to identify it; be lucid about it and you will be able to see it. Négritude is because it is said to be. It is identified with Negro Africans; but do Africans identify themselves with Négritude? That is the dilemma of Négritude as an ideology.[43]

This is an important consideration for our later discussion on Bediako, who, we will see, specifically rejects this practice as a Christian, striving to ensure that his research and writing remained relevant and accessible to the local community.

The fourth serious criticism of Négritude relates to its political connections and its reliance upon past colonial frameworks for its identity of alterity. Some critics see nothing further in Négritude than "a cultural ideology that could have no political effectiveness . . . [and] a petit bourgeois movement which could never serve the interests of Black people." It has

---

42. It should be recalled that this bicultural ambivalence did not begin with the Négritude movement; Blyden, for example, embodied this conflict decades earlier. See July, "Nineteenth-Century Négritude," 84–85.

43. Mbiti, *African Religions and Philosophy*, 268.

also been branded "a doctrine which reproduced the stereotypical images produced by the occident."[44]

This is clearly the antithesis of what the early Négritude writers perceived as their goals. However, perhaps it served a different purpose than these critics suppose. Rather than being simply "a tool of Western imperialism," we see it here as a significant stage within the emerging African study of African religions, and is therefore not an antiquated or irrelevant literary genre, but an important source for continued engagement with African scholars of African religions.

While criticisms of Négritude as reinforcing colonial ideologies, racial divisions, and cultural imbalances are valid, it is nevertheless an essential intellectual, political, and cultural link within this post-mission, pre-independence period. As evidenced in Senghor's work, "[i]t had been established that Africa was not an 'empty slate,' that great civilisations had flourished there. Africa could be reclaimed as the original source of art, innocence and beauty."[45] Perhaps the greatest criticism of Négritude is summed up in the often-quoted remark of Soyinka's: "a tiger does not proclaim its tigritude; it pounces."[46]

Négritude has unquestionably made a significant impact, the depths of which have yet to be fully explored. But as a movement, it is perhaps best understood as a catalyzing force rather than an end in itself. The remainder of this chapter takes up this challenge, arguing that Négritude makes an important contribution to the African study of African religions, as particularly evidenced by its impact upon Bediako's theological reflections.

Bediako and U Tam'si: Exploring Unexpected Influences

Tchicaya U Tam'si: Introduction and Biography[47]

In turning our attention back to Bediako's story, we might ask, just who was this Négritude poet who so strongly held his attention? Tchicaya U Tam'si (1931–1988) was born in what is now the Democratic Republic of Congo, but from adolescence onward he lived in Paris where his father was the first African deputy to the French National Assembly. Born Gérald-Félix

44. Césaire, *Notebook*, 49.
45. Ibid., 48.
46. Ashcroft et al., *The Empire Writes Back*, 124.
47. While I studied U Tam'si's poetry in the original French, I relied upon the English translation and commentary by Gerald Moore for further insight and linguistic clarification. However, for Bediako's master's and doctoral dissertations in French, I have provided my own English translation.

Tchicaya, he took the pen name Tchicaya U Tam'si, meaning *small paper that speaks for a country* in Kikongo. He began writing poetry in the early 1950s; and though he spent the greater part of his life in France, his poetry most frequently reflects the pain and challenges of life in his beloved Congo, grappling with the combined destructive effects of the past colonial history and tragic civil strife of the 1960s.

U Tam'si has been described as both the most prolific and most gifted of the second generation of African Francophone poets, but also the most difficult, with poetry that is "oblique, fluid, suggestive, and replete with private symbols and symbolic motifs which accumulate meaning as they appear in poem after poem."[48] In an interview from 1998, Bediako reflected thoughtfully that U Tam'si "has very beautiful poetry, but very dense poetry . . . Very, very dense poetry . . . extremely, in one sense, very difficult poetry . . . and yet very, very rich when one has meditated on it."[49] There are distinct challenges in trying to make sense of such esoteric writing; Bediako did admirably.

Key Themes

U Tam'si's poems are incredibly complex, with layers of religious images and symbols, political and colonial references, and frequent engagement with the natural world—rivers, oceans, trees, savannah; sun, moon, stars; blood, tears, sweat; birth, death. The emotional tone of his poetry ranges from nostalgia to despair, rage, lust, mockery, grief, despondency—and, occasionally, pleasure, though it is always fleeting. Some of the key themes which dominate U Tam'si's writing and which are of particular interest with Bediako in mind include the quest for identity, cultural authenticity, and religious tension. This is often displayed as unresolved ambivalence between primal religious traditions and Catholicism. Another significant theme is the belief that words—or one's intellect—provide the key to understanding the world. Gerald Moore, a leading U Tam'si translator and interpreter, offers the following initial impression of the poet:

> Asked in one of his own poems the nature of his destiny after death, the poet replies: 'To be pagan at the pagan renewal of the world' . . . The regenerative passion of that line has shaped all the poems in this collection. It is this momentum towards a new life which makes death both expected and accepted. Tragedy resides only in living basely or in dying without self-knowledge.

48. Knipp, "Négritude and Negation," 511.
49. Bediako, filmed interview by James Ault, 1998, DigiBeta Reel GB 105: 3–4.

Hence the urgency of the poet's unceasing quest for the roots of his being, for his lost ancestry. Hence also his continual self-examination . . .[50]

This intense search for identity, and an identification with the primal ("pagan at the pagan renewal of the world") are both hallmark features in U Tam'si's poetry and represent two key areas of affinity we will explore between his poetry and Bediako's later Christian theological work.

Bediako's Study of African Francophone Literature: An Atheistic Phase

After completing secondary school, Bediako studied for an honours degree in French at the University of Ghana, Legon. As his friend and former classmate, Alexander Glover-Quartey recalls, at that point, they both seriously pursued humanism and French existentialism. Glover-Quartey describes it in this way: "Among the authors we had to study . . . were those known as the Existentialists, who proclaimed that God was dead. I began to describe myself as an atheist at one point, even though I do not think I understood its full implications. Kwame was also tilting that way."[51]

Glover-Quartey elaborates on this comment, recalling that while he himself was asking questions like, "'where is God, and is He really alive?' Bediako was far more assured that God did not in fact exist."[52] In an unpublished interview, Bediako summarized his own position as follows: "You see, my studies in French, in the classics, in French literature, poetry in particular, I, I think increasingly turned me . . . to a more sort of humanist frame . . . of mind. And it wasn't so much that I was . . . anti-religious. It's just I was pro-humanist . . . you know, my view was, existentially life could be constructed on, on humanist principles, which is what I sought to do."[53]

When asked whether Bediako's views were typical in their university context, Glover-Quartey responded that although they were studying existential works and investigating humanism, Bediako was unusual among their classmates in calling himself an atheist. Few other students, Glover-Quartey noted, would have identified themselves as such in Ghana in the mid 1960s; not surprising, given the religiously electrified environment of the time.

50. Gerald Moore, introduction to U Tam'Si, *Selected Poems*, vii.
51. Glover-Quartey, "Tribute to the late Rev Professor Kwame Bediako," 19.
52. Glover-Quartey, interview by the author, April 22, 2010, Accra, Ghana.
53. Bediako, filmed by James Ault, 1998, DigiBeta Reel GB 105: 2.

Bediako further described his early atheistic position in an interview, acknowledging that during that early student period he believed his sense of intellectual superiority to be correct: "I was argumentative and, you know, I wouldn't take yes for an answer, I wouldn't take no for an answer. I mean I really set out to prove the Christians wrong! And I . . . appeared to win the argument each time, you know, really demonstrating how . . . intellectually feeble the Christian perspective was."[54]

After completing his Bachelor's degree, which included a year of study in Aix-en-Provenance, France (1967–68), Bediako was awarded a scholarship to pursue postgraduate work in France at the University of Bordeaux.[55] He pursued this opportunity eagerly, believing it would be an "excellent environment for intellectual growth."[56] Among his classmates in France, he was known "as one who thought religion was out-dated and [that] non-religious humanistic thinking was superior to philosophy that included religious aspects."[57] It is from this perspective, then, that Bediako began his research on U Tam'si.

"Négritude and Surrealism": Bediako's Masters Thesis

Bediako's first master's and doctoral theses—his *Maîtrise* and *Doctorat de troisième cycle* from the University of Bordeaux on the Congolese poet Tchicaya U Tam'si—represent his earliest scholarship engaging the questions of African history, identity, culture, and religion. Notably, there is a clear methodological and ideological shift between the two, which we shall consider in turn. His master's thesis is a relatively straightforward literary criticism in which he analyzes the key concepts of Négritude and surrealism, as well as U Tam'si's first four collections of poetry.

Significantly, in his *Introduction*, Bediako notes that for both African poets and novelists of the period, there was an increasing tendency to judge their own cultures from an insider's perspective and no longer from that of European colonialists, in keeping with what we have already noted with the Africanization of history and theology. In writing poetry reflective of their times, says Bediako, African poets did not give up being "black"; rather, they specifically affirmed Africa's contribution, which, effectively, was the basis

---

54. Ibid., 8.

55. Gillian Mary Bediako, interview by the author, April 27, 2010, Akrofi-Christaller Institute, Ghana.

56. Fotland, *Ancestor Christology in Context*, 22.

57. Ibid.

of Négritude ideology.[58] Here we see Bediako beginning to engage with the emerging Africanization of the study of African religion and culture within this literary movement.

Within his master's research, Bediako evaluates the two following tendencies and related concerns within U Tam'si's poetry: "the first comes from the fact that Tchicaya is a modern poet, has obviously read poets of his time, and . . . writes in French; the other, the fact that he belongs to a black culture. Furthermore, according to the significance of his name, he wants to speak at once about his country, and for his country. We note that if Tchicaya is a Négritude poet, his négritude consists not predominantly in an anti-racist revolt, but more so in the fact that almost all of his poetic landscape is composed of materials from his country of birth."[59]

From his earliest scholarship, Bediako interacts with and promotes the idea of Africans engaging with an African context: although U Tam'si was writing in Paris, Bediako notes that the poet's source of inspiration, and the substance of his poetry, comes from the Congo. This early concern for Africans to draw from their African context continues throughout his later theological writing, and is clearly evidenced in the curriculum and academic community at ACI.

It may be fairly stated that this master's research is not especially remarkable for its straightforward literary criticism. Bediako set out to define Négritude and Surrealist poetry and analyze a limited number of Tchicaya U Tam'si's poems, which he accomplished skilfully. What *is* remarkable, however, is that we begin to see the foundation of Bediako's later Christian scholarship in his careful engagement with concepts such as the "primal imagination" and U Tam'si's efforts to revalorise African history and identity, in this case through poetry. And even more remarkable, perhaps, is that his radical Christian conversion occurred in the midst of this research.

Bediako's Conversion: From Self as Saviour to Christ as Key

In contemplating the ways in which we develop or change a worldview, Walls offers the idea of a "mental world-view map" or "map of reality" as the way in which we understand and interpret the world, and argues that in becoming Christian we do not throw away our previous maps but rather adjust them. In fact, Walls argues, while worldviews are influenced and adjusted by a variety of factors, "it is very rare for a world-view to be entirely destroyed

---

58. Bediako, "Négritude et Surréalisme," 3.
59. Ibid., 7.

and replaced ... People rarely throw away a world-view map altogether, but tend to modify their maps of reality, correcting, adapting, altering the sizes of items on it."[60] Bediako's world-view—rooted in French humanism and the poetry of Tchicaya U Tam'si—was therefore already well formed when he encountered Christ; the resulting shifts and amendments to his "map" are what we see expressed in his extensive theological opus.

Bediako began this research as an atheist, connecting with U Tam'si on a profound level: as he describes it, having a "very strong feeling of affinity between myself and this poet."[61] However, partway into his master's degree he faced a personal crisis. Nine months into a twelve-month masters program, he had made little progress on his thesis, and feared he would fail. Glover-Quartey recounts that up to that point, Bediako had always been an exceedingly capable student, confidently giving persuasive speeches to large audiences, excelling at exams, and easily winning debates and arguments. However, in this period of personal and intellectual distress, he realized for perhaps the first time that his impressive intellect was fallible.

For someone like Bediako who had come to put his faith in his intellectual abilities, this was an extremely troubling experience.[62] Bediako himself admitted that during this period he "started to become conscious that things were not as coherent as they could be" and that "life was not as straightforward and intellectual as he thought." As a result, "[h]e went through a period of angst, though not depression, and had difficulties making a breakthrough in his thesis."[63]

It is interesting to speculate on how such in-depth study of U Tam'si's psychic and spiritual anguish may have impacted Bediako, perhaps even contributing in some measure to this period of malaise in his life, when we consider the deeply unsettling themes with which U Tam'si was wrestling. Glover-Quartey offered the following thoughts on this point:

> [W]hen people call themselves 'atheists,' sometimes you might think they've settled all issues with regard to God. But ... [there may be] moments when they ask themselves ... is this whole world without a creator? ... and what are we here for, where are we going? ... I believe that ... questions pop up, even though they may dismiss them ... But the questions remain; and that is perhaps what happened to Kwame: even though he referred to

---

60. Gillian M. Bediako, citing Andrew Walls in lectures given at Calvin College, July 2007, requoted in "Editorial" *JACT* 11/2 (December 2008) 2.

61. Bediako, "Doctoral Defence Introductory Remarks," 3.

62. Glover-Quartey, interview by the author, April 22, 2010, Accra, Ghana.

63. Fotland, *Ancestor Christology in Context*, 22.

himself as an atheist, yet there were issues he had not resolved and questions he had not really put to rest, and that would explain his identification with [U Tam'si] and [his] affinity with him. Here is someone who has been asking the questions I have been asking, you know?[64]

Bediako's conversion experience, which he dates to 10 August 1970, came as a surprise to him as well as to others.[65] As he reflected on this time of unsettledness in his life, he recalls, "it never occurred to me that I could find the solution in religion. That was an alien idea."[66] Indeed, he often quoted French mathematician and astronomer Pierre-Simon Laplace who, when asked why he made no mention of God in his work, purportedly replied, "*Je n'ai pas besoin de cette hypothèse*—I have no need for that hypothesis!"[67]

However, Bediako ultimately did experience, as he describes it, "Christ as key." As he has recounted on numerous occasions, on that particular August day in Bordeaux he was preparing to take a shower when he noticed with shock that he was crying. With this realisation, he recounts, "I just collapsed, fell to the floor like a sack of potatoes"; and, overcome with distress, wished for his life to be over.

But in that moment something pivotal changed. As he describes it, "suddenly I felt something new. I don't know where it came from, but it was a conviction that Jesus Christ was the source of life and the key to understanding . . . For me Christ became the integrating key of knowledge, the explanation, the light, the logic of life and science. Everything had its coherence and its meaning in and through Christ. From that point on intellectual life became very exciting."[68]

When asked to further analyze this experience in an interview, Bediako offered these thoughts, specifically in connection with his study of U Tam'si: "So I was working . . . on this poet. And what I think my experience in the summer did for me was that I . . . then began to read poetry through the eyes of Christian faith. Christian faith as an integrating element in the quest for . . . intellectual coherence in life . . . I think, perhaps this is what has stayed with me since . . . so that my conversion wasn't a sort of turning

---

64. Glover-Quartey, interview by the author, April 22, 2010, Accra, Ghana.

65. Gillian Mary Bediako, interview with the author, April 27, 2010, Akrofi-Christaller Institute, Ghana.

66. Fotland, *Ancestor Christology in Context*, 22.

67. Gillian Mary Bediako, interview with the author, April 27, 2010, Akrofi-Christaller Institute, Ghana.

68. Fotland, *Ancestor Christology in Context*, 22–23.

my back on intellectual life, turning my back on academic life, rather, it, it is now . . . asking how my intellectual life will find integration . . . in light of my faith."⁶⁹

Echoing Walls' earlier words, Bediako clearly identifies his conversion as a shift to his mental world-view map: a turning. Further elucidating the conversion process, Walls argues that becoming Christian is not a sudden discarding of the past and an appropriation of a new identity. Rather, "Christianity is about conversion. Conversion means turning. Conversion to Christ is turning towards him."⁷⁰ Furthermore, Walls clarifies, it is "about turning *what is already there*; it is more about direction than about content."⁷¹

This is precisely why it is critical to have an understanding of Bediako's pre-Christian life and thought: engaging with his Négritude scholarship helps us to see "what was already there" if we want to fully understand his post-conversion thinking. And more widely, this provides an example of the value in carefully exploring the history and context of African scholars of African religions: we do not know where we might find significant influences on their thinking. An examination of Négritude and Tchicaya U Tam'si offers us new insight into the impact of this movement on religious thought when we view this as a foundational part of "what was already there" in terms of Bediako's mental world-view map.

Immediately following his conversion experience, Bediako immersed himself in a student ministry led by American missionaries Bill and Mary Adams. He served in a variety of capacities including preaching, leading Bible studies, student work, and children's programs.⁷² In fact, his zeal was such that he had to be convinced to complete his doctoral studies, as he wanted to proceed directly with theological training. As Bill Adams recalls, "Kwame was really on fire for God. I had to remind him that he was there for his studies and that he was receiving aid for his studies and that he had better be faithful to that part of his life also. So he did back off a little [from ministry] to get his studies done."⁷³

After having struggled so seriously to make progress on his master's dissertation, he rapidly completed the bulk of the work in the remaining

---

69. Bediako, interview with James Ault, 1998, DigiBeta Reel GB 105: 4.

70. Walls, *The Cross-Cultural Process*, 67.

71. Ibid., 79; italics his.

72. Adams and Adams, "History of the Work," 8. The Adamses were American missionaries in Bordeaux with (what was then) Gospel Missionary Union, working with students, including Kwame and Gillian Bediako.

73. Adams and Adams, interview/personal correspondence with the author, February 22, 2010.

three months.[74] His thankfulness and relief are evident in his dedication: "To Him who saved me/ So that this year of scholarship/ Would be elevated to His glory."[75]

L'Univers Interieur de Tchicaya U Tams'i: Bediako's Apologia Pro Vita Sua

After experiencing this radical shift in his life, Bediako's doctoral thesis departs from literary criticism and emerges as nothing short of his Christian manifesto, a clearly delineated declaration of his evangelical Christian thought and doctrine that is heavily supported by biblical texts.[76] So much so, in fact, that it may be described as Bediako's apologetic for his newfound Christian faith, and a straightforward outline of his early theological positions on sin, salvation, atonement, reconciliation, and eschatology.

It is perhaps surprising to note that, while it was completed in a Department of French Literature in a secular French university, it was very well received and awarded high marks. Bediako stated forthrightly in his prepared opening remarks at his doctoral defence that he was departing from traditional literary analysis and taking quite a different approach to analyzing U Tam'si:

> Behind every authentic work there is an authentic author; what we mean is that the work has the ability to reveal profound and sincere truth about the man behind it. Perhaps we may be forgiven for having diverted, in some ways, from the field of literary criticism itself. For, far from having lost interest in the work, we have also been seized by the man [U Tam'si]. We hope, therefore, to take to a practical level our conviction that the literary critic must sometimes, and in fact often, come to the rescue of the author. And yet, this requires that the critic be enlightened![77]

If the work is intended to reveal the author and the source of the author's inspiration, Bediako's thesis clearly demonstrates that for him, the person behind this work is not the poet U Tam'si, but in fact Jesus Christ. He begins by dedicating his doctoral work "To All who confess / Jesus Christ,

---

74. Gillian Mary Bediako, interview with the author, April 27, 2010, Akrofi-Christaller Institute, Ghana.

75. Bediako, "Négritude et Surréalisme," n.p.

76. Immediately noticeable in this regard is the number of Scripture references Bediako includes, which he uses throughout to support his arguments and interpretation. Almost twenty percent of his references are for biblical citations.

77. Bediako, "Négritude et Surréalisme," 4.

Son of God / Saviour of the World / The Only Way / The Only Truth / The Only Life."[78] From there, he is bold in his apologetic approach, beginning with an Introduction entitled, "The Anguish of Man and the Peace of God." In it, he outlines his belief "in absolute truth in a world filled with relativism," together with "a sure and certain hope in a modern world filled with overwhelming pessimism."[79] He argues that he would be wrong to exclude the hope that he has in Christ from his intellectual life, since "this awareness is in part . . . the reason for this study."[80]

Before moving on to U Tam'si, Bediako proceeds with an outline of his Christian beliefs. Through written communication, spread across centuries, and inserted into human history, he argues, God has given a revelation of himself and has also revealed the origins of humanity and the future for all of creation. The mission of Jesus Christ is found in the centre of this plan, but humanity has revolted against him. It is clear from biblical analysis, Bediako concludes, that any human spirit that refuses to take account of this "God-who-is," is destined for obscurity and darkness.[81]

Bediako then elaborates upon what he views as the failures of the atheistic position, and outlines his understanding of the need for conversion and faith in Jesus. In doing so, he reveals the key to his thesis, and indeed to his faith perspective: "Man, in his fallen nature . . . cannot by himself recover the unity [with God] that has been lost. To realise a relationship with God is to acquire the life of God through 'new birth,' which is authentic conversion. This leads us, not to poetry, but to the person of Jesus Christ, and to His redemptive work."[82]

He finally engages with U Tam'si's poetry, drawing freely from psychology, sociology, history, and theology, in addition to literary criticism, as he analyzes the poet's *oeuvre*. His wide-ranging discussion includes an equally wide range of voices, from Freud and Fanon to Francis Schaeffer, A.W. Tozer, and the Bible, in addition to the expected Négritude writers and critics. In his bibliography, he also includes a list of a dozen "evangelical reviews and magazines," made up of publications such as *Africa Now*, *Decision*,

---

78. Bediako, "L'Univers Interieur." He is making reference to John 14:6: "Jesus answered, 'I am the way, the truth and the life. No one comes to the Father except through me."

79. Bediako, "L'Univers Interieur," 5.

80. Ibid. Here Bediako adds a footnote to explain that "the hope that he has" is based upon 1 Peter 3:15: "Always be prepared to give an answer to everyone who asks you to give the reason for the hope that you have."

81. Ibid., 6.

82. Ibid., 8. Here Bediako cites the biblical passages John 3:3 and 14:6 as the basis for his argument.

Encounter, Good News Broadcaster, and *The Gospel Message*, among others. To pre-empt any criticism for including such works, and to highlight his evangelical, and indeed evangelistic position, he adds the following note: "these evangelical publications are not listed here solely because of bibliographical requirements. To the contrary, they have constituted an important part of our general reading to the point that they inform, in a capital and decisive manner, our 'evangelical vision.'"[83]

The thesis continues, contrasting U Tam'si's poetic enterprise of "cosmic identification" with Bediako's understanding of sin and the need for salvation. Bediako lays out his argument thus: "So, in the context of the true nature of the universe and the glorious destiny of man—created in the image of God—the effort at cosmic identification in poetry takes on very important significance, in that its direction is contrary to divinely revealed thought. That is to say, instead of being elevated towards identification with the Person of the Saviour, the 'unregenerate' and rebellious man takes his thoughts inevitably and tragically to the lower echelons of creation."[84]

Here he demonstrates a sharp divergence from his master's thesis, critiquing U Tam'si's philosophical and creative perspective, with which he once so strongly identified. He further emphasizes his views on the insufficiency of surrealist and Négritude poetry to elevate humanity, again basing his argument on Scripture. He begins by quoting Psalm 8:3–8, ("When I consider your heavens, the work of your fingers, the moon and the stars, which you have set in place, what is man that you are mindful of him, human beings that you care for them? You have made them a little lower than the angels and crowned them with glory and honour . . . ") and offers the following assessment:

> This text is, for us, of paramount importance, given the statement that its makes of the dignity and honour of man. 'Surrealist mysticism' debases and diminishes man. If man did not have this particular place in the hierarchy of created beings, what right would he have to a life of liberty? What would be, then, the basis of the surrealist 'revolt'? And against whom would it be, anyway? It must be said that all atheistic thoughts, known as humanistic, come from equally erroneous bases, and lead, by the force of circumstances, to an impasse.[85]

Bringing together the ideas of mysticism and cosmic identification that he finds in U Tam'si, Bediako finally makes plain his argument that he

83. Ibid., 219.
84. Ibid., 96.
85. Ibid., 94.

sees the poet's error to be that of seeking "cosmic identification" on false grounds, or grounds which are apart from Christ. This leads further into Bediako's discussion on the fallen nature of humanity. He argues that when we begin to engage with the world around us, it is a sign of an awakening. This "awakening" leads us to discover what he calls "the anomaly in the universe," which, he argues, is brought about because of the sin of man.[86]

He sees U Tam'si's poetry as an effort at reconciling this anomaly, but deems it a futile exercise: "But, any effort at integrating with other elements of creation outside of the general context of a radical transformation of creation—on the human side as well as on the side of other created beings—is a seduction, and can only end in a distressing failure. To be able to enjoy true harmony with the surrounding world, we must await a new creation, what God has promised to His redeemed."[87]

Bediako's Christian apologetic—for this doctoral thesis is nothing less—is certainly vibrant, marked by the characteristic zeal of a new convert whose thinking and interpretation is bold and enthusiastic, though not yet mature. It represents Bediako's earliest Christian scholarship, and is therefore an important aspect of his opus that should not be overlooked.

Bediako and U Tam'si: Areas of Affinity

Quest for the Roots of an African Identity

Bediako began his opening remarks in his doctoral defence explaining that he had been studying U Tam'si for close to a decade, which in itself provides a strong argument for the poet's lasting influence in shaping Bediako's thinking. Bediako describes his attraction to this poet in the following words: "I was seized, then, with a very strong feeling of affinity between this poet and myself. From certain angles, in reading his poems, I believed I had found the verbalization of my own reactions in the face of a life that I did not understand; or, in the face of a life as I believed to understand it."[88]

In the midst of turbulent waters, U Tam'si stood out to him as a lighthouse, providing direction to Africans wrestling with rapidly shifting postcolonial realities and the enduring question, *what is my identity?* In seeking to answer this question, the motif of a *quest* can be found in both U Tam'si and Bediako. Négritude represented a type of spiritual and intellectual quest in the pre- and early post-independence decades; and as Moore so incisively

---

86. Ibid., 95.
87. Ibid.
88. Bediako, "Doctoral Defence Introductory Remarks," 3.

observes, U Tam'si's poetry demonstrates his "unceasing quest for the roots of his being." In Bediako's engagement with U Tam'si, we see a man on a similar quest, searching for a philosophy or paradigm by which to interpret the world. It seems almost unbelievable that from within this field, Bediako suddenly discovered his answer in Jesus of Nazareth.

Bediako introduces U Tam'si as "a man who is searching for himself, a man who constantly blames himself, who searches for his authenticity; and [whose] life as well as his work seem to be an effort at continual self-criticism."[89] Bediako continues, describing him as "an African; a Black . . . a Black Congolese who himself knows only a little of [the Congo], including only his childhood and adolescence. He is, then, a Black 'bastard' . . . searching for his roots."[90]

Capturing the challenges of making sense of this fragmented identity, U Tam'si cries out with pathos and frustration, "O my absurd ancestry! / Down from what tree? What flowers will that tree / let fall, before the funeral bell? Who will sound the knell? / A knell like an orphan's tear in the night!"[91] This cry takes us to the very heart of the matter: fully inhabiting one's present identity is dependent upon understanding one's origins.

As Walls states, "[i]t is our past which tells us who we are; without our past we are lost."[92] For Bediako and many Africans of this chaotic period, there was certainly no more urgent a question. Was an authentic African identity to be located in ancient African history? Modern French or British colonialism? African oral histories? European education? Christianity? Primal religion? Absurd ancestry, indeed!

The following phrases from U Tam'si's poem "Strange Agony" highlight the force with which the theme of identity emerges in his poetry: "body and soul naked / I am a man without history / one morning I came up black / against the light of setting suns / spitting out my heart / for every human . . ." Further in the poem, he expresses his profound identification with his country, saying, "but I go onwards / so long as I can meet with congolese / whose spirit is protestant catholic chinese / or negro / my nightmare is like myself."[93]

Underscoring his sense of deracination while simultaneously identifying with his homeland, U Tam'si concludes by saying, "I have indeed the

---

89. Bediako, "L'Univers Interieur," 2.

90. Ibid., 2–3.

91. U Tam'si, *Selected Poems*, "Summary of a Passion" from *Epitomé*, 37.

92. Walls, *Missionary Movement*, 13.

93. U Tam'si, *Selected Poems*, "Strange Agony," from *A Game of Cheat-Heart*, 18–19.

sickness of my land / but what land / the congo, the congo."[94] This poem is a helpful example of the raw and vulnerable quality of U Tam'si's poetry and demonstrates the familiar themes of painful loss, identity confusion, religious imagery, and longing for rootedness.

U Tam'si is a man searching for roots and identity in the midst of conflict and contradictions; a man deeply connected to, and yet paradoxically detached from, his African heritage and beloved country; and a man who grasps the importance of looking to the past in order to discover his identity. Reflecting on his situation, U Tam'si offers this poetic interpretation in a poem entitled "*The Dead*": "False growths upon the roots of my tree / poison my utmost branch / . . . I would speak if only I had memories. / Don't tell me what I was like yesterday / it is enough to be mortal now / very early tomorrow emptiness will invade my black forehead."[95].

Alongside of U Tam'si's search for his African roots and his professed affinity for his home country, his deeply held anti-colonial sentiments are also prominent in his poetry and references to the "blue-white-red" of the French flag are a recurring motif in his writing. We read, "How could I rejoice / to be born all of flesh / which is no coat of mail / nor this wind which raps at every door one opens / on the heart beating sky-blue sail-white blood-red? / I who know nothing / of the tree of my life / my disgrace has three colours."[96]

Religious Affinities: Primal, Christian, Humanist

The interaction between primal religion and Christianity is arguably the second most significant area of affinity between Bediako and U Tam'si; and an exploration of U Tam'si on this point suggests a significant influence on Bediako. A sizeable portion of U Tam'si's poetry is imbued with religious imagery, including elements from both Catholicism and African primal religions. As Susan Erica Rein says, his poetry conveys a transcendent religiosity constituting nothing less than a unique "Tamsien religion," which combines features of African traditional religions and Catholicism.[97] Rein expresses it more fully in these words: "[T]he elements of African religion co-exist with those of Catholic religion, not only at the level of the images but also with regard to ideas . . . In fact Tam'si is able to unite them at times in a sort of marriage of elements. This technique, which is rather typical

---

94. Ibid.
95. U Tam'si, *Selected Poems*, "The Dead," from *Epitomé*, 50.
96. Ibid., 47.
97. Rein, "Religiosity in the Poetry of Tchicaya U Tam'si," 240.

of our poet, consists of juxtaposing elements in order to create a new idea, born from the union of the two (unrelated) others..."[98]

However, U Tam'si's views on religion, whether Christian or primal, are extremely ambivalent, frequently negative, and even verging on hostile. At some points it seems clear U Tam'si's purpose is to shock and provoke. When engaging with Christianity, he uses language that at times is derisive, challenging, and rebellious, putting himself on equal footing with God and comparing his personal suffering to the suffering of the crucified Christ. The lines from the following poem, aptly titled "The Scorner," clearly displays these characteristics:

> Christ I laugh at your sadness
>
> oh my sweet Christ
>
> Thorn for thorn
>
> we have a common crown of thorns
>
> I will be converted because you tempt me
>
> Joseph comes to me
>
> I suck already the breast of the virgin your mother
>
> I count more than your one Judas on my fingers
>
> My eyes lie to my soul
>
> Where the world is a lamb your paschal lamb—Christ
>
> I will waltz to the tune of your slow sadness.[99]

Elsewhere, U Tam'si concludes that God (god) is altogether weak and certainly not powerful to save; he therefore confidently states, "I myself will be stage for my salvation!"[100] In his poem "Strange Agony," U Tam'si further demonstrates his unresolved conflict between primal religion and Christianity:

> a christian will never understand
>
> what is evoked in me
>
> by saint george and his intricate poetry
>
> shadow the pagan no longer remembers
>
> ... but love not being a christian virtue
>
> I have given joy to none

---

98. Ibid.
99. U Tam'si, *Selected Poems*, "The Scorner," in *Epitomé*, 72.
100. U Tam'si, *Selected Poems*, from "The Belly," 126.

> My face turned to the backs of men
> all christians tacitly
> thrusting at me the cross of a god betrayed
> who I betray to remain faithful
> to the shadow[101]

For U Tam'si, Christianity and colonialism are inextricably linked, rendering them both targets of mockery and opposition. In his view, they must be rejected if there is hope for reconnecting with an African primal religious outlook. The following lines capture his more vitriolic anti-Catholic, anti-colonial sentiments clearly:

> Those who came to us
> carried beneath their nostrils
> the cross and a banner
> which showed a christ
> crouching and somnolent
> over the flames of purgatory
> and I forgot, a vomitive
> in the chalices of either hand!
> You have come:
> Are you certain you have conquered?[102]

In contrast to U Tam'si's anti-Christian sentiments, there are more positive references to features of primal religion—"the shadow the pagan no longer remembers." He is clear that this offers a more authentic African anchor for his identity than the Catholicism that permeates his culture as a treacherous colonial import; though at times his regret and pain at feeling disconnected from this primal identity is evident. Often he portrays this through a sense of fruitlessly grasping for something that remains elusively just beyond his reach, or a memory or dream fragment that persistently teases and beckons from the inaccessible periphery of consciousness.

In a poem entitled "Viaticum," U Tam'si brilliantly portrays these two religious options set before him in dialectical tension. He sees Christianity and colonialism as untrustworthy schemers on the one hand, in contrast to

---

101. U Tam'si, *Selected Poems*, "Strange Agony," in *A Game of Cheat-Heart*, 16. The capitalization is U Tam'si's.

102. U Tam'si, *Selected Poems*, "Holding its navel in check," in *The Belly*, 125.

an African primal worldview as personified by a woman "who has poisoned his soul to love no one but her":

> The cross the banner of negritude in overalls
>
> who's taken in?
>
> As for knowing which path will bring me less regret
>
> Everything afflicts me in this vertebrate monologue
>
> . . .
>
> Am I quite sure that backbone was mine
>
> And then who was that woman I loved
>
> She had the blue scent of burnt grasses
>
> on the savannah at pitch of noon
>
> at noon when the cicada sings
>
> in the shadow of some murdered shade
>
> a woman with arms blackened by the sun
>
> a woman with empty cradled arms that rocked me
>
> poisoned my soul to love no one but her[103]

One example of his identification with the primal imagination is his imagery and engagement with the natural world: "the lightning which shatters the night / shows me the tree of my origin / it was written in fire and flames."[104] Expounding on the role of nature within the African cosmology, Bediako makes the following argument in his master's dissertation. Significantly, this is Bediako's first engagement with the idea of "primal imagination" in any of his written work; I therefore quote in full:

> Essentially the Black African ontology demonstrates the relation between man and his environment. It is therefore the Black that Senghor calls 'the man of nature' par excellence, distinguished from the White by his non-subjugation of nature, but rather by his harmonization with it. He achieves this harmonization by his participation in the force, the life, of nature. And this is where we find the foundation of what is called the Bantu philosophy of life-force. From this 'cultural heritage' the black-African poet writing in French tries to find a vision of beauty, a vision that

---

103. U Tam'si, *Selected Poems*, "Viaticum," in *Epitomé*, 68.

104. U Tam'si, *Selected Poems*, "Strange Agony," in *A Game of Cheat-Heart*, 13. For a detailed argument on the role of nature within primal religion, see Harold Turner's description of "kinship with nature" as one of the six features which he assesses within primal religion in "The Primal Religions of the World and Their Study."

> could be named the 'primitive imagination.' Without troubling ourselves over the pejorative connotation that the expression primitive imagination could convey, we see that the Black-African poet, as opposed to the academician from the Western literary tradition—which is already in doubt—must endeavour to recover its original quality . . .[105]

Clearly Bediako's later theological interest and thinking around a primal religious worldview go back much further than has previously been considered, with roots not in his Christian theology but surprisingly, in French surrealist poetry. And as Bediako states in the above quote, it is the black-African poet rather than the Western academician who has a significant role to play in recovering this primal imagination. From this point onward, we begin to see evidence of Bediako's Christian faith in his writing, an introduction to which we have previously noted. In a written introduction presented at his doctoral defence, Bediako gave this reflection on how he pursued his research, and how he perceived U Tam'si:

> It is only when I understood for myself the need for freedom, for liberation . . . in short, for redemption, that I understood the same for Tchicaya U Tam'si. Since then, I did not dare seek to establish a gap between the pressing, deep, and universal need for reconciliation with the God who created us in His image, and the literary malaise of a great number of poets of today who seem to want to entrust their feelings of alienation and anguish to movements of poetic imagination, and its fruit: that is, poems. In effect, it is out of the abundance of the heart that the mouth speaks![106]

While Bediako's doctoral research was in the field of French African literature, he in effect turned his work into a theological treatise on U Tam'si, outlining the Christian Gospel within the first ten pages of his thesis and subsequently critiquing the poet from a theological perspective throughout. As we noted when introducing his doctoral work earlier in this chapter, Bediako argued that U Tam'si's search for transcendence, or "cosmic identification," apart from Christ was an error that could only end in failure.

---

105. Bediako, "Négritude et Surréalisme," 21–22. In a footnote following that comment, Bediako refers the reader to C. Maurice Bowra's book *Chants et Poesie du Peuples Primitifs* for further discussion around the idea of "primitive imagination." We may speculate that this is where Bediako first encountered the expression which he eventually termed "primal imagination."

106. Bediako, "Doctoral Defence Introductory Remarks," 5.

In his conclusion, Bediako audaciously proclaims that Tchicaya U Tam'si "needs deliverance" from early traumatic experiences as well as from a past heavy with humiliating memories, and needs to be reconciled within himself. Bediako continues, saying that the poet needs to also be delivered from false beliefs about the person and work of Jesus Christ, saying that it is only Christ—and not poetry—that can give him eternal life.[107] From a man who so tenaciously defended his atheistic worldview—to the point that one of his close friends in Ghana did not believe him when Bediako wrote to share the news of his Christian conversion—this marks a most surprising and very dramatic shift indeed.[108]

From Poetry and Identity to *Theology and Identity*

It seems a logical continuation, then, that after nearly a decade spent analyzing the search for African identity within Négritude poetry, Bediako as a new Christian continued looking for answers to some of these questions from his perspective as an African Christian intellectual.[109] His second doctoral thesis, later published as *Theology and Identity*, casts this search in a new light. In his introductory remarks to this work, he traces his scholarly and spiritual itinerary in this way: "From quite early in my Christian conversion experience, I have felt the need to seek a clarification for myself of how the abiding Gospel of Jesus Christ relates to the inescapable issues and questions which arise from the Christians cultural existence in the world, and how this relationship is achieved without injury to the integrity of the Gospel."[110]

Completed in 1983 a decade after his first doctorate, and published another decade-and-a-half later in 1999, *Theology and Identity* represents an important example of Bediako's maturing theological reflection. Building on the concerns raised in Négritude literature for promoting a positive and authentic *African* identity, Bediako continues his quest but now seeks a foundation for a modern African *Christian* identity, which he finds in second-century Christian history. This work roots his scholarship clearly within the continuum of Christian history, an abiding theme for Bediako and one similarly emphasized later within the MTh program at ACI.

107. Bediako, "L'Univers Interieur," 210–12.

108. For his account of this event, see Bediako, filmed interview by James Ault, 1998, DigiBeta Reel GB 105: 8

109. In terms of chronology, from 1973–1976 Bediako pursued a BA at what was then London Bible College (now London School of Theology); returned briefly to Ghana where he was ordained as a Presbyterian minister (1978); and then went to Aberdeen to pursue his second doctorate with Andrew Walls (1978–1984).

110. Bediako, *Theology and Identity*, xi.

Within *Theology and Identity*, Bediako continues to examine the role of primal religion within African Christian discourse, and contrasts twentieth-century African scholarship and experience with second-century Christian thought. Bediako addresses the second-century voices of Tatian, Tertullian, Justin, and Clement of Alexandria with regard to the Christian gospel in relation to "barbarism" and the person of Christ within Hellenistic culture.

He then compares these second-century thinkers to four modern African Christian scholars. These include Nigerian Bolaji Idowo, who strongly advocates for continuity between African primal religion and Christianity. Bediako argues that Idowu's emphasis on the centrality of primal religion gives his theology "both a consistency and an ambiguity: a consistency, in that, more than any other African theologian of his generation he says clearly that African theology needed to give a theological interpretation of the old religion." However, "it seems to me," Bediako says, "[Idowu] never quite clarified what then constituted the 'newness' of Christianity . . . Idowu's theology, therefore, illustrates a very particular perspective, perhaps a *necessary* perspective, but also, in my view, an inadequate and a limited perspective."[111]

Idowu's Nigerian compatriot and ideological counterpoint is shown in Byang Kato, whose "deep roots in the conservative evangelical tradition—particularly of the North American variant" shaped his staunch views on the radical discontinuity between primal religion and Christianity.[112] In Kato, Bediako finds "the very antithesis of the basic positions" enunciated by the other African scholars whom he brings into this work.

For a more balanced perspective, Bediako turns to Kenyan John Mbiti. While Mbiti sees continuity between Christianity and primal religion, he brings to this discussion "a profoundly settled Christian self-consciousness which makes his vindication of African religious values free from anti-European polemic."[113] Mbiti remained a significant influence for Bediako both in terms of shaping his theological thought and later the curriculum at ACI.

Uniquely, Bediako also incorporates aspects of French African Catholic scholarship in this work, analyzing Congolese theologian Mulago gwa Cikala Musharhamina (Vincent Mulago), the only French and Catholic voice in the book. Bediako remarks that essays by Mulago were included in the seminal work *Des Prêtres noir s'interrogent* which he finds noteworthy because it was released under the auspices of "Présence Africaine," the

---

111. Bediako, "Bolaji Idowu," 16.
112. Bediako, *Theology and Identity*, 386–87.
113. Ibid., 304.

publishing house connected with French African intellectual thought in Paris, including a great deal of Négritude literature.[114]

This is noteworthy, argues Bediako, because "it indicated the extent to which this manifestation of African theological self-consciousness was related to the wider and intensifying 'cultural crisis of conscience' which had taken place among African francophone intellectuals in the previous two decades under the aegis of the Négritude movement . . . This convergence of the quest for an African theological identity on the one hand, and the more pervasive affirmation of an African cultural personality on the other . . . has continued, imparting a heightened degree of cultural awareness generally to the writings of francophone African theologians."[115]

In itself, the inclusion of this chapter is significant in that the French Catholic strand of the African study of African religions is rarely included in the wider, heavily Anglo-Protestant African literature. This again points to the influence of Négritude philosophy on Bediako's later thought and is another reason why a thorough study of his Négritude scholarship is important. Herein we begin to see how it prepared him for an ecumenical, pan-African approach to the African Christian study of African religions. The French Catholic component of Bediako's scholarship remains underexplored; but insight into his perspectives on the Négritude movement opens the door for fresh interpretation here.

A key focus in *Theology and Identity* is the process by which African Christian scholars grappled with issues of gospel and culture in order to establish identities that were equally African and Christian. Bediako argues that this concern was anticipated by early scholars of African religions. Here he points to Bengt Sundkler, who stated in 1960 that "a theologian who with the Apostle is prepared to become to the Jews as a Jew . . . and *therefore,* unto Africans as an African, must needs start with the fundamental facts of the African interpretation of existence and the universe."[116]

Bediako sees this as an effort at interpreting Christ within categories relevant to African thought: "what Sundkler's suggestion amounted to . . . was that the interpretation, albeit from a *Christian* stand-point, of the African pre-Christian heritage of ideas and wisdom, was an essential and integral part of the task of theology in the African Church." Furthermore, to the extent that this discourse "has been made as a self-consciously Christian and theological effort, it can be said to have been an endeavour to demonstrate

---

114. Présence Africaine, *Des Prêtres noir s'interrogent*.
115. Bediako, *Theology and Identity*, 347.
116. Sundkler, *The Christian Ministry in Africa*, 100; italics Sundkler's.

the true character of African Christian identity."[117] Here again are concerns which he first encountered in Négritude poetry.

Read against the backdrop of Bediako's Négritude scholarship and conversion experience, and recalling the zealously evangelistic, dogmatic emphasis of *L'Univers Interieur de Tchicaya U Tam'si*, the intellectual motivations underpinning *Theology and Identity* become much clearer. This is not a theological contribution in the narrow sense of addressing questions of Christian doctrine or biblical hermeneutics; indeed, his first doctorate covered that ground. *Theology and Identity* is instead a demonstration of Bediako's quest to root his African Christian intellectual itinerary in something concrete and quantifiable: history.

In the writings of these early Christians, Bediako finds their examination of the past to be paramount in their religious itinerary, noting, "[a] key was needed to interpret the past and stake claims on it, or to reject it as utterly unworthy."[118] It is difficult to miss the echoes of the Négritudinist agenda here, and especially the voice of U Tam'si seeking a key to interpreting the roots of his "absurd ancestry." Négritude writers struggled to overcome the imposed French colonial identities that they had inherited, but tried to do so by revalorising African history and religious cosmologies.

Similarly, Bediako saw a comparison in African Christians in the post-missionary, post-colonial era who sought to move beyond the European models of Christianity that had been bequeathed to them, seeking instead to root their faith authentically in African history and culture. In analyzing Bediako's lengthy immersion in Négritude ideology, it is easy to see the roots of his theological interest here: clearly, a motivating basis for his search for a key to interpreting African Christian history and identity lies squarely in his experience of the Négritude agenda.

U Tam'si tried to recover an African identity through images, poetic idiom, and surrealist thought—essentially, within the limitless, intangible expanse of the "primal imagination." But Bediako ultimately found this approach flawed. Grounding himself as an African Christian intellectual within a historical continuum of others like him provided a concrete framework from which to continue interrogating his questions of identity. Put more simply, history offered a much more "this-worldly" approach from the "other-worldliness" of U Tam'si's poetry. Furthermore—and perhaps this is a clue to the underlying motivation for the remainder of his academic career—as an intellectual, this historical approach gave him a basis for interpreting his intangible, unscientifically explainable conversion experience.

117. Bediako, *Theology and Identity*, 3; italics his.
118. Ibid., 49.

We will give the last word here to Bediako, as he explains the motivation behind *Theology and Identity* in an interview:

> What I learned from Andrew Walls ... is the ... ability to put one's experience in historical perspective. That my [conversion] experience wasn't in limbo, it wasn't simply hallucinatory, it wasn't just a trip. That what had happened to me in my quest for intellectual coherence through faith, in fact, could be documented, could be replicated, indeed, could be understood in the light of Christian history. It is Andrew Walls who helped me to begin to read the early second-century Christian writers ... and to read these as, well, as kinsmen, you know ... And so that led me to that doctoral work which I found fruitful, extremely fruitful. Early second century Christian thought and life, the quest for cultural integrity, cultural integration, intellectual integration, which in some ways I think is what I was myself feeling after, and modern African questions.[119]

Cultural integrity. Cultural integration. Intellectual integration. Through pursuing these themes within the context of modern African Christian theological thought, and seeking to affirm that there was a historical precedent for such discourse, Bediako discovered a more concrete approach to some of the irresolvable tensions of surrealist poetry and the Négritude movement. And, while he continued to pursue the intellectual concerns that strongly resonated with him in the Négritude movement throughout the remainder of his life—African identity, primal religion, vernacular language, proximity to one's homeland—his Christian perspective gave new shape and impetus to his scholarship and he never returned to Négritude poetry.

Afua Kuma, A New Poetic Muse

As we consider the abiding impact of Négritude scholarship on Bediako, one later figure brings this discussion full circle: Ghanaian poet Madam Afua Kuma, whom Bediako deeply respected and frequently used as a source in his theological writing. We have already read Bediako's argument that in the effort to recover an African identity, a participation in the "primitive

---

119. Bediako, interview by James Ault, 1998, DigiBeta Reel GB 105: 6. Bediako goes on to note that when *Theology and Identity* was published, it was among the top five finalists for the Harper-Collins award for theological books in the U.K., and was apparently the first time an African author was included as a finalist (7).

imagination" and the "Bantu philosophy of life force" is better done by the poets than by the academicians.

In the pre-Christian portion of Bediako's life, U Tam'si presented a paradigm to live by: a highly educated, French-speaking African poet expressing the deep pain of a lost identity, on a quest to recover his history and sense of Africanness. As a Christian, Bediako maintained the belief that the primal imagination lay at the heart of engaging an authentic African Christian identity; however, he finds a new poet with whom to identify.

Afua Kuma is in every way the antithesis of U Tam'si. In her we find a non-literate Ghanaian Christian woman who lived in the rural town of Obo-Kwahu in Ghana where she farmed, practised as a traditional midwife, and was a member of the Church of Pentecost.[120] Her poetry, expressed in the form of traditional chiefly Akan praise songs, is an example of joyful, extemporaneous praise offered to and about Jesus. Afua Kuma performed her praise poems in *Twi*, her mother tongue. While she became well-known for performing these praise songs extemporaneously, a small collection of her praise songs were transcribed and translated, published in Ghana in Twi and English as *Jesus of the Deep Forest: Prayers and Praises of Afua Kuma*, with translation by Jon Kirby, S.V.D.

U Tam'si's poems reflect a level of distress and conflict between primal religion and Christianity and highlight a deep desire to reconnect with a lost African identity by way of engagement with the primal. Afua Kuma, as Christian, instead dwells wholeheartedly in that African reality, seeing Jesus in nature and everyday life, experiencing him as protector, provider, and chief. The delight of this discovery leads to her "spontaneous adoration of Jesus," with praise songs in the tradition of those offered to a local chief.[121] A few lines of her words begin to illustrate these features:

> [Jesus is] The great Rock we hide behind:
>
> the great forest canopy that gives cool shade:
>
> the Big Tree which lifts its vines
>
> to peep at the heavens,
>
> the magnificent Tree whose dripping leaves
>
> encourage luxuriant growth below.[122]

Another image of Jesus which roots him firmly within her primal religious worldview: "O great and powerful Jesus, incomparable Diviner, / the

---

120. See Bediako, "Cry Jesus!," 9, and Afua Kuma, *Jesus of the Deep Forest*, 3.
121. Bediako, "Cry Jesus!," 9.
122. Afua Kuma, *Jesus of the Deep Forest*, 5.

sun and moon are your *batakari* [robe] / It sparkles like the morning star. / . . . all the nations see your glory."[123] One final example from both Tchicaya U Tam'si and Afua Kuma demonstrates their radically different perspectives on how they perceive themselves in relation to Jesus. In turn, this underscores the paradigm shift within Bediako.

As we read earlier, U Tam'si, disconnected from his African home and identity, writes, "Christ I laugh at your sadness / . . . / I will waltz to the tune of your slow sadness."[124] Afua Kuma, on the other hand, says this: "We are going to praise the name of Jesus Christ. / We shall announce his many [chiefly] titles: / they are true and they suit him well, / so it is fitting that we do this."[125] The contrast between them could not be more stark.

Bediako argues for the role of primal religion in engaging Christian theology and laments the fact that much of our present, and particularly Western, theological framework has lost touch with, or is unable to, engage with this worldview. A primal perspective, he argues, engages "the crucial issues which lie at the heart of human existence, issues which are essentially religious: questions of human identity, community, ecological equilibrium and justice. Because primal world-views are fundamentally religious, the primal imagination restores to theology the crucial dimension of living religiously for which the theologian needs make no apology. The primal imagination may help us restore the ancient unity of theology and spirituality."[126]

Bediako once saw U Tam'si providing guidance in this area; but concluded that by failing to acknowledge Jesus, he proved an inadequate guide. However, U Tam'si's lasting influence is evident as Bediako applied the same key themes to his Christian theological task. As he said, he was searching for a meaningful paradigm through which to make sense of the world. He found this in the person of Christ, and regularly commented that it was only in becoming Christian that he truly became African.[127] U Tam'si and Négritude poetry led him into this line of thinking; but ultimately he found the fullest expression of an African poet engaging with the primal worldview in the Christian praises of Afua Kuma.

Drawing this chapter to a close, it is helpful to bring these diverse strands back together. To return to our original focus on Négritude

---

123. Ibid., 6. The term *batakari* is defined in the glossary as "long flowing robe worn in the north of Ghana" (50).

124. U Tam'si, *Selected Poems*, from "The Scorner," 72.

125. Afua Kuma, *Jesus of the Deep Forest*, 5.

126. Bediako, "The Primal Imagination," 105.

127. Gillian Mary Bediako, interview with the author, April 27, 2010, Akrofi-Christaller Institute, Ghana. When I was at ACI in 2006, Bediako regularly referenced this comment in lectures, interviews and discussions.

literature, we see that these writers represent some of the first twentieth-century African scholars to contemplate the interactions of Africa's Old and New Religions. However, during these early decades (1930s–1950s) the themes of identity, nationalism, and anti-colonialism took precedence, with religion more often in the background.

As an ideological and literary movement, Négritude has raised many criticisms, some irreconcilable. Nevertheless, it cannot be easily dismissed, particularly in the African study of African religions. Beier comments that "those African poets who most strongly assert their *négritude* are often the most sophisticated and—on the surface at least—the most assimilated Africans."[128] In reading Senghor's poetry, Beier contends that while some might imagine Senghor's references to various African personages, places, and stories to be "merely picturesque trappings intended to provide atmosphere and an African flavour to his poetry," the opposite is true. In his opinion, the *Africanness* of Senghor's poetry is not an external, "folkloristic" imposition, but in fact is what makes his poetry "genuinely African, because it expresses genuine African attitudes on very basic questions."[129]

When we consider this as the intellectual and philosophical foundation upon which Bediako built his subsequent theological arguments, we can already see a pattern of looking to the past and to one's culture for a sense of authentic identity. Indeed, Bediako's value for using biography as a methodological approach began with his study of U Tam'si. He understood that analyzing U Tam'si's poetry apart from his context would have been of little value. Instead, to get a fuller sense of the man, he read U Tam'si within the wider context of the poet's family, his African community in Paris, and the emerging post-independence and war-torn Congo to which U Tam'si was looking. Text needs context. And, as we have seen, Bediako went on to apply this same approach to reading early and modern African theologians.

From this reading of Bediako's early research on Tchicaya U Tam'si alongside of *Theology and Identity*, it is evident that we can trace many significant roots of Bediako's later theological writing to this period of his life, making an argument for Négritude as a key influence on his Christian scholarship. Further, it highlights the contribution of Négritude literature to the wider African study of African religions. Significantly, this chapter uncovered the fact that Bediako was discussing the primal imagination (or "primitive imagination," as he called it then) prior to his conversion or Christian engagement with primal religion. Exploring this thought further in comparing the poetry of U Tam'si with Afua Kuma, it is clear that these

128. Beier, "L. S. Senghor," 95.
129. Ibid.

African poets made lasting but very different marks on Bediako. These important discoveries provide new and exciting keys to interpreting Bediako, and also point to poetry as an important but overlooked source within the study of religion in Africa.

Summarising U Tam'si and Bediako's perspectives on the roles of intellect, poetry, and religion, let us conclude this chapter with the following two quotes, the first, from U Tam'si:

> And if this harp cannot follow me
>
> there where the spirits wait
>
> This is my testament:
>
> I leave you the fire and the song.[130]

And from Bediako, a concluding statement from his first doctoral thesis: "Tchicaya U Tam'si is a very gifted poet. But he has yet to receive the most magnificent of gifts that he could desire, that of meeting the Giver himself. This Jesus Christ, in whom 'are hidden all the treasures of wisdom and of sciences (knowledge),' is 'the same yesterday, today, and forever.'"[131]

The Négritude movement, which gave dignity and ascribed worth to African history and identity, had a profound and lasting impact on Bediako: on his methodology, his subsequent theological work, and in his continued value for African poetry as an important medium for engaging with African religion.

While U Tam'si's cry of "oh my absurd ancestry, down from what tree?" remains unresolved, Bediako asks the same question but arrives at a specific answer. He identifies his ancestral source as being Jesus Christ, and argues that modern African Christian scholars can trace their identity through the "family tree" of second-century Christianity.

---

130. U Tam'si, *Selected Poems*, "Legs" in *Bow Harp*, 141.

131. Bediako, "L'Univers Interieur," 212–13.

Bediako is referencing two biblical passages here: Colossians 2:2–3: "My goal is that they may be encouraged . . . in order that they may know the mystery of God, namely, Christ, in whom are hidden all the treasures of wisdom and knowledge," and Hebrews 13:8: "Jesus Christ is the same yesterday and today and forever."

Chapter 6

Reading the Akrofi-Christaller Institute as Text
Bediako's Magnum Opus

Theology is an academic discipline, to be pursued, like other disciplines, with rigor; but its sources lie, not in the study or the library, but in the nature of Christian life. The mainspring of theology is in the decisions that Christians—all Christians— have to make; simply because they are Christians.[1]

—Andrew F. Walls

---

1. Walls, Foreword to *Re-Imagining African Christologies*, ix. Adinkra symbol *Dwennimmen*, or "ram's horns." This is a symbol of humility together with strength: the ram will fight fiercely against an adversary, but also submits humbly to slaughter, emphasizing that even the strong need to be humble. This symbol is used on the ACI

The Story of ACI

WALLS' QUOTE SETS THE scene for this chapter's focus on the Akrofi-Christaller Institute as the embodiment of Bediako's theological opus, which institutionally combines rigorous scholarship, historical continuity, and engagement with daily Christian life and thought; the mainspring of theology, as Walls puts it. Bediako's experiences studying in Ghana, France, and the U.K. highlighted for him the lack of relevant training opportunities for African Christian scholars that took seriously the African context and simultaneously valued a Christian perspective in rigorous intellectual engagement. This motivated him to creatively address this gap through the establishment of an institution focused on these values.

As we will see, it is in the creation of ACI that Bediako most vividly displays the wide-angled lens through which he examines, not only his own personal spiritual and intellectual journey, but that of Ghana and indeed Africa as a whole. Within the Institute's curriculum and academic community, Bediako models his preferred methodological approaches to the study of religions in Africa, an examination of which reveals new interpretative keys to his own theological conclusions.

Bediako's Road to ACI

Following from the conclusion of his first doctorate in 1973, Bediako identifies three pivotal events that ultimately led to the founding of ACI. Firstly, he points to his participation in the Lausanne Congress on World Evangelisation (1974) as a "defining moment." It was at this Congress that he first encountered other theologians whom he calls "other 'radical' Christians of evangelical persuasion from the Two-Thirds World."[2] These colleagues were wrestling with similar theological issues, and it became clear to Bediako that there was a need for greater scholarship, fellowship, and collaborative reflection. Subsequent to this Congress he began a file of ideas for a future "mission research centre" in Ghana.[3]

The second key event was Bediako's first encounter with Andrew Walls, whom he invited to speak at the London School of Theology in 1975. As Bediako recalls, Walls addressed "the modern shift in the centre of gravity of Christianity . . . and the significance of Africa's place in Christian history

---

crest, as the combination of strength and humility are values that they seek to embody in their scholarship and community.

2. Bediako and Bediako, "Ebenezer," 5.
3. Ibid.

as an emergent heartland of vital Christian life and thought." This made a profound impression upon Bediako. Nearly half a century later, these ideas are very well-known; but, Bediako recalls, "it was a notion that, at the time, was not found in any textbook on Church History, nor was it taught on the syllabus of any theological college."[4]

Significantly, this encounter began to clarify for Bediako that his engagement with African Christian scholarship needed to be based in Africa, and that it "was not to be the pursuit of an academic career in an ivory tower, isolated from the life and struggles of the church" but quite the opposite. Perhaps this was in response to his experience with the limited reach of Négritude scholarship as literature by and for the African intellectual elite. At any rate, his call was to be fully engaged with the mission of the Church, continuing his quest to understand how his Christian faith could interact positively with his Ghanaian cultural identity.[5] This vision for scholarship that was linked to the everyday concerns of African Christians was, and remains, a guiding force in the establishment of the Institute, as was his continued association with Walls.

The third key event occurred in 1983 when Bediako was a student in Aberdeen. He received a visit from the Rev. S.K. Aboa, a Presbyterian minister tasked with visiting all PCG scholars abroad. Bediako describes this meeting as "catalytic." By this point, he had an eleven-page memorandum entitled "The Idea of a Centre for Mission Research in Ghana," which he shared with Aboa, who responded enthusiastically. The PCG Synod Committee subsequently informed the Bediakos that they supported this vision, and in 1984 Kwame and Gillian Bediako returned to Ghana to begin this work.[6]

The Institute as Text

While Bediako's publications have primarily been evaluated theologically, his scholarly legacy as seen in the establishment of ACI has not been adequately examined for what it is; namely, his overarching contribution and an important example of an innovative paradigm for studying religion in Africa. An examination of the Institute as a whole, and particularly Bediako's unpublished course materials and his reflections on the vision behind ACI, reveals that his itinerary as an African Christian scholar goes far beyond familiar theological discourse.

4. Ibid., 6.
5. Ibid.
6. Ibid., 7–8.

Furthermore, as we shall see, even those scholars who have evaluated Bediako through engagement with his published opus have missed important aspects of his contribution by failing to recognize that the most comprehensive expression of his thought is found in the Institute and surrounding community—the laboratory in which he lived out and tested his methodological approaches. Through ACI, Bediako has made, and continues to make, a unique and abiding contribution to the African Christian study of African religions.

It is rightly said that Bediako's legacy includes "his thought, sermons, actions, writings, influences and the institution he built."[7] I would go so far as to argue that ACI may be seen as Bediako's magnum opus, the bringing together of his methodological, historical, theological, cultural, and pastoral concerns. We have already begun to see this academic itinerary in *Theology and Identity*. This chapter demonstrates that within the community and curriculum at ACI, Bediako crystalizes these concerns within the course themes for the MTh in African Christianity, as well as in the daily worship practices and community involvement that he instituted. Taken together, we see that Bediako's key concerns include biblical foundations for African Christian scholarship; African Christian history; primal religion; vernacular languages ("mother-tongue"); and the combined role that these all play in shaping African Christian identities.

The remainder of this chapter therefore offers an evaluation of ACI, including an analysis of the MTh curriculum and ACI's community life. As we will see, such an examination chronologically and thematically draws together the concerns of the previous chapters, including historical, geographical, and ideological links to the Basel Mission; the British colonial concern for rigorous academic engagement with African religion and culture; and the nationalistic and Négritude foci on the quest for authentic African identity and an affinity for primal religion. What we have seen so far should bring into sharper focus the methodological creativity and theological vision that Bediako most clearly displays through ACI. Within all of the complexities of this emerging religious discourse, ACI models a unique paradigm in African Christian scholarship, and simultaneously challenges accepted categorizations within Western theological scholarship and the study of religion in Africa.

---

7. Asamoah-Gyadu, "Kwame Bediako and the Eternal Christological Question," 39.

New Paradigms in the African Christian Study of African Religions

From my reading of Bediako's unpublished course materials and my participation at ACI, I find that ACI may be "read" as a tangible demonstration of Bediako's key theological concerns, manifest in the curriculum, physical location, name, and academic community that he designed and led. Here Bediako is revealed as a leading figure in this emerging discourse. An observation from Sierra Leonean theologian Harry Sawyerr in 1971 presciently pointed to the need for such an Institute a decade and a half before its inception:

> We would say that, certainly within the last thirty years, with the development of nationalism and the collateral dissemination of the unclear term 'African personality' and its French counterpart 'Négritude', the Church in Africa is faced with a clamant demand for an interpretation of the Christian faith, in a sanguine hope that such an interpretation, when produced, would provide a means of bringing home to Africans the truths of the Christian gospel in an idiom related to the African situation.[8]

Uniquely, Bediako interacted with both of these ideologies firsthand, concluding that both failed to offer a positive corollary for African Christian engagement with African religions. Sawyerr's observation was something of a prophetic word: he identified the gap in African Christian scholarship and concluded that a completely new approach was needed. In turn, Bediako brought his understanding of the goals and weaknesses of both the African personality and Négritude movement, as well as the "clamant need" for an interpretation of Christianity "in an African idiom" and developed something new: an institution designed to pursue African Christian scholarship in an idiom related to the African situation. Bediako defines his vision in this way:

> The nature of the field is theological and pastoral. While we are dealing with deeply theological questions, we are also being called to a pastoral challenge . . . The materials we study, once held to be the preserve of anthropologists, have theological significance, and we need courage to handle them theologically. We are looking at them in a new way, as "our" story, making us true participants and not merely participant-observers.
>
> We also need a new style of scholarship marked by collegiality, fellowship and collaboration (as against competition,

---

8. Sawyerr, "The Theological Method," 13.

individualism, careerism). Our task is Christian scholarship as ministry, so that it is not for ourselves alone.[9]

ACI: The First Two Decades (1985–2006)

Upon returning to Ghana, Bediako was posted as a pastor at Accra Ridge Church for two years. It was an important period for him to become more at home in the PCG and to make connections with those who would later support the Institute. In 1985, he was appointed by the PCG as Director of the Akrofi-Christaller Memorial Centre [sic] for Mission Research and Applied Theology.[10] By 1987, the Institute was established in former Basel Mission Buildings in Akropong, where it remains. In these early years, efforts were focused on programs and seminars supporting the work of the Church.

The shift from church-based programs to postgraduate research (graduate research in North American terms) began in 1995. ACI partnered with the University of Natal's School of Theology to offer the MTh in African Christianity, as well as doctoral research. By 2006, the Institute was accredited as a postgraduate research institution by the National Accreditation Board of the Ministry of Education (Ghana) with a Presidential Charter to award its own degrees. I was in fact present at ACI when they received this status, and recall having the issue raised as a topic of prayer in daily chapel times leading up to the decision, with much rejoicing following the successful outcome.

Scholarship from the Grassroots

As the Bediakos outline in "Ebenezer," the main focus of the first decade at ACI included *Twi* Bible studies; seminars for Catechists, Presbyters and Group Leaders; courses for teaching students in the Presbyterian Training College interested in lay ministry; Mission and Ministry Orientation for newly commissioned pastors; retreats for pastors and spouses; and Children and Youth Leaders' seminars.[11] But this had a direct impact on the Institute's subsequent transition into a postgraduate theological research center in that the concerns and challenges which Bediako encountered at a grassroots

---

9. Bediako, as referenced in "Editorial" *JACT* 11/2 (December 2008) 4.

10. The name was officially changed to the Akrofi-Christaller Institute for Theology, Mission, and Culture in 2006 when they received a full Presidential Charter.

11. See Bediako and Bediako, "Ebenezer," 14.

level ultimately provided "the essential resource and raw materials for the reflection, writing and action emerging from the [Institute]."[12]

While the Bediakos had benefitted from what they call "probably the best that the West could offer by way of theological training," their engagement with the Ghanaian Christian context, and specifically the *Twi* Bible studies, "provided the context for the new theological reflections that would ultimately feed into the publications that would come from the Centre."[13]

Gillian Bediako remarks, "[We realized] that it was possible to maintain a link between active participation in the life and ministry of the church and the task of scholarship, and that it was possible for the [Institute] to serve the church through research and Christian scholarship as its unique focus. It was then only a short step to seeing its implications for the development of academic programs."[14] This is in keeping with earlier remarks we have read by Bediako on the importance of his Christian faith being able to relate to everyday life, and of his desire to engage his intellectual questions in a more grassroots environment.

From the early days of the Institute's development and partnership with the University of (now) KwaZulu-Natal, the stated purpose was the provision of theological training in the African context "that equips young scholars to find Christian answers to African questions. This course has the potential for training a new generation of African theologians, and for eventually attracting students from the West who are open to learn in and from Africa."[15] We are only another decade further into the future, but already these goals are increasingly being realized.

The Basel Mission and ACI: An Enduring Legacy

The Town of Akropong

The foundation of ACI takes us back to the Basel Mission, with ACI being based in the town of Akropong in former Basel Mission buildings. The significance for Bediako of this geographical link is addressed when, while taking documentary filmmaker James Ault on a tour of Akropong, Bediako remarks, "For me it's always an emotional experience, this Hanover, as they

---

12. Ibid., 17.

13. Ibid.

14. Gillian Mary Bediako, "'Ebenezer, this is how far the Lord has helped us': Celebrating 25 years of God's faithfulness," 3–4. This is an updated version of the earlier "Ebenezer" document.

15. Visser and Bediako, Introduction to *Jesus in Africa*, ix.

call this part of Akropong. Not Hanover in Germany, but Hanover in Jamaica because that's where the Moravians came from."[16]

He further reflects upon the contribution of these West Indian missionaries and demonstrates his value for rooting the Institute, and this field of research, in African and Christian history: "These people who themselves, through the melancholic history of slavery . . . were now returning to Africa—in their mind they were returning to their own people, as missionaries. And what they brought was a sympathy, a fellow-feeling, and identification with our people, because these were their people. They came to settle, they didn't come to go back, they came to settle."[17]

Bediako's personal commitment to remaining in Ghana despite attractive offers to relocate partially echoes the actions of these Moravian Christians and gives a clue as to the depth of his sentiments here. After a painful sojourn abroad, the Moravians were returning in liberty as committed Christians with the desire to use their "insider" position to engage in the local community meaningfully. It is not a stretch to understand Bediako's emotional identification with them, as he himself returned from foreign countries with a newfound faith and commitment to settle and engage in Christian service as a member of the community. Like the Moravians, he first encountered Christ while living outside of Africa, struggling to connect with his African identity. And for Bediako, his faith proved to be a key to connecting with this identity, and living in Ghana was a critical aspect of nurturing it.

Bediako also identifies with the work of the Basel Mission when he comments on ACI's residence within former Mission buildings: "[w]e have entered into the labours of others."[18] Thus Bediako was increasingly seeing his new faith as being, in fact, an old faith—an African faith—with a history that included European and African missionaries.

Furthermore, in "Ebenezer," the Bediakos list all of those present for the launching of the Centre on Saturday, November 1, 1986, and mention the ambassadors of Switzerland and Germany and the High Commissioner of the United Kingdom, who "spoke about the human connections through the Christian histories of their respective countries with Ghana that the Centre symboliz[ed]."[19] Also represented were the Christian Council of Ghana, the Presbyterian Church of Ghana, the University of Ghana (through the

---

16. Bediako, "Kwame Bediako in conversation with James Ault during walk through the Hanover section of Akropong, 2006," GF 18, 1. Bediako is referring to the Moravian missionaries who revived Andreas Riis's efforts in Akropong.

17. Ibid., 2-3.

18. Ibid., 10.

19. Bediako and Bediako, "Ebenezer," 11.

presence of Kwesi Dickson) and *Oseadeeyo* Nana Addo Dankwa III, the Omanhene, "symbolic of the close connection between Christianity and traditional culture in Akuapem, a historic link he [Dankwa] saw the Centre as coming to enhance."[20] These connections not only tied Bediako to Ghanaian history, including the Basel Mission's nineteenth- and twentieth-century efforts, but to broader African history, world history, and to Christian history; all key themes ultimately reflected in ACI's curriculum.

The location and physical buildings of ACI can therefore be read an as outward, tangible sign of Bediako's sense of being a part of wider Christian history, a history which linked Ghanaians with Europeans and Africans in a common desire to make Christ known in that community. Underscoring this point, the title of the Bediakos' unpublished account of the history of ACI is itself significant: "Ebenezer" is traditionally a stone or memorial commemorating the Lord's faithfulness. They perceive the Institute itself as an ebenezer, an outward sign representing an important religious and scholarly itinerary, linking Bediako historically to the Moravians, Akrofi, Christaller and others in the continuum of African Christian history and experience.

"Akrofi-Christaller": What's In a Name?

The links between the Basel Mission and the Akrofi-Christaller Institute extend far beyond the physical location of the town of Akropong or the Basel Mission buildings. One immediately clear link is in the Institute's name. Bediako enumerates several reasons why he chose to honour J.G. Christaller and C.A. Akrofi by naming the Institute after them, which gives further insight into his understanding of his life mission and that of the Institute. Christaller and Akrofi shared a love for Christ; outstanding abilities in *Twi* translation; a vocational commitment to Christian scholarship; and, coincidentally, a home within the Basel Mission compound, though a century apart. To Bediako, these factors served as potent symbols of physical continuity, demonstrating unity of purpose and vision between himself and those who had gone before.

Bediako reflects that Christaller entered so deeply into the Twi language and thought patterns that his work served as a cultural witness of the Church, demonstrating affinities and pointing the way to further engagement between Akan thought and Christianity. The strength of Bediako's connection to Christaller is demonstrated when he says, "[i]n a sense, [Christaller's] work laid the foundation for the work which I dedicate my

---

20. Ibid.

life to doing here."[21] Bediako shows equally high regard for Akrofi's subsequent contribution, arguing that both men demonstrated a deep awareness of Akan culture and worldview to have been able to do such extensive translation work. This serves as a clear reminder that Bediako perceives his theological itinerary as following a well-established historical pattern of Christian scholarship.

ACI and Pietism

Another important link between Akrofi, Christaller, and Bediako is their pietism. Bediako acknowledges that these men set an example for earnestly holding to their Christian faith while simultaneously applying this faith to scholarship and public witness. For them, Bediako argues, Christian faith was necessarily lived out "in the public arena of scholarship, of thought, of one's participation in culture, with Christian tools, offering them to the community, offering them to society, offering them to the culture."[22] These are clearly values that Bediako embraces, and which continue to be lived out through the Institute within times of daily worship, community life and in the context of the classroom, which we will consider shortly. As Asamoah-Gyadu observes, Bediako's "combination of academic rigor with a deep personal evangelical faith, devotional interest in the Bible and pastoral heart were rare gifts," and he reflects that Bediako never planned or led academic conferences without beginning each day's activities with prayer and a reading of the Bible.[23]

A further critical point of affinity for Bediako is evidenced in a speech given by Akrofi in the 1960s. In it, Akrofi challenged the prevailing views of Christianity propagated by Nkrumah, including the suspicion of Christianity as a foreign and imperialist religion to discard in favor of Nkrumah's African Personality. Akrofi instead argued that Christianity was a universal religion, and stated that his daily engagement with the Bible through his translation work was both culturally and personally liberating.[24]

Bediako interprets Akrofi on this point when he says, "[b]eing Christian is not being less African . . . [it is being] even more so . . . And Christianity became [for Akrofi] the integrating element in one's life. Not that sort of naïve integration where everything was simply locked in or folded in, no. But it became a critical factor, sifting, sifting old and new, sifting and

21. Bediako, filmed interview by James Ault, 1998, DigiBeta Reel GB 109: 54.
22. Ibid., 55.
23. Asamoah-Gyadu, "Bediako of Africa," 9.
24. Bediako, interview by James Ault, 1998, DigiBeta Reel GB 109: 56–57.

creating a new ... unity of self."[25] This statement equally describes Bediako's understanding of his faith journey as an African Christian. His recognition of this perspective in Akrofi and his choice to name the Institute after him offer strong indicators as to the Christian and intellectual itineraries of Bediako personally and institutionally. Bediako concludes, saying that he finds it particularly interesting that both Christaller and Akrofi shared

> the same sense of the integration that comes when Christianity is seen for what it truly, in [their] understanding, is: as the critical element in every cultural integration. And so we named the [Institute] after these two men, because of their cultural witness to the Gospel in this place. Because, in a strange way, from modest beginnings [we see] their outstanding efforts in bringing together Christian faith and cultural integrity. And, a cultural integrity, not just an idea, not as an abstraction, but as a concrete focus of human existence ... you know, and a concrete existence which is meant to be shared.[26]

Here again we see Bediako's repeated focus on cultural integration, cultural integrity, and the search for a concrete existence for a faith perspective. He demonstrates here that his search was not unique; he was part of a historical continuum. Their search was his search.

The Institute was named for these two men because ultimately their religious itineraries—engaging Christ and the local language and culture on a deep level—resonated profoundly with Bediako's own search and sense of vocation. Christaller and Akrofi lived out their understanding of cultural identity as a "concrete focus," balancing rigorous linguistic scholarship with grassroots community engagement. In the same way, Bediako not only wrote about cultural integration but lived it out and demonstrated this same concrete focus within the life of the Institute.

To this end, both the name and location of the Akrofi-Christaller Institute can be read as outward signs of Bediako's methodological approach in locating the African Christian study of religions unequivocally within the wider trajectory of African and Christian history. And, by including a German missionary in the Institution's identity, Bediako makes a further statement about his inclusivity: ACI may be an Afrocentric institution, but this identity does not ignore or discount the efforts of some Western missionaries and colonialists whom he sees as having positively contributed to the African study of African religions.

25. Ibid., 57.
26. Ibid, 57–58.

However, his positive approach to European participation is certainly not shared by all African theologians. Maluleke, for example, offers a strong critique of both Bediako and Sanneh on this point when he says that, "while recognizing the possibility of positive implications in the calls of Sanneh and Bediako for a view of African Christianity that is not too thickly clouded by the mist of colonialism, the question is whether they do in fact make a compelling case with their particular proposal. I do not think they do. It is one thing to engage in what I have called the search for alternative histories of and for the oppressed. It is quite another to seek such histories in order to let the oppressors off the hook . . ."[27] Bediako chooses to class these individuals as ancestors rather than oppressors.

Translation and "Mother-Tongue Theology"

Recalling both Christaller and Akrofi's work, as well as the Mission's emphasis on language and education, the subject of vernacular language and translation must be considered. Indeed, this is arguably the deepest influence of the Basel Mission on the Institute and is a clear link with its pietistic history. It has been argued that in order to produce an intelligible theology, it is necessary "to use the language of the culture within which particular theologies are created."[28]

This is academically and practically evident in the life of ACI and is one example of Bediako's vision being expressed through the work of the Institute. However, this concern extended beyond Bediako's writing to the curriculum, program requirements, and community activities of the Institute. For example, we may note the use of *Twi* in the Institute's daily times of prayer, worship, and Bible study, which Fotland outlines in detail, and which I similarly encountered during my time there. These gatherings occur twice daily, at the beginning and end of the workday, and include students, faculty, and staff gathering for a time of worship together:

> Hymns are sung both in English and . . . Twi. Then there is a time for free prayer, either in English or one's own mother tongue. When the Scripture and comments to the Scripture are read, it is done in both English and Twi. After that there is time for comments and questions . . . Everybody is encouraged to participate . . . and all that is said is translated either to English or Twi . . . For Bediako . . . this is a very conscious way of worshipping together . . . in order to create an atmosphere for doing

27. Maluleke, "Black and African Theologies," 9.
28. Shyllon, "What Role?," 12.

grassroots theology in the mother tongue. It is an act of putting his theology into practice.[29]

Speaking to the significance of mother-tongue theological engagement, Asamoah-Gyadu, like Bediako, takes a positive approach to the missionary endeavour. He asserts that translation was "[o]ne of the major contributions of the Western missionary enterprise to the growth of the church in Africa," enabling Africans to encounter the Word of God in their own languages and contexts.[30] We will further consider the significance of language as it appears in the MTh program shortly.

Neither a University nor a Seminary: "ACI as Ashram"

From its historical connection, we need to understand the ontological nature of ACI as a unique training institution for the African study of African religions. Gillian Bediako clarifies that the vision behind ACI was for "an institution dedicated to pursuing Christian scholarship in Africa, on the understanding that a serious religious orientation, in this case focused on a vital communion with Jesus Christ, could contribute to the shaping of intellectual culture and to the renewal of academic excellence."[31]

To this end, ACI is neither a university nor a seminary, though retains certain characteristics of both as the above quotations intimate. Creatively, it combines Christian scholarship with an academically rigorous approach to the study of African religions in a pluralistic Ghanaian context. We have seen the importance of the early University Departments for the Study of Religions, which first included Parrinder's groundbreaking efforts at Ibadan in bringing "African Traditional Religion" into the academy. We further observed Nkrumah's efforts to secularize the study of religions in Ghana, reflective of the religiously plural environment of the country and of his desire to elevate African traditional religion and culture in a way not previously done under Christian leadership in the Department of Divinity. This was Bediako's academic inheritance as an emerging African scholar of religions.

But coming into his own as a scholar in the 1980s, there were no useful options in West Africa for Christian study of African religions, despite the fact that many of the leading African scholars of religions were themselves Christians—"the highly committed churchmen who constitute the body of Africa's academic theologians so far," as Bediako calls them.[32] While the

29. Fotland, *Ancestor Christology in Context*, 278.
30. Asamoah-Gyadu, "Kwame Bediako Memorial Lecture," 9.
31. Bediako, "Christian Universality," 362.
32. Bediako, *Theology and Identity*, 5. Here we might recall the number of African

universities placed significance on the study of African primal religion, they did so from a secular perspective; and seminaries, which upheld a Christian approach to scholarship, tended to minimize or exclude the study of primal religion, and furthermore, at times pursued more Western theological lines of thought. The serious infrastructural decline of West African universities during this period further limited research options. On this point, as Kalu reminds us, each year "[Walls] teaches at [ACI] in the belief that if Africans built academic ashrams, they would lick the desolation caused by the collapse of educational infrastructure and resources."[33]

The late Kwesi Dickson, a Ghanaian theologian and professor in the Department for the Study of Religions at Legon, observed in 1984 that with regard to theological study, the university departments in West Africa were in fact much more innovative than seminaries in their exploration of African culture and Traditional Religion. "It may be noted in this connection," Dickson states, "that the study of African traditional religion as a theological discipline was pioneered at the university Departments of Religion in contrast to which the seminaries may, with considerable justification, be described as bastions of Western orthodoxy, their systems being usually modelled after Western system with respect to the kinds of courses offered and their content."[34]

The seminaries typically maintained Church affiliations and were more focused on preparing students for the practical aspects of ministry, such as preaching and church administration. Unlike universities, they did not typically prepare their students for degrees.[35] Bediako noted that the exponential growth of churches in Africa throughout the latter decades of the twentieth century had led to the proliferation of Bible schools, "as if what was felt to be needed was simply a process of undergoing training, and as if models and methods imported wholesale from elsewhere could achieve the desired effects."[36] He goes on to say that at the start of the twenty-first century, it was increasingly recognized that these forms of theological education had proved to be ineffective, as they appeared not to connect "with the redeeming, transforming activity of the Living God in the African setting."[37]

Christian scholars who, in part for this very reason, pursued their higher degrees at Aberdeen, as we saw in chapter 2.

33. Kalu, preface, *African Christianity*, xi.
34. Dickson, *Theology in Africa*, 201.
35. Ibid., 209.
36. Bediako, "The African Renaissance," 29.
37. Ibid.

Noting the available choices, which seemed to include, on the one hand, less research-focused training for Christian service that did not successfully engage African culture, or the more academic, secular study of religions in university on the other, Dickson concluded that theological education in Africa was in many ways insufficient.[38] Bediako similarly observed these various pitfalls and limitations, and envisioned a different kind of academic environment, one simultaneously reflecting a deep commitment to rigorous scholarship and authentic Christian interaction with African culture and primal religion.

This raises the question: what sort of institution is ACI? Gillian Bediako offers one response to that question when she states that unlike typical theological institutions offering familiar courses, "ACI is concerned to research the intellectual roots of Ghanaian and African traditions, in a cultural matrix that recognizes the centrality of the transcendent in the whole of life. By pitching its accredited programmes at the graduate and research levels exclusively, ACI seeks to connect the indigenous insights that are summed up in the proverbial saying, 'Nsɛm nyinaa ne Nyame' (God is the foundation of all things), with the resources of Christian scholarship."[39]

Adding to this, Walls provides the enlightening suggestion that Indian ashrams, "where seekers after truth came together to live a simple common life of study and meditation," might be seen as a helpful comparison for this model of Christian life and scholarship.[40] In his essay entitled "Of Ivory Towers and Ashrams," Walls outlines the significant obstacles and inefficacies posed by importing the Western "ivory tower" approach to the academic study of theology in the African context, common to both the university and seminary models in West Africa.

As Walls argues, this is because the Western approaches, as products of the Enlightenment, are "highly indigenised, highly contextualised and represent a series of choices related to the cultural and religious history of the Western world."[41] As such, they do not effectively engage with the concerns of the African context. Furthermore, Walls notes the disconnect between the scholarly activity of the ivory tower and the grassroots concerns of the emerging African Church, an imbalance which Bediako was profoundly concerned to redress.

Perhaps most significant here is the observation that Christian scholarship in the West typically emphasizes the firm division between sacred

38. Dickson, *Theology in Africa*, 211.
39. Bediako, "Christian Universality," 364.
40. Walls, "Of Ivory Towers and Ashrams," 4
41. Ibid., 2.

and secular spheres, a division not widely recognized in the African context. Bediako was seeking to bring together the rigorous scholasticism of a university, the pastoral concerns of a seminary, and the primal imagination of the African context, all within a supportive Christian community; a unique endeavour in our present time. Indeed, he is quite conscious that he is attempting something different: he uses the term "unique" twelve times in the "Ebenezer" document with regard to the goals of the Institute, including the following phrases: "unique focus on African Christianity," "unique character," and "educational opportunity of a unique kind." Indeed, the phrase "unique focus" is used seven out of the twelve times! There can be no mistaking Bediako's conscious intention to break new ground through ACI. In this way, the institution aptly reflects the man: it does not fit easily into familiar categories.

One aspect of this distinct focus is seen in Bediako's depiction of the role of the scholar within the community, which similarly serves to indirectly challenge the Western academy. He notes that in African indigenous knowledge systems, knowledge is not the possession of an individual, "but is held in trust by and for the community, for the common good and for meeting community needs."[42] Not stopping there, Bediako hints at the negative associations to be made of the scholar who promotes him or herself above others: "In our societies, when the individual alone advances far ahead and no one knows how this was achieved, it could easily be assumed that such advancement was achieved through witchcraft or magic. Therefore, it becomes a very sensitive negotiation for the inspired individual who has something to share to be at the service of the community. For the person who is perceived to be self-serving, is believed to have 'bad' medicine, and the knowledge itself is held to be suspect, for the knowledge has not been put at the service of the community."[43]

This aspect of community participation in the African study of religions remains a key ontological component of ACI, demonstrated, for example, in Bediako's engagement with Nana Addo Dankwa III for insight into the religious and cultural functions of libation, and within Bediako's rationale for locating the Institute in the royal town of Akropong. An ashram is therefore a particularly apt metaphor for ACI, capturing the vision of the Institute as a community of scholarship and faithful reflection.

Here Walls' voice is again a helpful one, with a career spanning more than six decades with a foot in both "ashrams" and "ivory towers" in the U.K., U.S., and West Africa. From his experiences, he charges the Western

42. Bediako, "A New Era in Christian History," 6.
43. Ibid.

academy with being sick, "as sick as the Greek academy was in the early days of Christianity. The university developed in the west [sic] as a product of Christian concern. The earliest universities there were church institutions holding as sacred duties the preservation and promotion of learning and its impartation to new generations."[44] The original purpose for Western universities, he argues, was "the promotion of learning for the glory of God," but Western institutions have all but lost sight of this through becoming what Walls forthrightly calls "pensioners of global capitalism."

Instead, he calls for a cleansing and reorienting of the Western academy towards these early aims, which he suggests may come from institutions in the Global South: "We need a cleansing of theological scholarship, a reorienting of academic theology to Christian mission, a return to the ideal of scholarship for the glory of God, a return to the ideal of the academic life as a liberating search for truth. How can this come about? The Western academy is corrupted; in some areas, absolutely corrupted. Perhaps it will be in the non-western world that the scholarly vocation will begin anew."[45]

Another important element underlying this vision for a new and unique institution was Bediako's rightly-perceived need for fresh methodological approaches, which neither the university nor seminary sufficiently addressed. As he expresses it, identity was the driving force behind this search for a new methodological idiom, which we examined in greater detail in chapter 2: "At the heart of this unfolding method of African theology would be the issue of identity. This entailed not only confronting constantly the question as to how and how far 'the old' and 'the new' in African religious consciousness could become integrated in a unified vision of what it meant to be African and Christian."[46] This approach, and the process of engaging with these questions, may be seen in the curriculum that Bediako designed for ACI's MTh program.

The Masters of Theology in African Christianity: Bediako's Abiding Contribution to the African Study of African Religions

The lectures for the MTh program represent significant yet unstudied texts by Bediako, providing us with an outline of the themes he deemed foundational for African Christian scholarly engagement with African culture and religions. The Institute, and in particular the MTh curriculum, represent

---

44. Walls, "Christian Scholarship in Africa," 47.
45. Ibid.
46. Bediako, "The Genesis of African Theology (Lecture III)," 12.

a logical culmination of the preceding chapters in both chronological and ontological ways, bringing together the joint themes of the development of the African study of religions in twentieth-century Ghana and Bediako's unique contribution within this emerging religious discourse. The Institute itself has been described as one of the two "most comprehensive resource[s] for mission studies in Africa to be found anywhere"[47]; and its roots take us right back to Bediako's 1970 conversion in Bordeaux.

In a later interview, he reflected on his early Christian experiences such as studying with Francis Schaeffer at L'Abri, and remarked that this early period of Christian study furnished him with "a sense of confidence that the Christian faith wasn't what I had thought it was . . . a recipe for intellectual failures, which is what I had thought it was, quite frankly. I had said that loud and clear to my friends in Legon who had been Christians before me . . . [And] here was I now, investigating how, in fact, the Christian faith in Jesus, faith in God, faith in Christ, far from being an escape from reason . . . in fact . . . actually enabled an integration of faith into the whole of life."[48]

This paradigm shift was key for determining the course of Bediako's future vocation as well as his vision for the Institute. While many postgraduate research institutions focus predominantly on intellectual development, Bediako remained deeply committed to engaging with Christian faith holistically, understanding academic engagement as an integrated, not separate, part of life. We gain a sense of what prompted his academic shift from Négritude to Theology in his following recollection: "I wanted to be a, you know, a Christian intellectual, if you like . . . [T]hat's really what [I had] in mind, was to be a Christian . . . intellectual, who thought through his faith and who applied his faith in the area of . . . the academy."[49] The theme of conversion as an intellectual process is a recurring one for Bediako. He describes his intellectual and faith itinerary in the following way:

> Because I saw my conversion in intellectual terms . . . my concern was to see how it all tied together with intellectual integrity. I thought that was important, that, you know . . . coming to faith wasn't . . . to become a flight away from thought. From serious thought, from facing serious social, cultural and political issues

---

47. The second institution being referenced here is the former Centre for the Study of Christianity in the Non-Western World in Edinburgh. Balcomb, "Faith or Suspicion?," 5. It should also be noted that Diane Stinton later developed an MTh in African Christianity at Daystar University in Kenya along similar lines to that offered at ACI, with encouragement from Bediako. See Bediako, Quarshie, and Asamoah-Gyadu, *Seeing New Facets of the Diamond*, xiii.

48. Bediako, filmed interview by James Ault, 1998, DigiBeta Reel GB 105: 4–5.

49. Ibid., 6.

of life. These were the realities of life, these were the [realities] that faith must relate to . . . So that was something that was of concern to me.[50]

This also describes the vision of the MTh: a program in which faith and intellect are brought together in Christian community to engage with African religious concerns. And this is not for the personal gain of the scholar, nor for practical pastoral training, but to equip African Christian academics in the study of African religions and to engage with, and benefit, the wider community.

The Impact of Négritude on Bediako's Christian Thought: Integrating an Academic and Philosophical Past

As we have seen, so much of the Négritude movement and the poetry of Tchicaya U Tam'si in particular centered upon the quest for lost African roots and the sense that Christianity was a negative foreign imposition. To U Tam'si, Catholicism was the religion of the colonizer and a contributing factor to the cultural deracination that he experienced. We have already observed links between Bediako's in-depth understanding of Négritude and some of his later theological scholarship. However, Bediako only once explicitly reflected on how his study of Négritude literature and U Tam'si's poetry shaped his Christian thinking. These insights are especially valuable, because after completing his research on U Tam'si, we have no other record of Bediako writing about or discussing this poet or the impact of his early doctoral research apart from in this unpublished interview. He explains his academic itinerary in the following way:

> I felt my sort of, my pre-Christian era had some, had some significance in this. I needed to integrate, I needed to find, uh, I needed to find the integrated center of my life . . . culturally, part of my training in literature and poetry had made me conscious of, of cultural identity. Uh, now that I have come to faith, I need to see the Christian faith as not destructive of my cultural identity . . . perhaps you re-shape it, whatever, but not destructive of it. And that became . . . an important question for me for a long time.[51]

Bediako's question of how his Christian faith could interact with his culture in a positive way to develop a rooted, integrated center—in other

50. Ibid., 11.
51. Ibid., 12.

words, an identity that was both African and Christian—is reflected not only in his writing, which we have already seen in *Theology and Identity*, but in the vision and *raison d'être* of the Institute and the MTh. The earlier exquisite and often painful search for identity that we observed in U Tam'si, with whom Bediako so strongly identified for a period of time, is now replaced in Bediako's mind by a very different, and decidedly more joyful, quest. U Tam'si's search for a key to make sense of his fragmented ancestry proved futile; he determined that he alone was responsible for his own salvation. Bediako, however, concludes that Christ is the key; but, in turning to Christ that which was already part of his mental worldview, he continued on the quest for a coherent cultural identity— which meant a coherent African and Christian identity.

As Walls has argued, Christian conversion involves turning to Christ that which is already there; theology, he observes, is the intellectual part of this process.[52] In having this deeper understanding of Bediako's engagement with Négritude literature, his interest and commitment to establishing an institution dedicated to the study of Christianity and culture in Africa takes on added clarity and can be viewed as the intellectual "turning" of these fruits of Négritude literature to Christ.

Furthermore, it may be seen as Bediako's way of drawing together the historical concerns of previous scholars and providing a more helpful answer to the abiding question of African religious identity than what he found in Négritude, the African personality, or indeed in Western theological study. These concerns for the integration of Christian faith, culture and intellect remained key for Bediako and featured prominently within the course materials for the MTh program.

MTh Curriculum: Four Themes

Much of the course materials which Bediako wrote for the MTh program originated in lectures which he presented in the Duff Lecture Series at the University of Edinburgh in the late 1980s and early 1990s.[53] While there are other programs at ACI, the MTh remains the core program and arguably the Institute's most unique offering, and a key part of Bediako's opus. In addition to using Bediako's unpublished lecture notes and course outlines, I have

52. Walls, "Of Ivory Towers and Ashrams," 4.

53. In addition to the MTh program, ACI also offers several different degree options, including: Master of Arts in Theology and Mission, with specialisations in Holistic Mission and Development; Biblical Studies; Pentecostal Studies; and Mother-tongue Theology. In the Master of Theology program, options include African Christianity and Bible Translation and Interpretation.

completed the program, and have used both textual and participant-observation sources to provide analysis here.

The stated objectives of this two-year program include clarifying the significance of African Christianity; enabling African students to engage in Christian study that is directly relevant to their own context; providing an opportunity for cross-cultural Christian workers to explore the historical, religious and cultural context of their work; and the provision of cultural relevance for biblical exegesis and interpretation.[54]

In studying Bediako's unpublished Duff lectures, a clue to his thematic and curricular vision for the MTh is found in his exposition of Mbiti's doctoral research, and particularly in what Mbiti outlines as four critical components for African theology.[55] These include, firstly, a strong foundation in biblical theology. Bediako agrees with Mbiti, who says the Bible "must be the basis of any theological reflection, otherwise we shall lose our perspective and may not claim the outcome to be Christian theology."[56]

The second area is "Christian theology from the major traditions of Christendom," essential because it points African Christian scholars to "the mainstream of ecumenical and apostolic heritage" as well as to the catholicity of the Church. As Bediako notes, "all this rich heritage—in Biblical theology as in the theology from other Christian traditions—needed to be understood and translated into the African milieu and so be made relevant to the Church in Africa."[57]

The third and fourth areas offer "a uniquely African contribution to Christian theology" and include a study of African religions and philosophy—"in other words, the pre-Christian traditions of Africa in religion and thought—in dialogue with the Christian message as embodied in Christ himself." And finally, a theology of the living Church: that is, "the actual life and experience of African Christian communities."[58] These four align very

---

54. See Appendix B for the full MTh program outline and a complete list of Course Objectives.

55. Mbiti's doctoral thesis was submitted to Cambridge in 1963 and was finally published in 1971 as *New Testament Eschatology in an African Background: A Study of the Encounter between New Testament Theology and African Traditional Concepts* (London: Oxford University Press, 1971). Bediako addresses it in "Perspectives in African Theology (II): The Place of Christ in the African heritage in John Mbiti." It is not surprising to find a clear link between Mbiti's thought and Bediako's curriculum.

56. This quotation is taken from Bediako's unpublished lecture notes, and while he indicates that is comes from the conclusion to Mbiti's work, he does not indicate whether this is from the original thesis or the published work. See Bediako, "Perspectives in African Theology (II)," 7.

57. Ibid.

58. Ibid.

closely with the major themes in the MTh program, suggesting that Bediako has used, whether consciously or unconsciously, Mbiti's categories in the formulation of this program, at least to some degree.[59]

The MTh is divided into four core and six electives.[60] The core courses, reflecting Mbiti's four categorizations, are as follows: 1) *Gospel and culture—biblical, historical and theological perspectives;* 2) *World Christian history as mission history;* 3) *The roots of African theology in the twentieth century;* and 4) *Christian faith and primal religions of the world, with special reference to Africa—historical, phenomenological and theological perspectives.* The elective courses similarly fall into these same categories, with courses in history, African biblical hermeneutics; Christian expression in Africa; and Christian-Muslim relations in Africa.

Theme 1: A Biblical Foundation

Firstly, the importance of a biblical foundation is evidenced in further traces of the Institute's pietistic heritage, including its family-like community and twice-daily times of worship, prayer, and Bible reading. My time at ACI in 2006 gave me the opportunity to see Bediako functioning in his role as leader of the Institute. In studying the pietistic Basel missionaries and understanding the importance of the father-figure as spiritual leader of the community, it occurred to me that this was very much what I had observed with Bediako.

He functioned in just that capacity, providing pastoral care alongside of fulfilling academic and administrative duties, seen explicitly in the way in which he gathered the whole community together for these times of interactive worship. This built Christian community alongside of Christian scholarship, with a strong emphasis on the shared study of the Bible in both Twi and English. In this way, the Institute promotes not just Christian scholarship but Christian community life, which can be viewed as a legacy of its pietistic heritage and corresponds with Walls' metaphor as the Institute as ashram as opposed to an ivory tower.

Within the MTh curriculum, this biblical emphasis is explicitly evident in the required course on "Gospel and culture—biblical, historical and theological perspectives." This covers both Old and New Testaments, examining

---

59. This is suggested on the basis that Bediako was studying Mbiti prior to and during the time he was identifying his own key theological concerns and beginning to synthesize them into a coherent programmatic structure. It is possible, of course, that the similarities are entirely coincidental; however, the direct correlation would seem to reasonably suggest a line of influence.

60. See Appendix B for full program details.

the "religion of the Old Testament in the context of the Ancient Near East" followed by the role of Christ within the New Testament. Describing the course and its objectives, Bediako states that it is concerned with "the role of culture in shaping the biblical witness of the Old and New Testaments" and is intended to enable students to gain insight into the significance of understanding cultural background for biblical interpretation.[61]

Theme 2: African Christian History

Bediako's personal value for locating one's Christian experience within a historical context is similarly demonstrated in the MTh curriculum. Indeed, African Christian history may be seen as the key focus of the program: out of a total of ten courses, two core and two elective courses focus on aspects of Christian history in Africa.[62] Refuting the arguments of those like Nkrumah, p'Bitek, or U Tam'si that Christianity was a "foreign import," Bediako regularly emphasized in lectures and discussions that Christianity had strong roots in Africa, extending all the way back to Jesus' sojourn as a refugee in Egypt, an emphasis that continues to shine through in the program.

Through the historical emphasis of this program, Bediako offers scholars the opportunity to view Christianity in Africa not as colonial and chaotic, as U Tam'si suggests, or foreign and suspect, as Nkrumah and p'Bitek argue; but as indigenous and abiding: Jesus himself lived in Africa, and therefore African Christians may legitimately locate themselves within the historical continuum of Christian history.

Theme 3: Primal Religion

Primal religion is another key component of the MTh program, with one class dedicated to exploring the historical, phenomenological, and theological aspects of this religious phenomenon in Africa and the rest of the world.[63] This subject similarly emerges in other classes; for example, understanding the primal religious worldview of the Old Testament. It is arguably the most controversial component of the program, and certainly one of the most controversial aspects of Bediako's theology. Here it bears noting again

---

61. Bediako, "Issues of Gospel and Culture," 1–2.

62. See Appendix B.

63. The course is entitled "Christian faith and primal religions of the world, with special reference to Africa—historical, phenomenological, and theological perspectives."

that the term "primal" itself is crucial for Bediako, somehow more expansive and indicative of the transcendent reality that he is trying to engage than terms like African indigenous or traditional religion.

For teaching on primal religion Bediako relies significantly on the work of Harold W. Turner, whom he calls "a sure guide into the phenomenology of the world's primal religions."[64] Bediako regularly makes use of Turner's "six-feature framework for understanding primal religions as authentically religious, rather than as merely epiphenomena of the social organization of . . . preliterate societies."[65] Bediako argues that it was the last feature ("the physical as sacramental") that held the key to the wider argument; namely, "the primal conception of the universe as a unified cosmic system, essentially spiritual . . ."[66] In this we see a further example of an abiding impact of Négritude and U Tam'si's focus on nature as a conduit and expression of transcendence on Bediako's later Christian thought.

Bediako is particularly interested in the contention that primal religion has a special connection with Christianity, which he sees evidenced by the significant expansion of Christianity within primal religious societies. This includes "the Mediterranean world of the early Christian centuries, and tribal peoples of Northern and Western Europe and finally the primal societies of Africa, the Pacific, and parts of Asia."[67] Bediako recognizes this critical difference between a European and African Christian outlook, with the former rejecting any affinity with a primal worldview, and the latter encountering it daily. He therefore saw the need for African Christian scholarship to actively engage with the primal imagination at the Institute. He defends his rationale, arguing, "primal world-views are fundamentally religious, [therefore] the primal imagination restores to theology the crucial dimension of living religiously for which the theologian needs make no apology. The primal imagination may help us restore the ancient unity of theology and spirituality."[68]

In addition to being dealt with in classes at ACI, primal religion is also approached outside of the classroom within the wider community. One important example here is having students observe the annual *Odwira* festival,

64. Bediako, "The Primal Imagination," 93.

65. Ibid. Turner argued that the following six features were common to most, if not all, primal religions, and gave them the following labels: "kinship with nature," "human weakness and finitude," "man is not alone," "relations with transcendent powers," "man's afterlife," and "the physical as sacramental." See Turner, "The Primal Religions of the World and Their Study."

66. Bediako, "The Primal Imagination," 96.

67. Ibid., 95.

68. Ibid., 105.

a traditional festival celebrating the New Year in the community of Akropong. *Odwira* is "a festival of purification, reconciliation and renewal."[69] Students are encouraged to observe it and consider corresponding biblical festivals, evaluating how primal religious practices may undergird or parallel ancient and modern Christian practices. In extending the classroom to the "laboratory" of the surrounding community, Bediako refers to Akropong as "an ideal place to carry out this kind of work in Ghana, both because of its place in Ghanaian Christian history and because it is close to a still-vital Akan traditional culture."[70]

Theme 4: Theology of the Living Church

Drawing upon Mbiti's categories, Bediako calls this broad category "the actual life and experience of African Christian communities."[71] I have chosen to call this "theology of the living Church," and, as Kalu further explains, "this approach is lived Christianity, with the potential for mature growth."[72] Within both course content and community life, this theme emerges regularly and in many ways undergirds the broader vision of ACI. Within the MTh course offerings, this theme is seen in the following topics of engagement: the roots of African theology in the twentieth century; patterns of Christian ministry in Africa, including early prophetic movements and the emergence of African Initiated/Independent Churches; and studies in Christianity and Islam in modern Africa. Furthermore, the realities of African Christians are explored through community interactions, both within ACI and the wider community. For example, questions and pastoral dilemmas relating to traditional religious practices are regularly brought forward in lectures and in daily times of corporate worship; through class visits to various chiefs's palaces; participation in *Odwira*; and other similar events.

Mother-Tongue Theology: A Signal Interpretative Key

Bediako's emphasis on engaging with vernacular language, previously identified within the legacy of the Basel Mission, is a key focus that cuts across all of these themes and relates to biblical interpretation, history, primal religion, and daily life in Africa. This influence is so strong and so pervasive

69. Bediako, "'How Is It That We Hear in Our Own Languages,'" 71.
70. Ibid., 67.
71. Bediako, "Perspectives in African Theology (II)," 7.
72. Kalu, Review of *Jesus and the Gospel in Africa*, 49.

that it may be seen as an interpretative key underpinning Bediako's African Christian scholarship. Bediako underscores the central position of language and its inextricable link to both Scripture and culture when he observes that "[w]hen the Scriptures come into a language, they become an element of the culture, and can, therefore, serve as the hermeneutic, the interpreter, of that culture."[73]

Elias Bongmba identifies language as one of the critical factors that must be taken into account within his listing of six "Considerations for future accounts of African Christianity."[74] He argues that "future studies of African Christianity should wrestle with the challenge of language . . . While so much has been accomplished in this regard . . . serious research is needed so that scholars can continue to engage the literature that is available in many of the African languages that have been used by Christians to express their faith."[75] Through ACI, Bediako demonstrates some ways in which this charge may be put into practice. We have already seen some evidence of the significant role of vernacular languages at ACI. In part through Bediako's influence and the programs at the Institute, Asamoah-Gyadu is able to assert that "mother-tongue biblical hermeneutics, which affirm languages as God's means of talking to people, has emerged as a serious theological discipline [at ACI]. In pursuance of the mother-tongue project, MTh and PhD candidates of the . . . Institute are expected . . . to produce a short summary of the dissertations in their mother tongues. This may pose a formidable challenge to some, but it is a worthy exercise that consciously trains academic minds to think in the vernacular."[76]

Additionally, the Institute now offers an MTh in Bible Translation and Interpretation, reflecting an ongoing and deepening scholarly commitment to this task. Bediako deeply perceived the truth that language is not only a means of communication but an integral aspect of culture. He regularly encouraged students to engage their faith from within the language and thought-patterns of their home cultures, arguing that this would further elucidate their understanding of Christianity in their contexts.

He clearly expresses his view of the significance of how language brings all of these concepts together in a lecture entitled "New Ways of Experiencing Jesus." Herein he argues that language may be understood as "the experience of reality" and "religion as its expression."[77] Language for

---

73. Bediako, "Gospel and Culture: Guest Editorial," 1.
74. See Bongmba, "Writing African Christianity," 282–89.
75. Ibid., 288–89.
76. Asamoah-Gyadu, "Kwame Bediako Memorial Lecture," 9.
77. Bediako, unpublished notes for the course The Roots of African Theology in the

Bediako is therefore a way of apprehending and experiencing this truth, and here he sees Bible translation as connecting people with this experience of religious truth. Indeed, he says, "it is this which makes language itself into a theological category, giving it eternal significance and transcendent power." Taking this further, he highlights the significance of the Incarnation: the divine Word being translated into flesh.[78] It is helpful to hear him at length drawing these views together:

> Once we have understood that the Bible, through translation, is in fact bringing all languages and all cultures into contact with the Living God, and recognize . . . that God has always been speaking all these languages from creation, the Gospel becomes our story. It is no longer a question of trying to accommodate the Gospel in our culture. This kind of view is usually the cause of our fear of syncretism. Rather, our Lord has been from the beginning the Word of God for us as for all people everywhere. He has been the source of our life, and illuminator of our path in life, though, like all people everywhere, we also failed to understand him aright. But now he has made himself known, becoming one of us, one like us. By acknowledging him for who he is, and by giving him our allegiance, we become what we are truly intended to be, by his gift, that is, the children of God. Our response to him is crucial, because becoming the children of God does not stem from, nor is it limited by, the accidents of birth, race, culture, clan or even 'religious' tradition. It comes by grace through faith.[79]

Therefore, it is *language*, and particularly one's mother tongue, which makes the Bible accessible and enables us to encounter and acknowledge Jesus—the translated, incarnate Word—in an African idiom. This is nothing less than a signal interpretative key for engaging with Bediako's theology. As Hans Visser and Gillian Bediako cogently argue, Bediako's understanding of the significance of vernacular language extends beyond ACI and has implications for the Christian scholarship worldwide.

His argument is not without criticism, however. While a number of African theologians, as well as students at ACI, have found "mother-tongue theology" an important concept and relevant tool in their own contexts, others disagree. Maluleke offers perhaps the sharpest criticism on this point, disagreeing with both Bediako and Sanneh for equating the Bible with the Word

---

Twentieth Century: "New Ways of Experiencing Jesus: Lecture 5," 1. Here he references Pieris, *An Asian Theology of Liberation*, 70.

78. Ibid.
79. Ibid., 3.

of God: "It is on the basis of this equation," argues Maluleke, "that translation and vernacularization acquire such a lofty status in the arguments of both Bediako and Sanneh. What is being translated, according to them, is the very Word of God itself. So that in fact, properly speaking, it is not translation that is taking place; God through his Word, is translating himself, making himself available in the mother tongue of the people and in the process touching both the translator and the assimilator equally."[80]

Maluleke is right in his assessment of Bediako's "Bible = Word of God" equation, and in his understanding that Bediako's high view of translation comes from perceiving this as God translating himself into an African context: the Word indeed becoming flesh. But, rather than a criticism, this may be seen straightforwardly as Bediako's adherence to an evangelical Christian position which affirms the same, a view which he upheld from his conversion onwards. While overlooking the increasing challenges and inconsistencies inherent in the term, it is perhaps helpful to recall that Bediako regularly identified himself as an evangelical, as defined by his view of the Bible as the Word of God, and was widely recognised as such—humorously called a "rather leftish type of evangelical" by one theologian.[81]

Without belabouring the point here, Maluleke seeks to challenge Bediako's position on the charge of failing to appreciate that the very same Bible has been used oppressively to denigrate African religion and culture. Therefore, he finds Bediako's emphasis on the Bible as the Word of God "dangerous" and "naïve."[82] While there is no question that the Bible has at times been used very oppressively—and here Maluleke's South African context comes immediately to mind—it is hard to see his charge as being descriptive of Bediako's thought or Ghanaian context. Where Maluleke is right, however, is in highlighting the irony of various African Christian scholars each turning to the same Bible to uphold their pronouncements of other African Christian scholars as being biblically unfounded or dangerous.[83] And, I would add, when we perceive Bediako's commitment to the evangelical "Bible as the Word of God" position, it is equally ironic to find Western theologians who denounce his scholarship as "biblically unfounded." But, the intricacies of these theological debates are not our focus here.

Bediako stood by the conviction that "God speaks into the African context in African idiom, and that it is through hearing in African mother-tongues 'the great things that God has done' (Acts 2:11), that African

---

80. Maluleke, "Black and African Theologies," 10–11.
81. Van den Toren, "Kwame Bediako's Christology," 219.
82. Maluleke, "Black and African Theologies," 12.
83. Ibid., 11. Here he is specifically referring to John Mbiti and Byang Kato.

theology emerges to edify not only the African Church but the Church world-wide."[84] While this emphasis on mother tongue is evident in his published work, the weight of its significance is made most clear when seen as pervading essentially all aspects of the MTh curriculum and community life at ACI.

To demonstrate, vernacular language and translation is firstly dealt with regularly within biblical study and worship, with the twice-daily services conducted in both English and Twi. Secondly, it is an essential component to an apprehension of the primal worldview, with regular examples shown through the use of Twi poetry and songs from Afua Kuma and Ephraim Amu in lectures. Thirdly, within course materials and community issues relating to daily African life and experience, there is a high degree of overlap with primal religion and the role of language, as language, culture and religion were shown to be deeply interconnected. To this end, language has rightly been called "the shrine of a people's soul."[85] And fourthly, language is raised within historical courses with reference to biblical translation, Christian scholarship, and missionary activity in different parts of the world and at different points in history.

Additionally, with this emphasis on the use of vernacular language, we once again see glimmers of Bediako's Négritude study giving shape to his Christian thinking. He had seen the painful disconnect for African intellectuals who were unable to express their hearts' deepest cries in their mother tongue. In *Négritude et Surrealisme*, Bediako agrees with the criticism that Négritude poetry, being written in French, is only accessible to the educated elite and not to the majority of Africans. He identifies this as a significant disadvantage; however, he acknowledges that the main reason for this is that the poets themselves were not always capable of writing in *la langue maternelle* because their dominant language of study and expression had been French.[86]

Senghor claimed that the use of French language for Négritude poetry meant that it was "also" accessible to non-African French speakers in France, in addition to other Africans. Bediako challenged that statement, saying that the use of French meant that it was "instead" accessible to the non-African French community, while remaining inaccessible to the majority of Africans.[87] In this way, it may be argued that in his focus on "mother-tongue theology" at ACI, Bediako achieves what the Négritude poets never

---

84. Visser and Bediako, Introduction to *Jesus in Africa*, vii.
85. See Smith, *The Shrine of a People's Soul*.
86. See Bediako, "Négritude et Surréalisme," 18–20.
87. Ibid., 19.

could: making African thought accessible to, and authentically reflective of, local African communities.

The psycho-linguistic distance of the Négritude poets is now contrasted with the comfortable indigenous expression of poets such as Ephraim Amu and Afua Kuma, whose poetry embodies "mother-tongue theology." In Afua Kuma, we find someone who perceived the world through the idiom of her mother tongue, and who saw Christ as a welcome and familiar part of her African landscape: not at all distant, but very near. She is sharply contrasted against the African educated elite in Paris, who were writing sophisticated poetry for a narrow, French-speaking audience. This is not dissimilar to the tenor of much of the African study of African religions that Bediako observed, both in universities and seminaries: an intellectual discourse divorced from its context. As we have seen, this was one key reason why it remained so critical for him to remain rooted in the local Ghanaian community.

In this, he found an ally in Afua Kuma, who similarly understood her Christian faith in the language and cultural idioms of Ghana. Unlike U Tam'si, she was not searching for lost roots or struggling to reconcile "foreign" Christianity with "local" primal religion. Instead, through the combination of her primal worldview, interpreted through her Christian faith and mediated through her mother tongue, she perceived Jesus as present and accessible. In contradiction to the Négritude poets, whose work was really only accessible to the educated elite, Afua Kuma's poems are most easily understood by her Akan community, who immediately recognise her chiefly praise-song format, vivid descriptions, and idiomatic language.

This is a key reason why mother-tongue theology, and Afua Kuma in particular, were so important to Bediako, and why the issue of vernacular language was one that he took every opportunity to reinforce. From his study of Négritude literature, he had observed the cultural, spiritual, and psychic deracination that can occur when individuals lack the linguistic ability to express their faith and worldview in their mother tongue. In his efforts to demonstrate that Christianity was not "foreign," Bediako saw the necessity for students to engage with their vernacular languages in order to fully understand the nature of their faith as African Christians.[88] As he

---

88. When I first studied at ACI in 2006, there were no English-speaking church services in the town of Akropong. With several of us in residence whose first language was English and who did not speak Twi, Kwame and Gillian Bediako organized a weekly Sunday evening English service at the Institute so that we too might also worship in our mother tongue.

unequivocally states, "it is only through the vernacular that a genuine and lasting theological dialogue with culture can take place."[89]

Here again, Afua Kuma's poetry comes to the fore. Throughout Bediako's work, his joint concern for a Christocentric approach to Christian scholarship and his openness to engaging with primal religion shines forth most clearly in his engagement with Ghanaian poet Afua Kuma. Bediako first interacts with her at length in an essay entitled "Cry Jesus! Christian theology and presence in modern Africa." In it he says that rather than arguing further about Africa's significance within the future of Christianity, he will instead "present the evidence of a theological articulation within Ghanaian Christianity—I believe it exists elsewhere in Africa also—rarely mentioned in the usual discussions about African theology . . . It is the evidence of what I call a 'grassroots' theology."[90]

He goes on to quote from Afua Kuma's poetry, commenting that her words are an example of "theology which comes from where the faith lives and must live continually, in the conditions of life of the community of faith, the theology of the living church, reflecting faith in the living Lord as present reality in daily life . . . In this setting of ubiquitous forces and mysterious powers, the Christian who has understood that Jesus Christ is a living reality, can be at home, assured in the faith that Jesus alone is Lord, Protector, Provider, and Enabler."[91]

For Afua Kuma, Jesus does indeed represent all of these categories. Using her mother tongue and scenes and idioms familiar to her Akan context, she depicts Jesus simultaneously as the deep forest which provides the necessities of life; the elephant which feeds the community; and the hunter who bravely goes into that forest to kill the elephant, penetrating to the darkest corners to make it safe for others. In her words, "You [Jesus] are the deep forest which gives us tasty foods."[92] Going further:

> He is the Hunter gone to the deep forest.
>
> *Sasabonsam*, the evil spirit,
>
> Has troubled hunters for many years.
>
> They ran in fear,
>
> Leaving their guns behind.
>
> Jesus has found these same guns,

---

89. Bediako, "'How Is It That We Hear?,'" 73.
90. Bediako, "Cry Jesus!," 4.
91. Ibid., 5.
92. Afua Kuma, *Jesus of the Deep Forest*, 40.

And brought them to the hunters
To go and kill the elephant.
Truly, Jesus is a Man among men,
The most stalwart of men![93]

As Bediako observes, in Afua Kuma's remarkable overlaying of ideas and images, Jesus has not only created the forest but is seen to have become a Hunter himself, "in order to deliver his fellows; and in this striking association of images, the Incarnation and the victory of the Cross are brought together and made meaningful in the defeat of the terrors of the African world."[94] Jesus is further seen as the provision himself, becoming the elephant: "The great Elephant of the forest, / who knows its secrets, / and walks its arbors, without hindrance."[95]

As Bediako says, "the wider implications of all this are enormous for our subject; in that the relatively early possession of mother-tongue Scripture meant that many Africans gained access to the original sources of Christian revelation as mediated through African traditional religious terminology and ideas. Through these, Jesus Christ the Lord had shouldered his way into the African religious world, and was to be discovered there by faith, not invented by theology."[96]

It is clear that mother-tongue theology—and its earlier history in missionary translation efforts—alongside of the poetry of Afua Kuma are key themes for Bediako, which emerges clearly in ACI's curriculum. In "mother-tongue theology," Bediako sees a new and exciting paradigm for African Christian engagement with the African religious worldview expressed in very real, living images.

He sees in Afua Kuma, and others similarly practising this implicit theology, "clear evidence that Christianity in Africa is a truly African experience." And this is because Afua Kuma's "lively sense of spirituality in nature, which signifies the African side of her African Christianity, informs the Christian side of her African Christianity, her claim that Jesus presides over spiritualized nature. Jesus is Lord because he meets African people where they need him most; namely, in life's deep forest, highest among its principalities and powers, installing hope where fear once reigned."[97]

---

93. Ibid., 20.
94. Bediako, "Cry Jesus!," 10.
95. Afua Kuma, *Jesus of the Deep Forest*, 35.
96. Bediako, "Cry Jesus!," 17.
97. Middleton, *Mother Tongue Theologies*, 66

While poetry may seem a somewhat unconventional source within either Theology or Religious Studies, Bediako again demonstrates that within the African Christian study of African religions, interdisciplinary, multi-methodological, mixed-media approaches are all of value.

One final thought on this point is that Bediako reminds us that mother-tongue scholarship is not limited in relevance to an African context, but has important implications for the West as well. "So Western languages too, by depositing along the banks of African consciousness their freight of the Western interactions with the Christian faith, make it possible for Africans to share with the West the distinctive African interactions with the gospel."[98]

Evaluating Bediako through ACI: A Critique

As I have argued throughout, I find that analyzing Bediako on narrow theological points based upon scholarship of only a few of his published works and with no further attention to his wider context often leads to misinterpretations. Furthermore, as a study in intellectual history as opposed to traditional theology, I am concerned to interrogate the roots and scope of his contribution. To this end, I find that his scholarly itinerary may most fully be critiqued through an assessment of ACI, since, as has been demonstrated, its location, course content, and community structure incorporate all of his key concerns and represent the drawing together of various aspects of the African study of African religions.

We have already noted several positive aspects of ACI, particularly its uniqueness as an institutionalized forum for studying African religions and for training African Christian scholars for academic engagement in this emerging field. The MTh has been shown to be of particular importance as the Institute's core program, and indeed, as the most complete expression of Bediako's views on the essentials of the African Christian study of African religions. Within this program, we have seen that Bediako's concerns for vernacular language, history, culture, and primal religion all feature regularly, supported by a biblical focus maintained in the worshiping life of the community.

However, we must also take account of weaknesses within ACI and the MTh program. One immediate concern—which is not so much a criticism, but simply a reality—is that in its present capacity as a postgraduate research institution, it remains as yet relatively young and therefore must be

---

98. Bediako, "Editorial" *JACT* 12/1 (June 2009) 3.

evaluated as such. While it came into being in the mid-1980s, it was only given its own charter and sole degree-awarding powers in 2006. At the present time, the total number of graduates remains under 300 from across its MA, MTh, and PhD programs.[99] It is therefore not yet possible to thoroughly evaluate the depth of Bediako's impact upon the African Christian study of African religions, or determine the wider reach of ACI's scholarship, beyond beginning to note the interesting scope and high calibre of research emanating from the Institute.[100] We will need to continue evaluating these factors for a number of years to come in order to make such assessments; and it will likely only be in the next generation that we will begin to be able to properly analyze these outcomes.

While some have argued that Bediako's arguments (and by extension, ACI) are no longer relevant in twenty-first-century Ghana—like my interlocutor from chapter 1 who informed me that Bediako's views hold no value for Africans born after independence—Bediako's contributions are still so recent, and his contribution incompletely and at times ineffectively appraised, that we are in fact only in the early stages of assessing both the scholar and the institution. As Maluleke rightly argues,

> Construction, innovation and contextualization in African theology/Christianity should not be left entirely in the hands of each generation of African theologians as if African theology was a frivolous and merely cerebral activity that is unconnected either to African Christian life or previous African theologies . . .
>
> What about previous theologies? Am I suggesting that their usefulness consists only in terms of "the ground they have covered" so that they are of no direct relevance now? No. The issues that were being addressed by these theologies are far from finished.[101]

We may do well to consider that many concerns within Western Christian scholarship remain focused on debates of centuries and even millennia past. African Christian scholarship on African religions continues to grow,

---

99. This is an approximation based upon statistics provided to me by Gillian Bediako in personal correspondence, November 2016.

100. Here I am thinking of the great diversity of voices and subjects found within JACT, as well as the variety of research projects undertaken by masters and doctoral students. In addition to important ethnographic and archival studies, there have also been some quite creative literary and ethno-linguistic projects, for example. It is hoped that the combination of creativity and scholarly rigor will continue to grow and expand in years to come.

101. Maluleke, "Half a Century," 470, 493.

and Bediako's contributions through ACI are only just beginning to become clear. Time and patience are needed here to let the plant grow before we can assess what kind of fruit it is bearing.

Other criticisms of ACI that may be levied include its relatively small size and rural location, insofar as such factors limit it in some capacities. Issues of technology and practical living such as internet accessibility, water shortages, and power outages emerge on a regular basis, posing impediments to research activity and residential life. While Western students, myself included, often classed these challenges as being "a reality of studying in Africa," many African classmates rejected such views as being Afro-pessimistic and argued that amazing technology and development capacity exists on the continent, such that they were frustrated by such setbacks and looked forward to seeing progress on these fronts at ACI. In fact, it was often Ghanaian students who were the most disturbed by these challenges, as it was not necessarily the case that such resources were unavailable but rather unaffordable for the Institute. Certainly, most growing institutions face the challenges of balancing finance and infrastructure; ACI is no different.

However, as we have seen, these same qualities—its small community feel and specific location in Akropong—are also integral for the Institute's historical identity and research itinerary, as Bediako demonstrated. Therefore, some of these challenges must be patiently accommodated for the benefit of the rich research opportunities at hand. While these logistical challenges do represent some limitation to the Institution's life and impact, it is hoped that over time, finance, infrastructure, and ACI's global engagement will grow.

Another consideration related to its relatively small student body is that while critical research is emerging from the Institute, it is coming slowly and is not easily accessible for scholars outside of Ghana. A key example of this lack of accessibility is seen with the Institute's publication, the *Journal of African Christian Thought* (JACT). JACT contains a significant amount of Bediako's published scholarship but remains a very underused source for analyzing his thought, primarily because it is not yet available online. As a print-only resource available by subscription, scholars outside of Ghana are unlikely to stumble upon it in more generalized searches, and those who go looking for it are often not able to access it.[102]

102. As far as I am aware, outside of Ghana, it is available in full or partial runs in the following institutions: in the U.K., at the University of Edinburgh; Cardiff University; Liverpool Hope University; School of Oriental and Asian Studies; All Nations Christian College; and the Crowther Center (Oxford Centre for Mission Studies). Across the U.S., it is available in just over thirty universities/seminaries; and in approximately one library each in Denmark, Germany, Switzerland, the Netherlands, Australia,

Established in 1998, JACT is a critical voice for the Institute and provides a window into the scholarly concerns being addressed there, as well as serving as an important platform for diverse voices ranging from students to senior scholars. It is a resource that I have used extensively for further insight into Bediako's perspectives on the role of Christian scholarship in Africa, the vision of ACI, primal worldview, and Christianity and politics in Africa. But, in addition to Bediako's writing, it is also a resource which I gladly consult for a vibrant mix of fresh, new scholarly voices, alongside of other seasoned African scholars, many of whose work is less accessible (and sometimes totally inaccessible) to those of us based in the West.

Within the growing African Christian study of religions, JACT is a valuable resource; and for assessing ACI, it is essential. Therefore, making it more widely accessible through online subscription should be an urgent priority for the Institute. It would significantly expand scholarly discourse in the field and invite greater interaction between scholars at ACI and elsewhere, which in itself would be an important step towards widening ACI's scholarly reach. Particularly in this day and age, when academic and informal research relies heavily upon online resources in many parts of the world, this lack of online access to JACT hinders ACI's global engagement. However, online access should not be *instead of*, but in *addition to*, print subscriptions, so as not to disadvantage those for whom internet access is problematic. Like the infrastructural challenges above, it is hoped that this will be addressed as a matter of urgency so that ACI's unique contribution may develop a wider impact.

A more serious concern to consider is ACI's practice of having a high proportion of its alumni engaged in faculty, staff, and research positions. This is due in part to the related factors of small size, limited finances, and difficulty attracting new external faculty. On their website, for example, they list 10 out of 23 members of staff (including adjunct lecturers and research fellows, but excluding the Rector, Deputy Rector, and Librarian) as either graduates of ACI or in partnership with KwaZulu-Natal, or as doctoral candidates with the Institute.[103]

This is certainly a high percentage, and raises some concerns about academic innovation and scholarly diversity that faculty from outside might

---

New Zealand, and South Africa. I am not aware of any libraries carrying this journal in Canada. Over the years I have had a variety of students and scholars contact me with requests to borrow copies of JACT from my personal library, finding themselves unable to access it more locally.

103. This information was first noted on ACI's website on March 3, 2015. A check on May 22, 2017, showed the same details, though some changes are likely to have occurred. See "Academic Staff," http://www.acighana.org/site/academics/staff.php.

otherwise bring to the Institute. Some measure of balance may be seen in the fact that among the remaining members of faculty (nearly all of which are adjunct lecturers), there is significant institutional and cultural diversity, with lecturers having studied elsewhere in Ghana, and in Nigeria, Kenya, South Africa, Australia, the US, and the UK.

Gillian Bediako confirms the practice of hiring alumni/ae, but sees it as reflecting positively on the Institute: "It is also important that the growth of the Institute's own academic staff has been, to a considerable degree, a direct fruit of the Institute's postgraduate programmes, a new generation of African Christian scholars committed to developing a tradition of thought in close connection with vital Christian life and imparting it to others."[104]

While it may be a reflection of students' support for the scholarly itinerary at ACI, this continued practice may be seen as a weakness in the long-term for two reasons. Firstly, and the more serious concern, is that scholarship, and particularly that which includes the creative working out of new methodological approaches, is generally strengthened in contexts of debate and diversity. In my experience studying at ACI, the curriculum was indeed unique and academically rigorous, with students trained to use creative methodological approaches in the study of African religions. However, there was also some evidence of scholarly insularity: the methodological approaches emphasised at ACI reflect Bediako's methodological framework—which makes sense if we are to understand the Institute as an extension of his scholarly contribution. However, as we observed in chapter 2, there are diverse voices and contested methodologies within the African study of African religions.

Bediako's approach is an important one, and continues to be a relevant and helpful framework for emerging generations of African Christian scholars. Yet, with methodology being a critical but contested area within the African study of African religions, and with African Christian voices often marginalised in this discourse, some wider engagement could only be to ACI's benefit, and would further highlight the unique methodological approach which it offers. Indeed, if ACI is to remain faithful to Bediako's call for "greater scholarship, fellowship, and collaborative reflection," which he first sensed at the Lausanne Congress and which first prompted his vision for a research centre such as ACI, this would seem an important avenue to pursue.

The second disadvantage to having ACI graduates step into faculty positions is the argument that it may be seen as limiting it's potential impact on the wider field of the African study of African religions. To this end,

---

104. Bediako, "Christian Universality," 364.

one could argue that ACI might have a greater impact within this emerging discourse by encouraging graduates to take up positions in other institutions, carrying with them ACI's unique methodological approaches and pointing other faculty and students in this interesting direction. Gillian Bediako seems to affirm this when, in highlighting the unique nature of the scholarly community at ACI, she says, "It will be important to continue to foster and nurture this spiritual and intellectual freedom, so that future graduates . . . will have the sense of space and enabling to build upon, and develop elsewhere, what ACI gives them."[105]

Of course, the constraining realities of current postsecondary economies, whether in North America or Africa, come into play here. ACI may do all it can to encourage its graduates to go elsewhere; but the question will be, where will they go? My hope is that as ACI grows in stature and reputation, other institutions will be seeking out ACI graduates to take up positions as skilled academicians with important contributions to be made from an African Christian perspective.

Olademo supports such concerns from her observations of similar practices within Religious Studies departments in Nigeria, where exceptional students are frequently retained as lecturers. She upholds the argument that this practice has serious implications as far as potentially limiting creative engagement and diversity of thinking, and she similarly sees problems for methodological insularity. In her view, there are implications for both the institution and the scholars involved: "Such implications include the sustenance of an old status quo which may impede innovative initiatives in curriculum review. However, another implication is for innovative reviews suggested by such lecturers to be discounted because they are viewed as upsetting known methodologies in the study of religions."[106]

Furthermore, it is possible that such lecturers may struggle to throw off the identity of "student" within the institutional community and may struggle to have their new or different ideas gain acceptance. Therefore, for the benefit of the Institution in terms of broader academic acceptance, greater global visibility, and wider impact within African Christian scholarship, it would be hoped that in the future more ACI graduates would go further afield and that the Institute would take on more faculty from outside of their own ranks.

On a different note, one critique of the curricular focus of the MTh is that despite Bediako's regular and substantial engagement with modern socio-political concerns in his writing—even dedicating an entire JACT

---

105. Ibid., 366.
106. Olademo, "Gender," 70.

volume to its study, in addition to numerous other essays, as we have previously noted—this is not reflected in ACI curriculum to any meaningful extent. As such, it would seem helpful and appropriate to have, if not an entire course, at least a substantial portion of a course dealing with these important issues. This would support Bediako's argument that African Christianity has an important role to play in addressing social and political concerns, and in promoting the desacralization of politics in present-day Africa.

Valentin Dedji criticizes Bediako's focus on contextualised theology as not being sufficiently relevant to contemporary African concerns, failing particularly to address social and political realities. In fact, Bediako does engage extensively with political thought in relation to theology, though this is not the focus in *Theology and Identity*, Dedji's primary source. Nevertheless, while Bediako does address these issues in his writing, it is a missing element from ACI's curriculum and is one area in which ACI does not fully reflect the range of Bediako's concern for African Christian scholarship.

The importance of incorporating political elements into the curriculum is further supported by Bongmba when he argues that "there is need to continue to examine the relationship between church and state in Africa from a broad historical context. There is no uniformed story here . . . There is no doubt further studies are needed not only to understand the use of religion to supplant constitutional rule in many countries. Further studies of political theology are necessary to understand the belief systems that influence politicians who profess to be Christians . . ."[107] Since politics and historical engagement were of such importance to Bediako, and in view of Bongmba's argument for a continued need for the study of "political theology," this would seem a natural area of curricular and research development for ACI. Furthermore, in considering the important contributions of figures like Nkrumah and Busia to Church and State discussions in Ghana, ACI's location would similarly seem to support such a focus.

But another criticism of ACI is the more serious question of whether ACI has a life beyond its role as Bediako's magnum opus. On this point, the question that was in the minds of many was whether the Institute would in fact survive Bediako's untimely death in 2008. Gillian Bediako writes that while this was a period of "unexpected transition," the Institute emerged from it successfully, and, she argues, perhaps stronger, "because the vision and trail-blazing work of the founding pioneers are being built upon by a new generation of persons committed to consolidate and ensure the sustainability of the institution."[108]

---

107. Bongmba, "Writing African Christianity," 295.

108. Gillian Mary Bediako, "'Ebenezer, this is how far the Lord has helped us,' Celebrating 25 years," 6.

In the years since Bediako's death, ACI has indeed continued to grow and expand, a positive indication for a continued and fruitful future existence beyond Bediako's tenure. Overall, therefore, the Institute is not without its challenges, ranging from practicalities of finance and infrastructure to leadership and continuity. However, current signs point to an increasingly productive future.

Andrew Walls suggests eight key points necessary for what he calls the "theological revolution" presently before us within Christian scholarship, which may be helpful as a sort of rubric for continued evaluation of ACI's effectiveness.[109] Firstly, "a renewal of the sense of Christian vocation to scholarship, with the anchoring of Christian scholarship to Christian mission." Secondly, a research climate. As Walls rightly observes, "the southern continents are packed with the most amazing resources for research—historical, biblical, theological and phenomenological. But their institutions, often demoralised by the lack of funding and resources of another kind, are not always aware of the gold mines within their reach. They have the capacity to collect and preserve research materials, foster a sense of enquiry, develop forums for discussion and scholarly investigation." The third ingredient is exacting standards in scholarship. Fourthly, collegial attitudes. "The western academy is suffering from rampant individualism and built-in competitiveness. The *ashram* model is one of scholarly co-operation, of sharing resources and corporate responsibility..."

Fifthly, a pioneering spirit. Those who are innovators and willing to take risks, with the understanding, as Walls warns, that "such experimental scholarship is risky." Sixth, Walls calls for "dual education," with input from both biblical and Christian texts on the one hand, and local society on the other. Seventh, "a catholic attitude to knowledge." In contrast to the trend toward specialisation in scholarship, Walls argues, "this new situation needs scholars who, while maintaining and developing their own expertise, are willing to listen, learn and absorb Christian learning from every discipline, sacred and secular." And finally, "a lively interactive sense of world Christianity." Stressing the unity of the Church universal, Walls says, "The theological activity of Africa and Asia is not a matter of indifference to the church in the west. We are one Body and the health of the whole is involved. The discoveries about Christ that are made in the African, Asian, and Latin American heartlands will belong to us all." It will be helpful to continue returning to these points in order to evaluate developments at ACI in years to come.

---

109. See Walls, "Christian Scholarship in Africa," 51 for all eight points referenced here.

ACI: Significance for the Future

This chapter has demonstrated that Bediako's theological concerns, methodological approach, and intellectual itinerary may be seen most fully demonstrated in the curriculum and scholarly community of ACI: a creative embodiment of his scholarship and a logical progression from the concerns he first encountered in Négritude poetry. Evaluating Bediako within the historical context that shaped him—namely, African Christian history, and particularly Ghanaian Christian and mission history—together with "reading" ACI as text alongside of his other key unpublished and published works, reveals several important findings. Firstly, vernacular language emerges as a critical interpretive key to Bediako's contribution, seen both by understanding the impact of Négritude scholarship on his later theology, and by seeing the repeated emphasis on mother-tongue theology throughout both the curriculum and Christian community at ACI.

Secondly, by understanding Bediako's position as an African Christian scholar within the wider field of the African study of African religions, where we have already noted the controversies around methodology, and the call for further African contributions, Bediako's unique and open approach to African Christian scholarship pioneered at ACI serves as an important contribution to this wider field.

Thirdly, we see again the lasting impact of Négritude scholarship on Bediako's Christian theology in several areas: through his insistence on the use of vernacular languages for theological reflection, his admiration for the poetry of Afua Kuma, and his understanding of the primal worldview, as well as in his sensitive engagement with French African Catholic theologians.

In ACI we see a unique institutional model for Christian scholarship on African religions in an African context that brings us full circle. The legacy of the Basel Mission has proved to be an important feature here: the physical location and name of the Institute, in addition to a pietistic approach to Christian community, are ways in which Bediako further sought to express his theological agenda and situate himself as a Christian scholar in the clear trajectory of the historical continuum of Christian history in Africa. Within this historical continuity we most clearly see Bediako, and ACI, coming full circle, from the early engagement with African religions by European missionaries to African Christians leading this field of study—in former Mission buildings, no less.

In chapter 3, we observed some of the consequences resulting from European Christians who engendered serious cultural disruption through, for example, the creation of segregated salems and boarding schools. In various ways missionaries regularly conveyed negative messages about African culture, often deeming it incompatible with Christianity. While large numbers of Africans embraced the Christian message, this disconnect between faith and culture proved to be painful and confusing, evidenced both in Négritude literature as well as in the religio-political conflicts of the 1960s. In deliberately linking ACI with the former Basel Mission, Bediako demonstrates a radical revalorisation of African culture and religion and, while claiming continuity with historical Christianity in Ghana, he wholeheartedly does so from a thoroughly African perspective, thereby redeeming and completing the work of these early missionaries and achieving what Négritude poetry never quite managed.

In reflecting on his envisioned itinerary for ACI, Bediako comes to the following conclusion: "We are seeking our way towards a scholarship of spirituality, in which we need to grow in trusting God, grow in confidence, courage, sensitivity and willingness to think in new ways. God has brought us into deep intellectual engagement, for which we need spiritual sensitivity. We are called to a scholarship of spirituality—to something prayerful, deep and reflective, where human words do not say everything, and one needs to hear with the spirit."[110]

One final point must be made about the significance of ACI to the African Christian study of African religions. Walls states that "[t]he primary responsibility for the determinative theological scholarship for the twenty-first century will lie with the Christian communities of Africa . . ." This point must be stressed, because apart from a few local specialities, "theology will be the only major field of scholarship where this is the case. In most of the scientific, medical and technological spheres, leadership will remain with the west, or with East Asia in those departments where East Asia can outstrip the west. And in the humanities and social sciences, the stockpiled resources of the west will continue to give it great strength . . . But authentic theological scholarship must arise out of Christian mission and, therefore, from the principal theatres of mission."[111]

For the fields of Christian theology and particularly African Christian scholarship, ACI remains an institution and community that merits ongoing attention. Bediako affirms his vision for the Institute, as well as its unique contribution to this field of study, in this way: "In stressing theological formation, our concern is not the production of a caste of theological professionals set apart from the day-to-day life of ordinary Christian people. Rather, it is a way of underlining and recapturing the central place

---

110. Bediako, as referenced in the "Editorial," *JACT* 11/2 (December 2008) 3.
111. Walls, "Christian Scholarship in Africa," 47.

of theological reflection and insight in their deep and broad dimensions for the nurture of Christian lives and minds, and for the equipping of the people of God and the transformation of society."[112]

At his death Bediako left much work unfinished. As Walls rightly indicates, his "all too few writings will continue their influence, as will his institute's *Journal of African Christian Thought*, to which he so often contributed. There are other books he never completed, rich material lying in those electrifying lecture courses and biblical expositions." But perhaps even more importantly, "much of his finest work has been written in the lives and thinking of his students, colleagues, and friends [and] in the concept of the institution he founded."[113] It will remain for future generations to continue assessing Bediako's abiding impact on the African Christian study of African religions as achieved through ACI.

---

112. Bediako, "The African Renaissance," 29.
113. Walls, "Kwame Bediako and Christian Scholarship in Africa," 193.

Chapter 7

Their Past, Our Present

Bediako's Abiding Significance for African Christian Scholarship

"We returned to our places, these Kingdoms,
But no longer at ease here, in the old dispensation . . ."[1]

—T. S. Eliot, "The Journey of the Magi"

---

1. These lines are taken from T. S. Eliot's poem "The Journey of the Magi" published in 1927. The Adinkra symbol *aya* means "fern," and is used to denote endurance or resourcefulness.

One Part of the Story Comes to an End: Kwame Bediako, 1945–2008

"KWAME BEDIAKO WAS ONE of those people who, if you're lucky, you may come across once or twice in your lifetime. Brilliant, engaging, charismatic, warm, generous, funny, the real deal: a Christian thinker, teacher and writer of the very highest order who lived what he preached. It was a tremendous shock to discover that he'd died a few months back at the age of 63. Although I'd not seen him for some years, Kwame has always loomed large in my mind as an example, an inspiration, a friend."[2] Such are the reflections of his friend and former classmate, theologian Iwan Russell-Jones.

One part of Bediako's story came to an end on June 10th 2008, when he passed away suddenly after a brief but serious illness. As Russell-Jones says, his death was a shock for many, myself included. I had been in correspondence with Bediako a number of months earlier about beginning this research project, which was to take the form of a PhD. As ever, he was warmly encouraging. I arrived in the UK on June 9th to begin my studies, and awoke the following morning to news of his death. I had envisioned spending more time studying with him at ACI, discussing his Négritude scholarship, prodding him on what exactly he was getting at with the primal imagination, and hearing what he dreamed of for the future of ACI. But, that was not to be.

However, as he has demonstrated, many important clues are waiting to be found in what has gone before, if we have the patience to explore carefully. In following Bediako's lead by using a historical-biographical approach, significant aspects of Bediako's scholarly itinerary have become clear, while simultaneously elucidating the emergence of an important African Christian discourse in twentieth-century Ghana.

African Christian Scholarship As Emerging Discourse

In exploring Bediako's voice within emerging African Christian discourse in twentieth-century Ghana, several important things have become clear. One is that Bediako's academic itinerary may more accurately be described as an African Christian intellectual approach to Christianity and primal religion in Africa. His concerns are quite distinct from those of Western theology, and we have engaged them here from the perspective of intellectual history. This has revealed that in many ways, the consistent trajectory of his academic career from Négritude scholarship, through to *Theology and Identity*,

---

2. Russell-Jones, "Following the Footprints of God," para. 1.

to the foundation of ACI, may be seen as seeking creative approaches to engaging questions of African Christian identity on the one hand, and clearly articulating responses to African intellectual critiques of Christianity on the other. More broadly, we have seen that the African study of African religions in Ghana and beyond is truly an interdisciplinary and emerging discourse, with contributions coming from a variety of unexpected corners, with African Christian voices making an important contribution.

A brief summary of some of the key developments in the late-nineteenth and early-twentieth century may be helpful to keep in mind. We noted that a number of European missionary, colonial, and academic figures played important roles in laying a foundation for this discourse. This included the pioneering efforts of Basel missionary J.G. Christaller in Twi translation, and the unexpectedly positive approach of Governor Guggisberg in seeing the significance of studying African religion and culture within the academy and looking ahead to the development of the University of Ghana. Moving towards the mid-to-later-twentieth century, we noted the important efforts of missionary-scholars Geoffrey Parrinder and Andrew Walls in further perceiving the significance of African indigenous religions as an important field of study alongside of Christianity and Islam, and in developing university departments in Nigeria and the U.K. that continued to foster such inquiry.

From the mid-twentieth-century onwards, we observed African scholars increasingly taking the lead in this area, from the re-translation efforts of C.A. Akrofi to Nkrumah's establishment of Legon's Department for the Study of Religions. Within the African Christian cohort, Bediako emerges as a pioneering figure primarily through his institutionalization of this discourse at ACI. Here, he most fully displays his scholarly and spiritual itineraries, creating space for African Christian intellectual inquiry and designing a community and curricular model for training future generations of African Christian scholars.

In his writing and through ACI, Bediako demonstrates that creative links between his Christian faith and a primal religious worldview, mediated through the use of vernacular language and given shape by the underlying, unresolved concerns of Négritude poets, have fostered positive expressions of an African Christian identity and opened up rich areas of scholarship for himself and for others. He draws upon the pietistic and linguistic legacies of Basel missionaries, builds upon the educational systems established by British colonial officials and Ghanaian politicians, and attempts to address the probing questions of African poets, intellectuals, and theologians in his efforts to demonstrate the historical and theological roots for an African Christian identity.

In this process, he demonstrates unequivocally that the African Christian study of African religions exceeds the narrow boundaries typically perceived by Western theology, while also challenging the marginalization of Christian voices within the wider African study of African religions. And his approach of situating African scholars within their historical contexts—both in his writing and through the physical location of the Institute—proves to be a fruitful one for analyzing him, and appears to be a useful approach to apply to other African Christian scholars. Indeed, in Bediako's writing and within the community and scholarship emerging from ACI, this historical-biographical approach emerges as a preferred "African tradition" in the study of religion in Africa.

Through ACI, he creatively draws the diverse strands of this emerging discourse together and brings his intellectual itinerary full circle. He builds upon the linguistic efforts of the Basel Mission; offers a Christian institutional response to Nkrumah's secularized Department for the Study of Religions; and replaces U Tam'si's painful laments with Afua Kuma's joyful praises. As Walls prompts us to see and as Bediako further demonstrates, in looking to the past, we often find patterns and themes that help us to clarify the present and intuit future trajectories. While Bediako brought his intellectual itinerary full circle personally and historically, it is regrettably a smaller circle than what it might have been, had it not been cut so short.

Methodological Divisions Reconsidered

Bediako's argument for placing scholars within the historical continuum that has produced them, as we have seen here, offers a dual focus: it elucidates the scholar, on the one hand, and the context, on the other. Within this book, I have sought to maintain this balance, focusing on Bediako the scholar, while opening up twentieth-century Ghana and the wider African Christian study of African religions as the geographical, historical, and disciplinary context in which he is located. Viewed in this way, we see that Bediako is part of a wider emerging religious discourse in which Africans are taking the lead and in which African Christian voices form a growing and significant component. In using this approach, the overall picture of the motivations and concerns of both the scholar and his context, and of their interrelated nature, has been brought into sharper focus. In order to ensure that the resulting image is clear after moving between these macro and micro views, I wish to briefly return to some of these discussions in order to highlight where further scholarship is needed.

Attending to the Voices of African Christian Scholars

This location of Bediako as an African Christian scholar within the African study of African religions was set against the backdrop of divisions between Western theology, African Christian scholarship, and non-confessional approaches to the study of religion in Africa. As we saw in chapter 2, there are complex reasons for these divisions. One is that emerging African Christian discourse often finds itself at odds with Western theology—if by theology we mean discussions about doctrine and dogma, or debates about "orthodox" and "heretical." Walls points us here to the Western theological inheritance of Enlightenment thinking, in which a clearly demarcated frontier between the empirical world of reason and the world of spirit is fundamental.

As Walls argues, the Christian Enlightenment "accepted the frontier between the worlds, but asserted that there were identifiable crossing-places: the Incarnation, the Resurrection, revelation, prayer, perhaps miracles. But these were recognized crossing points on a frontier that was generally closed; and theological activity was sometimes a matter of deciding where the bona fide crossing points were to be found. Theology, in effect, policed the frontier."[3]

Bediako is surveying the territory across the border, as it were. As he has said, he holds many Christian creeds and formulations in abeyance. They are not his focus as a scholar; neither are they for many other African Christian scholars. Yet many Western theologians continue to look to him on these points, leading to some of the responses we have seen among theologians and missiologists who interpret Bediako as being insufficiently biblically based, or as promoting syncretistic beliefs when they do not find what they are looking for in his writing. If we seek to interpret him along Western theological lines, it obscures his broader intellectual itinerary and can mislead us about his focus. As we saw in chapter 2, classifying African Christian scholars as theologians while failing to clarify what we mean by the term can be unhelpful and misleading; instead, care should be taken to ensure we are clear on our definitions and on the expectations that we bring to bear on such scholarship.

But this emerging African Christian discourse equally finds itself in a position of unresolved tension with Religious Studies. While African Christian scholars continue to move in new and creative directions as they explore religion in Africa, a commitment to privileging a Christian perspective—essential for a scholar like Bediako—typically renders them unwelcome guests

---

3. Walls, "Christian Scholarship in Africa," 49.

at the methodologically agnostic Religious Studies table, where many other scholars of religion in Africa are seated.

African Christian scholarship needs to be examined in its own right. It is not an African response to Western theology. As Bediako says, "the era of African theological literature as reaction to Western misrepresentation is past."[4] It is also distinct from methodologically agnostic approaches to the study of religion in Africa. Nevertheless, it shares some overlapping concerns and methodological frameworks with both, and as such, we need to consider those different voices. With Bediako, the result of doing otherwise is misinterpretations and missed opportunities for scholars on all sides.

Bediako saliently addresses this when he explores the misunderstandings that have followed the work of African Christian scholars in their attempts at shaping new methodological approaches:

> The failure in some criticisms of African theology may be traced to a misconception about what the tasks of these African Christian writers ought to be. When John Mbiti's *Concepts of God in Africa* is objected to for its 'primary theological purpose,' as 'attempting to lay the basis for a distinctively African theology by blending the African past with the Judeo-Christian tradition' . . . or when his *The Prayers of African Religion* is judged to be 'unsatisfactory' because 'it tends to blur the distinctiveness of African spirituality by seeking a praeparatio evangelica rather than the integrity of the cult-group' . . . such criticisms obscure the contributions that these African theologians could be making towards the understanding of what is, after all, their own religious heritage; which is, indeed, a proper task of theology. In both these instances, the critics rightly interpret the intention of the African theologian. It just so happens that they do not approve of what they find.[5]

To this end, it is a sign of encouragement that a number of important, large-scale reference works that specifically address African approaches to the study of religion in Africa, including those of African Christian scholars, are beginning to come out. This is helpful in understanding the wider contours of this emerging discourse, and of the particular contributions of African Christian scholars. But, there is little as yet which traces the emergence of this discourse in specific African countries, or which locates African Christian scholars in their more specific historical and cultural

---

4. Bediako, "Understanding African Theology" [*Jesus in Africa*], 57.

5. Ibid., 53. Here he references, in order: Ray, *African Religions*, 15; McKenzie, Review of *The Prayers of African Religion*; and Fasholé-Luke, "The Quest for an African Christian Theology," 268.

contexts, or which creates space for greater cross-disciplinary discussion. This remains an important area of scholarship to develop, and will require important interdisciplinary collaborations between fields such as history, politics, sociology, literary studies, theology, religious studies, and others.[6]

Bediako: Relic, Relevant, or Relative?

In this book, I have sought to offer a more holistic picture of Bediako's intellectual and spiritual itinerary. And, in observing the breadth and scope of his scholarship, and the ways in which he institutionalizes this discourse at ACI, he does indeed emerge as a pioneering figure within the African Christian study of African religions. Nevertheless, we are left with the following questions: what relevance does Bediako have for the study of religion in Africa, or for current world Christian scholarship? Is his work solely to be viewed as a response to the post-independence period—a historic relic, as one of my early interlocutors charged? As we have seen, Bediako's scholarship reaches across historic and disciplinary boundaries; and in many ways, we are only just beginning to discern the continuing significance of his contribution.

"Their past, our present": Implications for Christian Historiography

In an account that Bediako has written about and shared with some regularity, he recalls what for him was a pivotal encounter with John Mbiti in mid-1980 that was to shape the course of his continued scholarly focus. Bediako asked Mbiti "how it was that he, a scholar trained in Biblical Studies, author of a highly regarded Cambridge University doctoral thesis on New Testament eschatology, and a member of the international Society of New Testament Studies . . . had devoted such a sizeable portion of his academic career to the exploration of the theological meaning and significance of African traditional religions and their cultural worlds." Mbiti, he recalls, reflected silently for some time, "then asked me for my copy of his book, *African*

---

6. In a chapter entitled "Studying African Christianity: Future Trajectories," Bongmba outlines a number of areas for continued study in this field. His suggestions include globalization; African Christian missions; Christianity and the political economy in Africa; Christianity and the arts; and Christianity and human rights in Africa as key examples (Bongmba, "Studying African Christianity," 559–62).

Religions and Philosophy, wrote on the title page the statement: 'Their past is also our present,' and returned the book to me."[7]

This proved to be an encounter of lasting significance for Bediako, formative for his methodological approach, and points to a critical implication of his intellectual itinerary for world Christianity. He continues in his reflection:

> That, for me, was a moment of insight, borne upon me with singular clarity, showing me that no significant theological development in the history of Christian thought had ever proceeded on the basis of a religious vacuum. As my research had to do with exploring the possible thematic and analogical connections between early Hellenistic Christians, on the one hand, and modern African Christian theology, on the other . . . I was keen to apply that insight across the full range of my investigations. The more closely I looked at the early Christian developments and related them to the modern African efforts, the more it became evident to me that all Christians, in every place and time, not only need to have a past, but indeed, do have a past, a pre-Christian past that connects with the present.[8]

With this insight, it shifts discussion away from the polemical debates over Bediako's theology and reveals that his methodological approach—his underlying framework and intellectual motivation—is, arguably, the area in which we have the most to learn from him. He demonstrates the modern relevance of an ancient practice and offers a template for Christian scholars to engage with their culture and their past as a source for present understanding. Seen in this light, his Jesus-as-Ancestor discussion becomes, not the focus in itself, as a contentious Christological debate, but a creative demonstration of a possible line of thinking for him as an Akan Christian scholar looking to his historical, cultural, and religious past for current theological interpretative guidance. While Jesus-as-Ancestor will not have equal relevance or resonance for all, we miss Bediako's wider point if we leave our focus there.

Scholars of world Christianity may similarly find unexpected treasures and renewed theological resources by looking into their pre-Christian pasts to help illuminate present realities. This may hold especially true for scholarship in the West, where the Western pre-Christian past has essentially been given over to fields such as history, anthropology, and religious studies

---

7. Bediako, "'Why has the summer ended?,'" 8.
8. Ibid.

(when it is engaged with at all), and is not typically viewed as a relevant source for Christian scholarship.

Bediako further clarifies the significance of looking to the past for the West: "It is this re-location of African primal religions 'at the very centre of the academic stage' which may prove a benediction to Western Christian theology . . . For the African vindication of the theological significance of African primal religions . . . also goes to affirm that the European primal heritage was not illusory, to be consigned to oblivion as primitive darkness. The nature of the meeting of Christianity with European primal religions may hold more significance for understanding the modern West than it may have been assumed."[9]

Bediako signals the importance of this discussion when he argues that, while European pre-Christian religions seemed to be quickly overtaken by Christianity, Christians nevertheless continued to name the days of week after pre-Christian deities, as well as incorporating pre-Christian elements into the celebration of Christian festivals. This, argues Bediako, "indicat[es] that the old beliefs had not entirely lost their hold upon people's minds." "It may be," he continues, "that in Africa the opportunity lost in Europe for a serious and creative theological encounter between the Christian and primal traditions, can be regained."[10]

Community and Curriculum: Methodological implications

Another important aspect of Bediako's legacy is his model of scholarship undertaken in community. Within the community and curriculum at ACI, Bediako offers a template for institutional life, and a critical challenge to the Western academy and theological training in particular. When we perceive the task of theology as engagement primarily with doctrine and dogma, we risk missing much of what is vital. As this book demonstrates, the richness of the historical context, political thought, poetry, or as we have just seen, a pre-Christian religious past, are areas in which we may discern important sources for Christian intellectual engagement. Bediako as an African Christian scholar sees his theological task as building upon and engaging such sources.

---

9. Bediako, "Understanding African Theology" [*Themelios*], 10. Note that this statement is used in part, but altered, in Bediako's chapter by the same title in *Jesus in Africa* (see 59).

10. Ibid.

However, much theological discourse, in seeking responses to the "heretical or orthodox" questions, misses this. This can lead us to incomplete or inaccurate conclusions and may cause us to miss out on fresh approaches to Christian scholarship, which, perhaps especially in the West, could inject much-needed vitality into increasingly dry, well-trod terrain. As we have heard from Andrew Walls, the Western academy is sick and in need of rescuing. It is precisely the creative approaches and materials found within the African Christian study of African religions that may offer the salvific revitalization necessary here.

Furthermore, as we have noted, the "community" approach to scholarship as demonstrated at ACI may be seen in sharp contrast to the Western academy, which is all too often competitive, non-collegial, and as Walls puts it, "a pensioner to global capitalism."[11] Engagement with African Christian scholarship may offer new paradigms—which in fact are old paradigms—for scholarship which prioritizes rigorous scholasticism but not at the expense of Christian spirituality nor the good of the wider community.

In an essay entailing the way forward for theological education in Africa, Bediako speaks directly to this issue. He notes that when we take this view of scholarship, we are in fact connecting with an ancient vision for theological training, where "the whole focus was the training of the person, to make one Christ-like, to bring one into union with Christ, the Master." Among the early Church Fathers, Bediako reminds us, the model of theological formation was in fact a "quest for holiness and moral transformation within the student, who would then also become a model for others seeking their own liberation." Interpreting this, Bediako argues that in such a case, "one embarked on theological training not to receive information to pass on, not to acquire status through diplomas and degrees, not even to acquire skills for ministry, but to be changed inwardly. Only when one had learnt the secret of the holy life, was one recognized as being . . . a teacher to others."[12]

One of the reasons why Western theological scholarship differs so significantly from African theology relates to the Enlightenment models that have been passed down; the "policing of the frontier," as Walls describes it. The real harm here, charges Bediako, is that the Enlightenment theological model has trained us to "separate knowledge from character, intellectual development from spiritual growth, and, therefore, to produce scholars and intellectuals, theologically trained people, who are left morally weak because they have not been taken through the disciplines of being changed."[13]

---

11. Walls, "African Christian Scholarship," 47.
12. Bediako, "The African Renaissance," 32.
13. Ibid.

On the other hand, the point of ACI's community-based model of scholarship-as-spiritual-formation is "to feel after components of Christian formation that make for transformation of life, to provide the exposure to fields of knowledge that assist self-understanding and liberate the mind, and generate larger and deeper human sympathies on the basis that Christ is the key to all the treasure of wisdom and knowledge (Col. 2:3)."[14] Of course, ACI does not always meet its own standards in striving to be a scholarly, collegial, and faithful Christian community. Every model will fall short. However, what Bediako seeks to demonstrate through ACI holds important keys for scholars in and beyond Africa.

Implications for the Study of Religion in Africa

The question may rightly be asked: if Bediako's primary contribution is to African Christian scholarship, does it hold anything of value for non-confessional scholars of religion? As we will recall from chapter 2, African Christian scholars make important contributions within the wider African study of African religions, sharing some concerns in common with a variety of academics. Non-confessional scholars may not seek to engage with Bediako on the intricacies and outcomes of his Christian arguments. Indeed, some will argue that their methodological agnosticism specifically precludes or dissuades them from engaging with such concerns. This brings to mind the rather circular debates between Olabimtan, as a Christian scholar, and van Rinsum and Platvoet, as methodologically agnostic scholars, wherein both essentially reiterated the distinct positions of Christian and non-confessional scholars in the study of religion in Africa. Their extended discussion failed to identify meaningful common ground in their respective scholarly itineraries, and ultimately just further demarcated the boundaries between African Christian scholarship and religious studies within an African context.

Nevertheless, while it is understandable that Christian and non-confessional scholars do not always, or perhaps often, share a scholarly itinerary, in a growing and highly interdisciplinary field such as the African study of African religions, new approaches and greater dialogue is necessary. Non-confessional scholars have much to learn from African Christian academics, and likewise bring enriching insights from neighbouring disciplines to this growing field. The two areas that we have just considered, Bediako's historical approach and his template for scholarship-in-community, have implications for both Christian and non-confessional scholars alike. Both

14. Ibid.

of these may arguably be seen as "African traditions" in the study of religion in Africa, and require further engagement by a wider variety of scholars, not just African Christian scholars.

In particular, Bediako's concept of scholarship-in-community stands in stark contrast to the competitive, economically-based, individually-motivated scholarly approaches more common to the West, and is an approach requiring further testing.[15] As Bediako has already reminded us, in his context, any scholarly achievements attained by the individual alone, apart from the wider community, may be judged as suspect and perhaps classed as witchcraft. Therefore, part of his approach at ACI may be seen as endeavouring to allay such concerns by modelling scholarship done in community: at a transparent, grassroots, and not ivory tower, level. This is not limited to Christian approaches to scholarship; indeed, the "ashram" model itself is borrowed from Indian religious traditions. To this end, any of us engaged in the study of religion in Africa would do well to reconsider the broader significance and spiritually formative aspects of scholarship-in-community, both for the benefit of the individual as well as the wider community. While not an easily replicable methodological model, Bediako's example may prove to be a valuable one particularly for the health and integrity of ailing Western academic institutions.

In considering the diverse voices and wide-ranging concerns within the study of religion in Africa, we will all benefit if we choose to adopt more open and attentive postures in listening to and engaging with one another. Indeed, this will be an essential component for strengthening and expanding scholarly engagement with religions in Africa.

Future Directions for African Christian Scholarship

African Christian scholars, while sharing a faith perspective and some concerns with Western theologians, typically range far beyond Western theological "borders," with a keener sense of the importance of giving consideration to cultural, historical, and pre-Christian religious identities within their theological scholarship. We have also heard repeatedly, and would readily affirm, that we are now in a time when African scholars must take the lead in the study of religion in Africa, with non-African scholars

---

15. I use the term "scholarship-in-community" here in a broad sense to capture the various aspects of Bediako's community emphasis at ACI that we have already seen. This includes the small, tight-knit community of ACI itself, with daily rhythms of study, worship, and recreation by students, staff, and faculty; student participation and observation in the local surrounding community; and the emphasis on students bringing personal, pastoral, and wider questions to bear on lectures and research.

working collaboratively to contribute important counterpoints and alternate perspectives.

With this in mind, one would expect to find growing African Christian scholarship critically engaging Bediako, both theologically and methodologically; yet such engagement, for the most part, has been less than robust. Certainly, there are increasing numbers of masters and doctoral students analyzing Bediako, with mother tongue theology and African Christology being key areas of research, and a growing body of essays and journal articles that engage him on various theological points.[16] But much of this research remains relatively superficial, predominantly relying on Bediako's key published works (i.e., *Theology and Identity*; *Jesus in Africa*; and *Christianity in Africa*), and failing to offer a critique of his wider scholarly itinerary, his extensive unpublished material, or methodological approaches.

One interesting exception to this is the lively debate on Bediako's Jesus-as-Ancestor question, as seen in the writings of several African Christian scholars including South African theologian T.S. Maluleke and Ghanaians Charles Sarpong Aye-Addo and the late Nana Addo Dankwa III. To illustrate the range of perspectives very briefly, Maluleke affirms Bediako's proposal, but argues that he does not go far enough. In his opinion, the possibility is not just for Jesus to become the Supreme Ancestor, but to join the ranks of other ancestors at the service of the Supreme Being in Africa, according greater value to African indigenous religions as distinct from Christianity.[17]

Aye-Addo is sympathetic to Bediako's effort to pursue Christological categories reflective of the African context. However, he concludes that this attempt to make Jesus "'at home' in the African spiritual universe" is in fact reflective of the failed Anglo-European approach to do the same. And this, he argues, "is identified by African theologians as the source of the problem in the first place."[18] With yet another perspective, Dankwa, who, we may recall, was a traditional chief and committed Christian, argues that Jesus may *not* be viewed as an ancestor in Akan cosmology because his physical body did not suffer decay, and is therefore in a superior category to the ancestors. In his words, "The spirit of Christ which is part of the Trinity cannot be considered as an ancestor."[19] It is hoped that future generations of African Christian scholars will continue to engage critically with Bediako's theological arguments, as these three model.

16. See Appendix A for an overview of research on Bediako consulted here.
17. Maluleke "Black and African Theologies," 16.
18. Aye-Addo, *Akan Christology*, xi.
19. Dankwa, *Christianity and African Traditional Beliefs*, 221–22.

It will also be important to hear African Christian voices that interrogate Bediako's proposed methodological approaches. Olabimtan takes up the cause; but further discussion is necessary. How do African Christian scholars perceive Bediako's argument for adopting a historical-biographical method, or for the importance of scholarship-in-community, for example? Can these be considered "African approaches," or are they more specific to Bediako? How might such approaches function for African scholars in diaspora, or more broadly for the study of religion in Africa? African Christian responses on these and other questions would be instructive.

And of course, Bediako's substantive unpublished opus is another important area in which we would hope to see further analysis from African Christian scholars. Asamoah-Gyadu picks up on this, but there is more gold to be mined in Bediako's Négritude scholarship, his sermons, lectures, and unfinished research. Seen in this light, critical African Christian scholarship on Bediako is only just beginning.

African Christian scholars also have an important role to play within the wider African study of African religions. Bediako speaks to this when he argues that a key part of the future agenda for African Theology includes scholarship "engag[ing] creatively with the developing African intellectual opinion which interprets African reality differently to the point of setting aside the very principle of religion itself." He underscores the importance of this intellectual undertaking when he says, "How African Theology responds to this *African* philosophical and intellectual atheism must certainly be one of the most crucial issues in the theology of the future."[20] With regard to the scholarly itinerary that Bediako has outlined for African Christian scholarship, it would seem that while the harvest is plentiful, the workers remain too few. We will all be enriched as African Christian scholars continue to take up these challenges and expand scholarship in these areas.

With this in mind, it is helpful to recall here the six key considerations for future accounts of African Christian scholarship that Elias Bongmba has put forward, which we examined in chapter 2. All six of his recommendations offer useful points of departure for future scholarship analyzing Bediako, though as previously discussed, his latter three recommendations are especially apt for scholarship engaging Bediako. These include Bongmba's call for further engagement with transcendence, or "the religious factor," within the study of African Christianity; the "claims and challenges of culture"; and the contribution of literature published in African languages.[21]

---

20. Bediako, *Theology and Identity*, 439; italics are Bediako's.

21. See chapter 2 of this book, and see Bongmba, "Writing African Christianity," 282–89.

For those seeking to heed Bongmba's call and develop African Christian scholarship in these areas, Bediako's opus proves to be an important resource; a clear contradiction to those who argue that he only has limited, historical relevance.

In an interview that I conducted with U.K.-based Ghanaian Christian scholar Daniel Eshun, he similarly pointed to Bediako's relevance for future African Christian scholarship. Eshun identifies himself as a fourth generation African Christian academic with a scholarly focus in anthropology and sociology of religion. He recalled the formative impact of first hearing Bediako preach and lecture when he (Eshun) was a young student, and seeing in Bediako an example of being an African Christian academic. He suggests we might hear Bediako's voice as prophetic, but wonders whether current scholarship may have moved on from him without ever having properly engaged him.

In terms of Bediako's intellectual trajectory, and particularly issues relating to culture, primal religion, and identity, Eshun says, "He started us off, and we didn't take him seriously. He started a conversation, but we haven't carried it forward. The charismatic movement diverted and distracted us away from the conversation Bediako was trying to force us to have, but it is a conversation that needs to be revisited."[22]

We have seen some of the key areas highlighted as critical for future African Christian consideration; and we have further seen that Bediako's opus, published and unpublished, holds much of value for contributing to this emerging discourse. It is hoped that African Christian scholars will take the lead in opening up what is already a rich area of study.

Concluding Remarks

This book, it is hoped, has furthered our understanding of Kwame Bediako as an African Christian scholar with a unique intellectual itinerary, while further elucidating the emergence of African religious discourse in twentieth-century Ghana. As we have seen, scholarship that consigns itself to a limited review of certain aspects of Bediako's published opus, or that fails to take into account his historical and intellectual context, often leads to incomplete or inaccurate readings of this scholar. Kwesi Dickson affirms this when he states that "[the theologian who] fails to recognize the structures of religion as revealed by the historian of religion . . . may not notice the absence of religion from his theology. In the context of Africa, Christian

---

22. Eshun, interview by the author, May 28, 2013, Whitelands College, University of Roehampton, U.K.

theology must of necessity take account of that understanding of religion which bears the stamp of an authentic African contribution."[23]

Significantly, Maluleke perceives Bediako's scholarly itinerary more accurately than many theologians when he says, "The Africanisation sought by Bediako should not be confused with the indigenisation of the Christian faith and Gospel into African forms. Such indigenisation has already been achieved in the African Independent Churches, for example. According to Bediako, what is at issue is no longer a religious matter but an intellectual one of 'how African Christianity, employing Christian tools, may set about mending the torn fabric of African identity and hopefully point the way to a fuller and unfettered African humanity and personality.'"[24]

Bediako himself makes his intellectual focus clear. While he affirms the work of earlier generations of African theologians to "secure the roots of Christianity in the full African context by appropriating and integrating the pre-Christian primal cultural tradition," he unequivocally states that there is something different to be addressed. "The residual question now is this," Bediako begins. "[W]ill African Christianity be able to find viable *intellectual* grounds upon which to validate and secure its *African* credentials? In other words, following the 'Christianisation' of African tradition, African Christianity must achieve an *Africanisation* of its Christian experience, and this latter may well prove the more demanding task."[25]

When this is perceived, it takes us clearly out of the Western theological or religious studies trajectories and places us squarely within the wider discourse of the African study of African religions. Here it takes on a different focus altogether and includes a much wider compendium of questions and sources that lead us, not into doctrine or dogma, but into the ephemeral realms of Négritude and Surrealist philosophy; the "deep forest" portrayed by Afua Kuma; Akan systems of traditional chieftaincy; political propaganda; and European mission history. Not necessarily typical sources for Western theological or even religious studies discourse; but essential sources for engaging with Bediako and the African Christian study of religions in Ghana and beyond. As Bediako rightly argues, such scholarship "calls for a wider range of critical tools and criteria for scholarship than are usually allowed for, as well as levels of sacrifice, that are not generally required."[26]

---

23. Dickson, *Theology in Africa*, 46.

24. Maluleke, "Black and African Theologies," 6, citing Bediako, *Christianity in Africa*, 5.

25. Bediako, *Christianity in Africa*, 4.

26. Bediako, "A New Era in Christian Scholarship," 7.

Within all of this, it becomes clear that there are some important implications for scholarship in general. Within the humanities, much of our scholarship has become increasingly narrow and specialized, a practice that in some cases has left us polarized and insulated from wider scholastic discourse, unable to benefit from the insights of colleagues in cognate disciplines. Similarly, in current world affairs we are presently seeing and experiencing examples of such tensions and polarizations on various fronts. Bediako serves as a positive example to follow, within and beyond the study of religion in Africa.

When I reflect on what I have gained from my personal and textual interactions with Kwame Bediako, I am reminded again of my first encounters with him in 2006, and of his expansive welcome to all at ACI. To students from Ghana and other African countries; to those of us from North America, Australia, Europe, and the U.K; to women and to men; to gardeners, researchers, cooks, librarians; to young volunteers and senior guests. He had time to stop and speak with the ladies selling pineapple near ACI's front gates, time for students, for the local Omanhene, for church leaders and lay members, and time to meet and pray with politicians.

He viewed everyone as not only worthy of respect, but worthy of his time and attention. In all of this, it was not a sense of duty or busyness that he conveyed, but of keen interest. He believed that people's stories and lived experiences held something of value, and he was willing to be challenged, surprised, encouraged and at times discouraged, by these interactions. His scholarly thought was continually shaped by his community and the diversity of individuals therein, as much as by the scholarly texts with which he engaged. Furthermore, Bediako saw the importance for African Christian scholarship of engaging a variety of disciplines. As a challenge to many narrower approaches to theology, he demonstrates that for Christian scholars, no discipline is "out-of-bounds": he found value and continued to utilize certain frameworks he encountered in surrealist poetry and African literature alongside of his training in both theology and religious studies.

While we may point to a number of outstanding twentieth-century African Christian scholars, it is Bediako who is regularly referred to as the leading theologian of his generation. This strikes me as an important reminder that scholarship that is informed by a wide variety of sources, and a scholarly itinerary that creates space for such open engagement, emerges as holistic and robust. His work was strengthened, not weakened, by his wide-ranging interactions, and he remains an example for academics in any discipline of the benefits to be gained by maintaining an open and listening posture.

However, it must be said that many have rightly warned of the dangers of what might be called lazy interdisciplinarity, in which we approach different disciplines like a buffet: selecting bits from here and there, taking things out of context, and failing to thoroughly address scholars or their wider contexts. This is not the kind of "openness" that Bediako advocated or demonstrated. His was not "anything goes" openness, nor did it equate to uncritical agreement with all. Indeed, as we have seen, he is unequivocal in his rejection of some views, as his doctoral thesis on U Tam'si demonstrates. But his criticism emerges out of a deep level of thoughtful engagement, demonstrating both a thorough understanding of the poet's humanistic framework as well as his [Bediako's] own Christian convictions, while also acknowledging the areas where he agrees and resonates with U Tam'si. To extend the metaphor, far from critiquing items selected easily from a buffet, Bediako has studied the culinary traditions of others and tested their recipes himself before offering feedback—demonstrating the wider range of critical tools, criteria, and greater levels of sacrifice necessary in this field, to which he alludes. As we have already noted, Bediako sees this openness as a key feature of Christian scholarship, and what "Christian witness to the divine incognito in Christ requires."[27]

As those engaged with African Christian scholarship and more broadly with the study of religion in Africa, Bediako illustrates the larger discoveries that remain to be found for those willing to cross scholarly frontiers to explore less familiar terrain. As we have been reminded, however, this path is not necessarily the most straightforward or smooth; but the rewards to be gained make the journey worthwhile. As the Akan proverb reminds us, "when two people carry a heavy load, it does not hurt." There is indeed much of academic and spiritual significance to be gained here—more than any one tradition or scholar can "carry." As one who goes before us, Bediako's life and work continue to illuminate the way forward for those willing to follow his lead and continue the conversations that he has started.

---

27. Bediako, "How Is Jesus Christ Lord?," 44.

Appendix A

Current Scholarship Engaging with Bediako

THE FOLLOWING REFERENCES INCLUDE scholars who engage either entirely, or significantly, with Bediako. This list is not exhaustive, but reflects the breadth of scholarship of which I was aware for this research. I have arranged it chronologically within the following categories: books, articles/chapters in books, and unpublished masters and doctoral dissertations. This is intended to provide an accessible overview of who has been engaging Bediako, on what points, and in what formats.

Books

Gillian Mary Bediako, Benhardt Y. Quarshie, and J. Kwabena Asamoah-Gyadu. *Seeing New Facets of the Diamond: Christianity as a Universal Faith—Essays in Honour of Kwame Bediako.* Akropong-Akuapem, Ghana: Regnum Africa, 2014.

Aye-Addo, Charles Sarpong. *Akan Christology: An Analysis of the Christologies of John Samuel Pobee and Kwame Bediako in Conversation with the Theology of Karl Barth.* Eugene, OR: Pickwick, 2013. This is a revision of "Akan Christology: An Analysis of the Christologies of John Samuel Pobee and Kwame Bediako in Conversation with the Theology of Karl Barth." PhD diss., Drew University, 2010.

Articles/Chapters in Books

Edu-Bekoe, Yaw Attah. "Describing an African Dancing Without Hearing His Music: Kevin Howard Has Generally Misunderstood Kwame Bediako." *Global Missiology* 3/12 (April 2015). http://ojs.globalmissiology.org/index.php/english/article/viewFile/1787/3965.

Asamoah-Gyadu, J. Kwabena. "Kwame Bediako: Mr. African Theology." In *Mission as Transformation: Learning from Catalysts*, edited by David Cranston and Ruth Padilla DeBorst, 11–21. Eugene, OR: Wipf & Stock, 2014.

Howard, Kevin. "Kwame Bediako: Considerations on the Motivating Force Behind His *Theology and Identity*." *Global Missiology* 3/10 (April 2013). http://ojs.globalmissiology.org/index.php/english/article/viewFile/1186/2734.

Asamoah-Gyadu, J. Kwabena. "Bediako of Africa: A Late Twentieth Century Outstanding Theologian and Teacher." *Mission Studies* 26 (2009) 5–16.

Cox, James L. "The Globalization of Localized African Religions: The Case of Kwame Bediako." In *World Christianity in Local Context*, edited by Stephen R. Goodwin, 56–65. London: Continuum, 2009.

Walls, Andrew F. "Kwame Bediako and Christian Scholarship in Africa." *IBMR* 32/4 (October 2008) 188–193.

Ferdinando, Keith. "Christian Identity in the African Context: Reflections on Kwame Bediako's *Theology and Identity*." *Journal of the Evangelical Theological Society* 50/1 (March 2007) 121–43.

Fotland, Roar G. "The Christology of Kwame Bediako." *JACT* 8/1 (June 2005) 36–49.

Thomson, Alan. "Learning from the African Experience: Bediako and Critical Contextualization." *Evangelical Review of Theology* 30/1 (January 2006) 31–48.

Dedji, Valentin. "Kwame Bediako and African Christian Identity." In *Reconstruction and Renewal in African Christian Theology*, 166–219. Nairobi: Acton, 2003. This is a revision of "Reconstruction and Renewal in African Christian Theology," PhD diss., University of Cambridge, 1999.

Wagenaar, Hinne. "Theology, Identity and the Pre-Christian Past: A Critical Analysis of Dr. K. Bediako's Theology from a Frisian Perspective." *International Review of Mission* 88/351 (October 1999) 364–80.

Balcomb, Anthony. "Faith or Suspicion? Theological Dialogue North and South of the Limpopo, with Special Reference to the Theologies of Kwame Bediako and Andrew Walls." *Journal of Theology for South Africa* 100 (March 1998) 3–19.

Van den Toren, Benno. "Kwame Bediako's Christology in Its African Evangelical Context." *Exchange* 26/3 (September 1997) 219–32.

Maluleke, T. S. "In Search of the True Character of African Christian Identity: A Review of Kwame Bediako." *Missionalia* 5/2 (1997) 210–19.

———. "Black and African Theologies in the New World Order: A Time to Drink from Our Own Wells." *Journal of Theology For Southern Africa* 96 (1996) 3–19.

Masters and Doctoral Dissertations

Ayoola, Bernard. *Jesus in African Culture: The Contributions of Kwame Bediako to African Christianity*. (Masters thesis, printed in Germany by Lap Lambert Academic Publishing, 2011).

Ngodji, Martin. "The Applicability of the Translatability and Interpretation Theory of Sanneh and Bediako: The Case of the Evangelical Lutheran Church in Namibia, in Northern Namibia." PhD diss., University of Kwazulu-Natal, Pietermaritzburg, 2010.

Pulei, Moses S. "The Word-Faith Movement in Kenya: A Transnational Religious Culture and African Identity." PhD diss., Fuller Theological Seminary, 2009.

Maxey, James. "Bible Translation as Contextualization: The Role of Oral Performance in New Testament and African Contexts." PhD diss., Lutheran School of Theology at Chicago, 2008.

Fotland, Roar G. "Ancestor Christology in Context: Theological Perspectives of Kwame Bediako." PhD diss., University of Bergen, 2005.

Mdegella, Owdenburg Moses. "Authenticity of Christian Conversion in the African Context: An Investigation on the Rationale for the Hehe to Convert to Christianity with Special Reference to the Iringa Diocese of the Evangelical Lutheran Church in Tanzania (1899–1999)." PhD diss., University of KwaZulu Natal, Pietermaritzburg, 2005.

Musasiwa, Roy. "The Quest for Identity in African Theology as a Mission of Empowerment." PhD diss., University of Kwazulu-Natal, Pietermaritzburg, 2002.

Fon, Wilfred Tatah Wirsiy. "The Influence of African Traditional Religions on Biblical Christology: An Evaluation of Emerging Christologies on Sub-Saharan Africa." PhD diss., Westminster Theological Seminary, 1995.

Appendix B

The Akrofi-Christaller Institute's Master of Theology in African Christianity

THIS INFORMATION HAS ALL been taken from the official ACI website.[1] The MTh in African Christianity program objectives and courses are outlined below.

Objectives for the MTh Program:

1. To provide opportunity for understanding the significance of African Christianity.

2. To enable graduates from African countries undertake an advanced study of Christianity directly related to their own setting.

3. To provide opportunity for graduate Christian workers, lay or ordained, committed to ministry in cross-cultural situations, to examine the historical, religious and cultural context in which they operate and to reflect theologically on their experience.

4. To help prospective candidates of theological research involving cross-cultural or inter-religious study who do not have specialized training in these fields, to bridge the gap between previous academic study and the new material.

---

1. "Academic Programmes: MTh in African Christianity (Postgraduate Research Degree)." http://www.acighana.org/site/contents/academics/index.php?parentpage=academics&page=mthcourse1.

5. To provide cultural relevance in exegesis and interpretation.

Program Structure:[2]

In this two-year program students take a total of six taught courses, including four core subjects and two electives. At the end of the taught portion participants are assessed through an "Integrating Presentation." For this assessment, they are assigned a topic and given twenty-four hours to prepare a paper that addresses the question by integrating themes and details from all of their courses. The paper is orally presented before the Academic Board and students must be prepared to answer questions from Board members. In the second year researchers must submit a dissertation of 30,000 words; this must also include an abstract in their mother tongue (if that is not English).

Core Courses:

- The roots of African Theology in the Twentieth Century
- Christian Faith and Primal Religions of the World, With Special Reference to Africa: Historical, Phenomenological, and Theological Perspectives
- World Christian History as Mission History
- Gospel and Culture: Biblical, Historical and Theological Perspectives

Electives:

- The Bible in African Christianity: Aspects of African Biblical Hermeneutics
- Early African Christianity of the First Six Centuries
- Christian Faith and Islam and Christian-Muslim Relations in Africa
- Modern African Instituted Churches
- Aspects of the Christian History of Africa
- Patterns of Christian Ministry in Africa

---

2. Paraphrased from the website.

Bibliography

Achebe, Chinua. "The Education of a British-Protected Child." In *The Education of a British- Protected Child: Essays*, by Chinua Achebe, 3–24. Toronto: Anchor Canada, 2010.
Adams, Bill, and Mary Adams. "History of the Work of the Gospel Missionary Union at Pessac, France: 1960–1983." N.p., n.d.
Addo, Ebenezer Obiri. *Kwame Nkrumah: A Case Study of Religion and Politics in Ghana*. New York: University of America Press, 1999.
Adogame, Afe, Ezra Chitando, and Bolaji Bateye, eds. *African Traditions in the Study of Religion in Africa: Emerging Trends, Indigenous Spirituality and the Interface with other World Religions*. Surrey: Ashgate, 2012.
Agbeti, J. Kofi. *West African Church History*. Vol. 1, *Christian Missions and Church Foundations: 1482–1919*. Leiden: Brill, 1986.
Agyemang, Fred. *Amu the African: A Study in Vision and Courage*. Accra: Asempa, 1988.
———. *We Presbyterians: 160th Anniversary of the Presbyterian Church of Ghana, 1828–1988*. Ghana: Presbyterian, n.d.
Akrofi, C. A. *Twi Kasa Mmara: A Twi Grammar in Twi*. Accra: Scottish Mission Book Depot, 1937.
Asamoah-Gyadu, J. Kwabena. "Bediako of Africa: A Late Twentieth Century Outstanding Theologian and Teacher." *Mission Studies* 26 (2009) 5–16.
———. "Kwame Bediako and the Eternal Christological Question." In *Seeing New Facets of the Diamond: Christianity as a Universal Religion—Essays in Honour of Kwame Bediako*, edited by Gillian Mary Bediako, Benhardt T. Quarshie, and J. Kwabena Asamoah-Gyadu, 38–55. Akropong-Akuapem, Ghana: Regnum, 2014.
———. "Kwame Bediako Memorial Lecture: 'Who Do You Say That I Am?' Revisiting Kwame Bediako's Responses to the Eternal Christological Question." Memorial Lecture to Celebrate the First Anniversary of Kwame Bediako's Death, July 7, 2009, British Council Hall, Accra, 2009.

———. "Kwame Bediako: 'Mr. African Theology.'" In *Mission as Transformation: Learning from Catalysts*. Eugene, OR: Wipf & Stock, 2014.

———. "Renewal Within African Christianity: A Study of Some Current Historical and Theological Developments Within Independent Indigenous Pentecostalism in Ghana." PhD diss., University of Birmingham, 2000.

Ashcroft, Bill, and Pal Ahluwalia. *Edward Said*. New York: Routledge, 2001.

Ashcroft, Bill, Gareth Griffiths, and Helen Tiffin. *The Empire Writes Back: Theory and Practice in Post-Colonial Literatures*. New York: Routledge, 1989.

Ault, James. "Kwame Bediako." In "Educational Extras," *African Christianity Rising*, documentary by James Ault. 0:01–0:55 seconds. https://vimeo.com/61770717.

Austin, Dennis. *Politics in Ghana: 1946–1960*. London: Oxford University Press, 1964.

Aye-Addo, Charles Sarpong. *Akan Christology: An Analysis of the Christologies of John Samuel Pobee and Kwame Bediako in Conversation with Karl Barth*. Eugene, OR: Pickwick, 2013.

Balcomb, Anthony. "Faith or Suspicion? Theological Dialogue North and South of the Limpopo with Special Reference to the Theologies of Kwame Bediako and Andrew Walls." *Journal of Theology for Southern Africa* 100 (March 1998) 3–19.

———. "Theology and the Quest for the African Renaissance—Journeying into an African Horizon." *JACT* 6/2 (December 2003) 3–5.

Barnes, Leonard. *African Renaissance*. Indianapolis: Bobbs-Merrill, 1969.

Bartels, F. L. *The Persistence of Paradox: Memoirs of F. L. Bartels*. N.p.: Lulu, 2006.

———. *The Roots of Ghana Methodism*. Cambridge: Methodist Book Depot Ltd, Ghana: 1965.

Bediako, Gillian M. "Christian Universality: Christian Scholarship and Institution Building—Kwame Bediako on a Vision in Process." In *Seeing New Facets of the Diamond: Christianity as a Universal Religion—Essays in Honour of Kwame Bediako*, edited by Gillian Mary Bediako, Benhardt T. Quarshie, and J. Kwabena Asamoah-Gyadu, 361–69. Akropong-Akuapem, Ghana: Regnum, 2014.

———. "'Ebenezer, this is how far the Lord has helped us': Celebrating 25 years of God's faithfulness to Akrofi-Christaller Institute of Theology, Mission and Culture, Akropong-Akuapem." Unpublished (updated) handbook. Akropong-Akuapem: ACI, 2012.

———. "Editorial." *JACT* 11/2 (December 2008) 1–4.

———. "Editorial." *JACT* 12/1 (June 2009) 1–2.

———. "Primal Religion and Christian Faith: Antagonists or Soul-mates?" *JACT* 3/1 (June 2000) 12–16.

Bediako, Gillian M., Benhardt Y. Quarshie, and J. Kwabena Asamoah-Gyadu, eds. *Seeing New Facets of the Diamond: Christianity As a Universal Faith—Essays in Honour of Kwame Bediako*. Akropong-Akuapem, Ghana: Regnum Africa, 2014.

Bediako, Kwame. "Africa and Christianity on the Threshold of the Third Millennium: The Religious Dimension." *African Affairs* 99 (2000) 303–23.

———. "The African Renaissance and Theological Reconstruction: The Challenge of the Twenty-first Century." *JACT* 4/2 (December 2001) 29–33.

———. "Biblical Christologies in the Context of African Traditional Religions." In *Sharing Jesus in the Two-Thirds World*, edited by Vinay Samuel and Chris Sugden, 81–121. Grand Rapids: Eerdmans, 1984.

———. "Biblical Exegesis in the African Context—The Factor and Impact of the Translated Scriptures." *JACT* 6/1 (June 2003) 15–23.

———. "Bolaji Idowu: The Continuity of God in African Experience." Unpublished notes, Duff Lecture Series, Centre for the Study of Non-Western Christianity, New College, Edinburgh, 1987.

———. "Christian Religion and African Social Norms: Authority, Desacralization and Democracy." In *Christianity in Africa: the Renewal of a Non-Western Religion*, by Kwame Bediako, 234–51. Maryknoll, NY: Orbis, 1997.

———. *Christian Witness in the Public Sphere: Some Lessons and Residual Challenges from the Recent Political History of Ghana*' in *Public Witness*. An occasional publication of Akrofi-Christaller Memorial Centre, September 2002.

———. "Christianity and African Liberation: Reaffirming a Heritage." In *Christianity in Africa: The Renewal of a Non-Western Religion*, by Kwame Bediako, 39–58. Maryknoll, NY: Orbis, 1995.

———. *Christianity in Africa: The Renewal of a Non-Western Religion*. Maryknoll, NY: Orbis, 1997.

———. "The Church in the African State: Some Biblical Reflections." *JACT* 1/2 (December 1998) 58–60.

———. "Cry Jesus! Christian Theology and Presence in Modern Africa." In *Jesus in Africa: The Christian Gospel in African History and Experience*, 3–19. Ghana: Regnum, 2004.

———. "Doctoral Defence Introductory Remarks." PhD diss., L'Université de Bordeaux, 1973.

———. "Editorial." *Journal for African Christian Thought* 5/1 (June 2002) 1–3.

———. "The Genesis of African Theology (Lecture III): A Hermeneutic of Identity." Unpublished lecture notes, Duff Lecture Series, Centre for the Study of Non-Western Christianity, New College, Edinburgh, 1987.

———. "Gospel and Culture: Guest Editorial." *JACT* 2/2 (December 1999) 1.

———. "Gospel and Culture: Some Insights For Our Time From the Experience of the Earliest Church." *JACT* 2/2 (December 1999) 8–17.

———. "The Gospel and the Transformation of the Non-Western World." In *Christianity in Africa: The Renewal of a Non-Western Religion*, 172–88. Maryknoll, NY: Orbis, 1997.

———. "A Half Century of African Christian Thought: Pointers to Theology and Theological Education in the Next Half Century." *JACT* 3/1 (June 2000) 5–11.

———. "How Is Jesus Christ Lord? Evangelical Christian Apologetics amid African Religious Pluralism." In *Jesus in Africa: The Christian Gospel in African History and Experience*, 32–45. Ghana: Regnum, 2004.

———. Interview by Iwan Russell-Jones. *All Things Considered*. BBC Radio Wales. January 29, 1989. Transcript published online at http://www.shipoffools.com/features/2008/kwame_bediako_interview.html

———. Interview (filmed) by James Ault. 1998. *African Christianity Rising* project. Akropong, Ghana. Unpublished transcripts. DigiBeta Reel GB 105; 108; 109. Copyright James Ault and James Ault Productions, 2006.

———. Interview ("In conversation with") James Ault. 2006. Akropong, Ghana. Unpublished transcripts. Copyright, James Ault and James Ault Productions, 2006.

———. "Issues of Gospel and Culture—Biblical, Historical and Theological Perspectives." Unpublished course notes, MTh program, ACI, Ghana, n.d.

———. *Jesus in Africa: The Christian Gospel in African History and Experience.* Ghana: Regnum, 2004.

———. "Jesus in African Culture: A Ghanaian Perspective." In *Jesus in Africa: The Christian Gospel in African History and Experience,* 20–33. Ghana: Regnum, 2004.

———. "The Making of Christian Africa: The Surprise Story of the Modern Missionary Movement." In *Christianity in Africa: The Renewal of a Non-Western Religion,* 191–209. Maryknoll, NY: Orbis, 1997.

———. "Négritude et Surréalisme: Essai sur L'Oeuvre Poétique de Tchicaya U Tam'si [Négritude and Surrealism: A Study on the Poetic Works of Tchicaya U Tam'si]". Master's thesis, L'Université de Bordeaux, 1970.

———. "A New Era in Christian History—African Christianity as Representative Christianity: Some Implications for Theological Education and Scholarship." *JACT* 9/1 (June 2006) 3–12.

———. "New Ways of Experiencing Jesus—Towards an African Biblical Christology: Lecture 5." Unpublished course notes for "Christian Faith and Primal Religions," MTh program, ACI, Ghana, n.d.

———. "Perspectives in African Theology (Lecture II): The Place of Christ in the African Heritage in John Mbiti." Unpublished notes, Duff Lecture Series, Centre for the Study of Christianity in the Non-Western World, New College, Edinburgh, 1987.

———. "The Primal Imagination and the Opportunity for a New Theological Idiom." In *Christianity in Africa: The Renewal of a Non-Western Religion,* 91–108. Maryknoll, NY: Orbis, 1997.

———. "Roots of African Theology." *International Bulletin of Missionary Research* (April 1989) 58–65.

———. "The Roots of African Theology in the Twentieth Century." Unpublished course notes for "The Roots of African Theology in the Twentieth Century," MTh program, ACI, Ghana, n.d.

———. *Theology and Identity: The Impact of Culture upon Christian Thought in the Second Century and in Modern Africa.* Cumbria: Regnum, 1999.

———. "Understanding African Theology in the Twentieth Century." In *Jesus in Africa: The Christian Gospel in African History and Experience,* 49–62. Ghana: Regnum, 2004. First published in *Themelios* 20/1 (October 1994) 14–20.

———. "Understanding African Theology in the Twentieth Century." *Bulletin for Contextual Theology in Southern Africa and Africa* 3/2 (1996) 1–11.

———. "Understanding the Unity of the Church." Zondervan Ministry Videos, May 7, 2008. http://www.godtube.com/watch/?v=PGLK7NNX.

———. "L'Univers Interieur De Tchicaya U Tam'si [The Interior Universe of Tchicaya U Tam'si]." PhD diss., L'Université de Bordeaux, 1973.

———. "'Why has the summer ended and we are not saved?' Encountering the Real Challenge of Christian Engagement in Primal Contexts." *JACT* 11/2 (December 2008) 5–8.

———. "The Willowbank Consultation, January 1978—A Personal Reflection." *Themelios: An International Journal for Theological Students* 5/2 (1980) 25–23.

Bediako, Kwame, and Gillian Mary Bediako. "'Ebenezer, this is how far the Lord has helped us (1 Samuel 7:12)': Reflections on the Institutional Itinerary of Akrofi-Christaller Memorial Centre for Mission Research and Applied Theology (1974–2005)." Unpublished booklet. May 2005.

Beier, Ulli. "L. S. Senghor: The Theme of Ancestors in His Poetry." In *Introduction to African Literature: An Anthology of Critical Writing on African and Afro-American Literature and Oral Tradition*, edited by Ulli Beier, 95–99. London: Longmans, Green, 1967.

Beti, Mongo, and Odile Tobner. *Dictionaire de la Négritude*. Paris: L'Harmattan, 1989.

Boahen, Adu. *African Perspectives on Colonialism*. Baltimore: Johns Hopkins University Press, 1989.

———. "A New Look at the History of Ghana." *African Affairs* 65/260 (July 1966) 212–22.

Bongmba, Elias Kifon. "Studying African Christianity: Future Trajectories." In *The Routledge Companion to Christianity in Africa*, edited by Elias Kifon Bongmba, 555–63. New York: Routledge, 2016.

———, ed. *The Wiley-Blackwell Companion to African Religions*. Malden, MA: Blackwell, 2012.

———. "Writing African Christianity: Perspectives from the History of the Historiography of African Christianity." *Religion and Theology* 23 (2016) 275–312.

Bourret, F. M. *Ghana: The Road to Independence: 1919–1957*. London: Oxford University Press, 1960.

Bowra, C. Maurice. *Chants et Poesie du Peuples Primitifs*. Paris: Payot, 1966.

Busia, Kofi Abrefa. *Africa in Search of Democracy*. London: Routledge and Kegan Paul, 1967.

———. "The Ashanti of the Gold Coast." In *African Worlds: Studies in the Cosmological Ideas and Social Values of African Peoples*, edited by C. D. Forde, 190–209. London: Oxford University Press, 1954.

———. "The Functions of West African Universities." In *The West African Intellectual Community: Papers and Discussions of an International Seminar on Inter-University Co-operation in West Africa, held in Freetown, Sierra Leone, 11-16 December 1961*, edited by J. R. Saunders and M. Dowuona, 78–85. Nigeria: Ibadan University Press, 1962.

———. *The Position of the Chief in the Modern Political System of Ashanti: A Study of the Influence of Contemporary Social Changes on Ashanti Political Institutions*. London: Frank Cass, 1968.

———. *Urban Churches in Britain: A Question of Relevance*. London: Lutterworth, 1966.

Call to Glory: Rev. Professor Kwame Bediako, FGA: 1945–2008. Funeral brochure. Ghana: privately printed and distributed, 2008.

Césaire, Aimé. *Notebook of a Return to My Native Land [Cahier d'un retour au pays natal]*. Translated by Mireille Rosello, with Annie Pritchard. Newcastle upon Tyne: Bloodaxe, 1995.

Chitando, Ezra. "African Christian Scholars and the Study of African Traditional Religions: A Re-evaluation." *Religion* 30 (2000) 391–97.

Clarke, Clifton R. *Pentecostal Theology in Africa*. Eugene, OR: Pickwick, 2014.

Connolly, Peter, ed. *Approaches to the Study of Religions*. London: Cassell, 1999.

Cooksey, J. J., and Alexander McLeish, eds. *Religion and Civilization in West Africa: A Missionary Survey of French, British, Spanish and Portuguese West Africa, with Liberia*. London: World Dominion, 1931.

Cox, James L. "The Classification 'Primal Religions' As a Non-Empirical Theological Construct." *Studies in World Christianity* 2 (1996) 55–76.

———. "From Africa to Africa: The Significance of Approaches to the Study of African Religions at Aberdeen and Edinburgh Universities from 1970 to 1998." In *European Traditions in the Study of Religion in Africa*, edited by Frieder Ludwig and Afe Adogame, 255–64. Wiesbaden, Germany: Harrassowitz, 2004.

———. *From Primitive to Indigenous: The Academic Study of Indigenous Religions*. Burlington, VT: Ashgate: 2007.

———. "The Globalization of Localized African Religions: The Case of Kwame Bediako." In *World Christianity in Local Context*, edited by Stephen R. Goodwin, 56–65. London: Continuum International, 2009.

Cox, James L., and Gerrie ter Haar, eds. *Uniquely African? African Christian Identity from Cultural and Historical Perspectives*. Trenton, NJ: Africa World, 2003.

Dankwa, Nana Addo. *Christianity and African Traditional Beliefs*. New York: The Power of the Word, 1990.

Danfulani, Umar Habila Dadem. "African Religions in African Scholarship: A Critique." In *African Traditions in the Study of Religion in Africa*, edited by Afe Adogame et al., 17–34. Surrey: Ashgate, 2012.

Darkwo, D. W. "Akrofi, Clement Anderson." In *Dictionary of African Christian Biography*. http://www.dacb.org/stories/ghana/akrofi_clement2.html.

Dedji, Valentin. "Kwame Bediako and African Christian Identity." In *Reconstruction and Renewal in African Christian Theology*, 166–219. Nairobi: Acton, 2003.

Diamond, Larry. "Fiction as Political Thought." *African Affairs* 88/352 (July 1989) 435–45.

Dickson, Kwesi A. *Theology in Africa*. Maryknoll, NY: Orbis, 1984.

Edu-Bekoe, Yaw Attah. "Describing an African Dancing Without Hearing His Music: Kevin Howard has Generally Misunderstood Kwame Bediako." *Global Missiology* 3/12 (April 2015). http://ojs.globalmissiology.org/index.php/english/article/viewFile/1787/3965.

Ezigbo, Victor I. *Re-Imagining African Christologies: Conversing with the Interpretations and Appropriations of Jesus in Contemporary African Christianity*. Eugene, OR: Pickwick, 2010.

Fasholé-Luke, E. "The Quest for an African Christian Theology." *The Ecumenical Review* 27/3 (1975) 259–69.

Ferdinando, Keith. "Christian Identity in the African Context: Reflections on Kwame Bediako's *Theology and Identity*." *Journal of the Evangelical Theological Society* 50/1 (March 2007) 121–43.

Fotland, Roar G. "Ancestor Christology in Context: Theological Perspectives of Kwame Bediako. " PhD diss., University of Bergen, 2005.

Gibellini, Rosino. *Paths of African Theology*. Maryknoll, NY: Orbis, 1994.

Glover-Quartey, Alexander. "Kwame Bediako's Political Leaning." Personal correspondence with author, June 25th, 2013.

———. "Tribute to the late Rev Professor Kwame Bediako, Rector of Akrofi-Christaller Institute." In *Call to Glory: Rev. Professor Kwame Bediako, FGA: 1945–2008*. Funeral Brochure. Ghana: privately printed and distributed, 2008.

Graham, C. K. *The History of Education in Ghana from the Earliest Times to the Declaration of Independence*. London: Frank Cass, 1971.

Haar, Gerrie ter. *Faith of Our Fathers: Studies on Religious Education in Sub-Saharan Africa*. Utrecht: University of Utrecht Publications, 1990.

Hanciles, Jehu J. "Missionaries and Revolutionaries: Elements of Transformation in the Emergence of Modern African Christianity." *IBMR* 28/4 (October 2004) 146–52.

Hastings, Adrian. "African Christian Studies, 1967–1999: Reflections of an Editor." In *European Traditions in the Study of Religion in Africa*, edited by Frieder Ludwig and Afe Adogame, 265–74. Wiesbaden, Germany: Harrassowitz, 2004.

———. *The Construction of Nationhood: Ethnicity, Religion and Nationalism*. Cambridge: Cambridge University Press, 1999.

Hopkins, Daniel. *A Study in Nineteenth-Century African Colonial Geography*. Leiden: Brill, 2013.

Horton, Robin. "Judaeo-Christian Spectacles: Boon or Bane to the Study of African Religions? [Les lunettes judéo-chrétiennes: aubaine ou fléau pour l'étude des religions africaines?]." *Cahier d'Études Africaines* 24/96 (1984) 391–436.

Howard, Kevin. "Kwame Bediako: Considerations on the Motivating Force Behind His *Theology and Identity*." *Global Missiology* 3/10 (April 2013). http://ojs.globalmissiology.org/index.php/english/article/view/1186/2735.

Idowu, E. Bolaji. "'The Predicament of the Church in Africa': A Paper Given at the Seventh International African Seminar in Ghana, 1965." Later published as *Christianity in Tropical Africa*, edited by C. G. Baëta. International African Institute. Oxford: Oxford University Press, 1968.

Irele, Abiola. "A Defence of Négritude: A Propos of *Black Orpheus* by Jean Paul Sartre." *Transition* 13 (March–April 1964) 9-11.

———. "Negritude or Black Cultural Nationalism." *The Journal of Modern African Studies* 3/3 (October 1965) 321–48.

Ischinger, Barbara. "Négritude: Some Dissident Voices." *Journal of Opinion* 4/4 (Winter 1974) 23–25.

Isichei, Elizabeth. *A History of Christianity in Africa: From Antiquity to the Present*. Grand Rapids: Eerdmans, 1995.

Jenkins, Paul. "The Ghana Archive of the Basel Mission, 1829–1917: Contents of the Microfilm Collection with an Introduction by Dr. Paul Jenkins, Archivist to the Basel Mission." West Yorkshire: Microform Academic Publishers, 2005, Publication no. R97040. http://www.microform.co.uk/guides/R97040.pdf.

———. "A Short History of the Basel Mission." *Texts and Documents* 10 (May 1989). Basel: Basel Mission, 1989.

Jones, D. H. Review of *A Political History of Ghana: The Rise of the Gold Coast Nationalism, 1850–1928* by David Kimble. *Bulletin of the School of Oriental and African Studies* 27/2 (June 1964) 490.

Jules-Rosette, Bennetta. "Jean-Paul Sartre and the Philosophy of Négritude: Race, Self and Society." *Theory and Society* 36/3 (June, 2007) 265–85.

July, Robert W. "Nineteenth-Century Négritude: Edward W. Blyden." *Journal of African History* 5/1 (1964) 73–86.

Kalu, Ogbu, ed. *African Christianity: An African Story*. Pretoria: University of Pretoria, Department of Church History, 2005.

———. Review of *Jesus and the Gospel in Africa* by Kwame Bediako. *IBMR* 29/1 (January 2005) 48–49.

Kesteloot, Lilyan. *Les écrivains noirs de langue française: naissance d'une littérature* [*Black French Writers: Birth of a Literary Tradition*]. Brussels: l'Institut de Sociologie de l'Université Libre de Bruxelles, 1971.

———. *Négritude et Situation Coloniale [Négritude and the Colonial Context]*. Yaoundé, Cameroon: CLE, 1968.

Kimble, David. *A Political History of Ghana: The Rise of Gold Coast Nationalism 1850–1928*. Oxford: Oxford University Press, 1963.

Knipp, Thomas R. "Négritude and Negation: The Poetry of Tchikaya U'Tamsi [sic]." *Books Abroad* 48/3 (Summer 1974) 511–15.

Kuma, Afua. *Jesus of the Deep Forest: Prayers and Praises of Afua Kuma*. Translated by Jon Kirby. Accra: Asempa, 1981.

Langley, J. Ayodele. Review of *Négritude et Situation Coloniale* by Lilyan Kesteloot. *Journal of Religion in Africa* 4/1 (1971–72) 74–76.

Laryea, Philip T. *Ephraim Amu: Nationalist, Poet and Theologian*. Ghana: Regnum, 2012.

Le Baron, Bentley. "Négritude: A Pan-African Ideal?" *Ethics* 76/4 (July 1966) 267–76.

Ludwig, Frieder, and Afe Adogame. *European Traditions in the Study of Religion in Africa*. Wiesbaden, Germany: Harrassowitz, 2004.

Makulu, H. F. *Education, Development and Nation-building in Independent Africa: A Study of the New Trends and Recent Philosophy of Education*. London: SCM, 1971.

Maluleke, Tinyiko Sam. "Black and African Theologies in the New World Order: A Time to Drink from our Own Wells." *Journal of Theology for Southern Africa* 96 (1996) 3–19.

———. "Half a Century of African Christian Theologies: Elements of the Emerging Agenda for the Twenty-First Century." In *African Christianity: An African Story, Perspectives on Christianity Series*, edited by Ogbu Kalu, 468–93. Pretoria: University of Pretoria, Department of Church History, 2005.

———. "In Search of 'The True Character of African Christian Identity.' A Review of the Theology of Kwame Bediako." *Missionalia* 25/2 (August 1997) 210–19.

Maxey, James. "Bible Translation as Contextualization: The Role of Oral Performance in New Testament and African Contexts." PhD diss., Lutheran School of Theology at Chicago, 2008.

Mazrui, Ali. *Political Values and the Educated Class in Africa*. London: Heinemann, 1978.

Mbiti, John S. *African Religions and Philosophy*. London: Heinemann, 1969.

———. "Challenges Facing Religious Education and Research in Africa: The Case of Dialogue Between Christianity and African Religion." *Religion and Theology* 3/2 (1996) 170–78.

McIntire, C. T. *The Ongoing Task of Christian Historiography*. Toronto: Institute of Christian Studies, 1974.

McKenzie, P. R. Review of *The Prayers of African Religion* by John Mbiti. *The Expository Times* 87 (1975–76) 220–21.

McWilliam, H. O. A. *The Development of Education in Ghana: An Outline*. London: Longmans, 1959.

Melady, Thomas Patrick, and Margaret Badum Melady. *Ten African Heroes: The Sweep of Independence in Black Africa*. Maryknoll, NY: Orbis, 2011.

Mensah, Ephraim Kofi. "A Narrative Study: The Meaning of Western Colonial/Missionary Education for Contemporary Ghanaians." PhD diss., University of Saskatchewan, 2005.

Middleton, Darren. *Mother Tongue Theologies: Poets, Novelists, Non-Western Christianity*. Eugene, OR: Pickwick, 2005.

Middleton, John. "One Hundred and Fifty Years of Christianity in a Ghanaian Town." *Journal of the International African Institute* 53/3 (1983) 2–19.
Miller, Jon. *Missionary Zeal and Institutional Control: Organizational Contradictions in the Basel Mission on the Gold Coast, 1828-1917*. Studies in the History of Christian Missions. Grand Rapids: Eerdmans, 2003.
Minkin, L. *Exits and Entrances: Political Research as a Creative Art*. Sheffield: Sheffield Hallam University Press, 1997.
Ngũgĩ wa Thiong'o. *Something Torn and New: An African Renaissance*. New York: Basic Civitas, 2009.
Nicol, Davidson. Introduction to *The West African Intellectual Community: Papers and Discussions of an International Seminar on Inter-University Co-operation in West Africa, held in Freetown, Sierra Leone, 11-16 December 1961*, edited by J. R. Saunders and M. Dowuona, 1–6. Nigeria: Ibadan University Press, 1962.
Nkrumah, Kwame. *The Autobiography of Kwame Nkrumah*. London: Thomas Nelson, 1957.
———. "Primitive Education in West Africa." *Educational Outlook* 15/2 (January 1941) 87–92.
Oduyoye, Mercy Amba. "African Culture and African Development: A Critical Reappraisal." In *Seeing New Facets of the Diamond: Christianity as a Universal Religion—Essays in Honour of Kwame Bediako*, 315–24. Ghana: Regnum, 2014.
———. "The African Experience of God Through the Eyes of an Akan Woman." *Cross Currents* 47/4 (Winter 1997–98) 493–505.
Ofosu-Appiah, L. H. "Christaller, Johann Gottlieb 1827–1895, Basel Mission, Ghana." In *Dictionary of African Christian Biography*. http://www.dacb.org/stories/ghana/christaller_j.html.
Olabimtan, Kehinde. "'Is Africa Incurably Religious?' A Response to Jan Platvoet and Henk van Rinsum." *Exchange* 32/4 (2003) 322–39.
———. "The Study of African Christianity: Trajectories and Prospects." In *Seeing New Facets of the Diamond: Christianity as a Universal Religion—Essays in Honour of Kwame Bediako*, 285–97. Ghana: Regnum, 2014.
Olademo, Oyeronke. "Gender and the Teaching of Religious Studies in Nigeria: A Primary Overview." In *African Traditions in the Study of Religion in Africa: Emerging Trends, Indigenous Spirituality and the Interface with other World Religions*, edited by Afe Adogame et al., 67–76. Surrey: Ashgate, 2012.
Olupona, Jacob K. Foreword to *The Wiley-Blackwell Companion to African Religions*, ix–xxi. Malden, MA: Blackwell, 2012.
Owusu, Robert Yaw. "Toward a Recovery of Kwame Nkrumah's Liberation Philosophy and the Role of Religious Advocacy in Contemporary Ghana." PhD diss., Baylor University, 2003.
Parratt, John. *Reinventing Christianity: African Theology Today*. Grand Rapids: Eerdmans, 1995.
Parrinder, Geoffrey. *In the Belly of the Snake: West Africa Over Sixty Years Ago*. Peterborough: Epworth, 2000.
———. "The Religious Situation in West Africa." *African Affairs* 59/234 (January 1960) 38–42.
P'Bitek, Okot. *African Religions in Western Scholarship*. Nairobi: East African Literature Bureau, 1971.

———, ed. *Decolonizing African Religions: A Short History of African Religions in Western Scholarship*. New York: Diasporic, 2011.

———. *Song of Lawino*. Nairobi: East African, 1966.

Phillips, Claude S. *The African Political Dictionary*. Santa Barbara, CA: ABC-Clio, 1984.

Pieris, Aloysius. *An Asian Theology of Liberation*. Maryknoll, NY: Orbis, 1988.

Platvoet, Jan. G. "From Object to Subject: A History of the Study of the Religions of Africa." In *The Study of Religions in Africa*, edited by Jan Platvoet et al., 105–38. Cambridge: Roots and Branches, 1996.

Platvoet, Jan G., and Henk van Rinsum. "Is Africa Incurably Religious? III: A Reply to a Rhetorical Response." *Exchange* 37 (2008) 156–73.

Pobee, J. S. "Bible and Human Translation." *Mission Studies* 1 (1984) 3–12.

———. "Christian Goncalves Kwami Baëta–A Personal Appreciation." In *Religion in a Pluralistic Society: Essays Presented to Professor C. G. Baëta*, 1–4. Leiden: Brill, 1976.

———. "Identity, Religion, Nation. Asante-Opoku-Reindorf Lecture for 2010." *JACT* 14/1 (2011) 20–29.

———. *Kwame Nkrumah and the Church in Ghana 1949–1966*. Accra: Asempa, 1988.

———. *Religion and Politics in Ghana*. Accra: Asempa, 1991.

Présence Africaine. *Des Prêtres noir s'interrogent*. Paris: Cerf, 1957.

Pym, David. "'Primal Religions': Appropriate Religious Designation or Inappropriate Theological Imposition?" *JACT* 11/1 (June 2008) 60–69.

Quartey, Seth. *Missionary Practices on the Gold Coast, 1832–1895: Discourse, Gaze and Gender in the Basel Mission in Pre-Colonial West Africa*. Youngstown, NY: Cambria, 2007.

Quist, Hubert Oswald. "Secondary Education and Nation-Building: A Study of Ghana, 1951–1991." PhD diss., Columbia University, 1999.

R. R. [R. S. Rattray?]. Review of *Africa in Search of Democracy* by Kofi Abrefa Busia. *African Affairs* 68 (April 1969) 271.

Ray, Benjamin C. *African Religions: Symbols, Ritual and Community*. Englewood Cliffs, NJ: Prentice Hall, 1979.

Rein, Susan Erica. "Religiosity in the Poetry of Tchicaya U Tam'si." *Journal of Religion in Africa* 10/3 (1979) 234–49.

Reindorf, Carl Christian. *History of the Gold Coast and Asante: Based on Traditions and Historical Facts, Comprising a Period of More Than Three Centuries from About 1500 to 1860*. Basel: Printed for the author, 1895.

Rinsum, Henk J. van. "'They became slaves of their definitions': Okot p'Btek (1931-1982) and the European Traditions in the Study of African Religions." In *European Traditions in the Study of Religion in Africa*, edited by Frieder Ludwig and Afe Adogame, 23-38. Wiesbaden, Germany: Harrassowitz, 2004.

Rooney, David. *Kwame Nkrumah: The Political Kingdom in the Third World*. London: Tuaris, 1988.

Russell-Jones, Iwan. "Following the Footprints of God: Kwame Bediako (1945–2008)." http://www.shipoffools.com/features/2008/kwame_bediako.html.

Sanneh, Lamin. "The Horizontal and Vertical in Mission." *International Bulletin for Missionary Research* 4 (October 1983) 165–71.

———. *Translating the Message: The Missionary Impact on Culture*. Maryknoll, NY: Orbis, 1989.

———. *West African Christianity: The Religious Impact*. Maryknoll, NY: Orbis, 1990.

———. "The Yogi and the Commissar: Christian Mission and the African Response." *IBMR* 15/1 (January 1991) 2–12.

Sawada, Nozomi. "The Educated Elite and Associational Life in Early Lagos Newspapers: In Search of Unity for the Progress of Society." PhD diss., University of Birmingham, 2011.

Sawyerr, Harry. "The Theological Method: What Is African Theology?" In *A Reader in African Christian Theology*, edited by John Parratt, 12–27. London: SPCK, 1987.

Schweizer, Peter A. *Survivors on the Gold Coast: The Basel Missionaries in Colonial Ghana*. Accra: Smartline, 2000.

Schwimmer, Brian. "Ghana History Population Politics: Political Life." 2012. https://www.modernghana.com/ghanahome/ghana/default.asp?menu_id=6&sub_menu_id=0&section=6.

Shenk, William. "Challenging the Academy, Breaking Barriers." In *Understanding World Christianity: The Vision and Work of Andrew F. Walls*, edited by William R. Burrows et al., 35–50. Maryknoll, NY: Orbis, 2011.

"A Short Biography of Dr. K. A. Busia." Photo Exhibit of Dr. K. A. Busia. http://ruafrica.rutgers.edu/events/media/0708_media/intro_busia.pdf.

Shyllon, Leslie E. T. "What Role Do Institutions of Theology and Religious Studies Play in the Engagement with African Cultural Dynamics?" In *Uniquely African? African Christian Identity from Cultural and Historical Perspectives*, edited by James L. Cox and Gerrie ter Haar, 9–24. Trenton, NJ: Africa World, 2003.

Smith, Edwin W. *The Shrine of a People's Soul*. London: Edinburgh House, 1928.

Soyinka, Wole. "The Writer in an African State." *Transition* (1997) 350–56.

Stinton, Diane B. *Jesus of Africa: Voices of Contemporary African Christology*. Maryknoll, NY: Orbis, 2004.

Sundkler, Bengt. *The Christian Ministry in Africa*. London: SCM, 1962.

"Symposium to Commemorate Busia's 95th Birthday Anniversary." *The Statesman*, July 14, 2008.

Thompson, Alan. "Learning from the African Experience: Bediako and Critical Contextualization." *Evangelical Review of Theology* 30/1 (2006) 31–48.

Turner, Harold W. "The Primal Religions of the World and Their Study." In *Australian Essays in World Religions*, edited by Victor C. Hayes, 30–32. Bedford Park: Australian Association for the Study of Religion, 1977.

———. "The Way Forward in the Religious Study of African Primal Religion." *Journal of Religion in Africa/Religion en Afrique* 12/1 (1981) 1–15.

Ukpong, Justin S. "Current Theology: The Emergence of African Theologies." *Theological Studies* 45 (1984) 501–36.

U Tam'Si, Tchicaya. *Selected Poems*. Translated by Gerald Moore. London: Heinemann, 1970.

University of Ghana. "Department for the Study of Religions: Overview." http://www.ug.edu.gh/index1.php?linkid=686&sublinkid=576.

Van den Toren, Benno. "Kwame Bediako's Christology in Its African Evangelical Context." *Exchange* 26/3 (1997) 218–32.

Visser, Hans, and Gillian Bediako. Introduction to *Jesus in Africa: The Christian Gospel in African History and Experience*, by Kwame Bediako, vii–xiii. Ghana: Regnum, 2004.

Walls, Andrew F. "Alexander Gordon Fraser." In *Dictionary of African Christian Biography*. https://dacb.org/stories/ghana/fraser-a2/.

———. "A Bag of Needments for the Road: Geoffrey Parrinder and the Study of Religion in Britain." *Religion* 10 (1980) 141–50.

———. "Christian Scholarship in Africa in the Twenty-first Century." *JACT* 4/2 (December 2001) 44–52.

———. *The Cross-Cultural Process in Christian History*. Maryknoll, NY: Orbis, 2007.

———. "The Discovery of 'African Traditional Religion' and Its Impact on Religious Studies." In *Seeing New Facets of the Diamond: Christianity As a Universal Religion—Essays in Honour of Kwame Bediako*, edited by Gillian Mary Bediako, Benhardt T. Quarshie, and J. Kwabena Asamoah-Gyadu, 1-20. Akropong-Akuapem, Ghana: Regnum, 2014.

———. Foreword to *Re-Imagining African Christologies: Conversing with the Interpretations and Appropriations of Jesus in Contemporary African Christianity*, by Victor I. Ezigbo, i–xii. Eugene, OR: Pickwick, 2010.

———. "Geoffrey Parrinder (*1910) and the Study of Religion in West Africa." In *European Traditions in the Study of Religion in Africa*, edited by Frieder Ludwig and Afe Adogame, 207–15. Wiesbaden, Germany: Harrassowitz, 2004.

———. "Kwame Bediako." In *Dictionary of African Christian Biography*. 2008. https://dacb.org/stories/ghana/bediako-kwame/.

———. "Kwame Bediako and Christian Scholarship in Africa." *IBMR* 32/4 (October 2008) 188–93.

———. *The Missionary Movement in Christian History: Studies in the Transmission of Faith*. Maryknoll, NY: Orbis, 2007.

———. "Of Ivory Towers and Ashrams: Some Reflections on Theological Scholarship in Africa." *JACT* 3/1 (June 2000) 1–4.

———. "The Scottish Missionary Diaspora." In *The Cross-Cultural Process in Christian History*, 259–72. Maryknoll: Orbis Books, 2007.

Ward, Graham. *Theology and Contemporary Critical Theory*. 2nd ed. New York: St. Martin's, 2000.

Westerlund, David. *African Religion in African Scholarship: A Preliminary Study of the Religious and Political Background*. Stockholm: Almqvist & Wiksell, 1985.

Whaling, Frank. "Theological Approaches." In *Approaches to the Study of Religion*, edited by Peter Connolly, 226–74. London: Cassell, 1999.

Williams, A. N. "Assimilation and Otherness: The Theological Significance of Négritude." *International Journal of Systematic Theology* 11/3 (July 2009) 248–70.

Williamson, Sydney George. *Akan Religion and the Christian Faith: A Comparative Study of the Impact of Two Religions*. Accra: Ghana Universities Press, 1965.

Wiredu, Kwasi. "Decolonizing African Philosophy and Religion." In *Decolonizing African Religions: A Short History of African Religions in Western Scholarship*, edited by Okot P'Bitek, xiv–xv. New York: Diasporic, 2011.

Wright, Marcia. "African History in the 1960s: Religion." *African Studies Review* 14/3 (December 1971) 439–45.

Index

Achimota, 72, 73–76, 80, 88, 95
  See also Guggisberg, education
Adams, Bill and Mary, 128
Addo, Ebenezer Obiri, 83, 85, 86, 87, 90, 91, 92, 96, 97, 98, 99
Adinkra symbols, 1, 23, 58, 82, 109, 148, 191
Adogame, Afe, 16, 20, 27, 28, 29, 30, 31, 36, 40, 42, 50
  African Traditions in the Study of Religion in Africa (2012), 20, 30, 36
African Christian scholarship, 3, 5, 7, 8, 13, 64, 195, 196, 200
  African religions, of, 7, 9, 10, 12, 13, 15, 16–18, 204
  Bediako, 10, 12, 13, 151, 152, 171, 173, 186, 188, 189, 191, 201, 204
  emerging discourse, 13, 47, 107, 150, 181, 192–94
  future trajectories, 24–26, 42, 44, 46, 56, 185, 201, 202–5
  gender and ethnicity, problematization of, 18–22
  missions, 66, 68
African Christian Studies Series, Wipf & Stock, ii, 24–25
African identity. *See* identity, African

African Personality, x, 44, 152, 167
  See also Nkrumah
African religions, ii, x, xii, xiii, 4, 5, 6, 7, 39, 44, 48, 83, 89, 95
  Akrofi-Christaller Institute and the study of, 160–66, 168, 180, 184, 189, 190
  Bediako, 12, 13, 15, 40, 54, 84, 86, 102, 177, 180, 181, 188, 195, 197
  Hellenization of, 51, 54, 56
African religions, the study of, 48, 49, 85, 93, 103, 168, 193, 201–2
African, the, 7, 15, 19, 28–30, 39, 40, 41, 42, 46, 47, 52, 55, 57, 60, 66, 70, 72, 73, 77, 83, 84, 87, 92, 97, 111, 117, 121, 128, 146, 158, 184, 193, 196, 201, 206
African Christian, the, 9, 10, 11, 12, 13, 15, 16–18, 21, 23–30, 34–35, 50, 51, 64,102, 141, 151, 152–53, 160, 166, 181, 189, 190, 194, 197, 200, 201, 202–5
  Bediako, 125, 141, 147, 164–80, 188, 195
  emerging discourse, as, 11, 22, 34–35, 45, 80, 102, 108, 121
  European pioneers, 30–34, 188

African religions, the study of (*continued*)
- methodology, 35–38
  - African approaches, 38–44
  - African Christian approaches, 44–48, 180, 184, 188, 196
  - interdisciplinary, xiii, 2,9,12, 24, 26, 46, 48, 180, 193, 197, 201, 208
  - Non-confessional approaches, 48–57
  - *See also* Bediako, methodology
- future trajectories, 173, 194, 202–5
- *See also* African Christian scholarship; Nkrumah; primal religion

African Traditional Religion, ii, 17, 18, 29, 31, 32, 33, 34, 77, 107, 134, 160, 161, 197
- *See also* African religions; primal religion

Afua Kuma, 143, 206
- Bediako, 143, 144, 177, 188, 194
- Christology, 144, 145, 178
- *Jesus of the Deep Forest: The Prayers and Praises of Afua Kuma*, 144, 145, 178 179
- mother tongue theology, 177, 179
- poetry (*see* poetry, Afua Kuma)
- primal imagination, 145, 176, 177

Akrofi, C. A. [Clement Alexander], 65–66
- Akrofi-Christaller Institute, connection to, 42, 156–57
- Basel Mission, 60
- Bediako, 157, 158
- translation, 65, 66, 74, 159, 193

Akrofi-Christaller Institute of Theology, Mission and Culture (ACI), ix, x, xvi, 2
- ashram, as, 26, 160–64
- Basel Mission (*see* Basel Mission, Akrofi-Christaller Institute, historical links)
- Bediako (*see* Bediako, Akrofi-Christaller Institute)

Journal of African Christian Thought (JACT), 102, 181, 182–83, 185, 190
- Master of Theology in African Christianity (*see* Bediako, Akrofi-Christaller Institute)
- methodology, 164, 184, 185, 188–90, 199–202
- mother tongue theology, as a center for, xii, 167, 188
- Négritude (*see* Bediako, Négritude, lasting influence of)
- Pietism, 15, 157–60, 169, 188, 193
- Presbyterian Church of Ghana, partnership with, xii, 150, 153
- primal religion, curricular focus and, 169, 170–72, 176, 180
- *See also* grassroots theology

Akropong, Ghana, xii, xvi, 2, 9, 15, 16, 65, 172, 177, 182
- royal capital, 101, 163
- *See also* Basel Mission, Akrofi-Christaller Institute, historical links and Basel Mission, Akropong

Asamoah-Gyadu, J. Kwabena, 3, 10, 35, 45, 151, 157, 160, 165, 173, 204

Ault, James, xvi, 14, 15, 53, 154

Aye-Addo, Charles Sarpong, 47, 102, 203

Balcomb, Anthony, 27, 165
Basel Mission, 15, 59, 70, 73, 75, 78
- Akrofi-Christaller Institute, historical links, 15, 16, 60, 153, 154–60, 163, 172, 188, 189, 194
- Akropong, 15, 62, 63, 65, 67, 153, 154–55, 156
- Asante, David, 65
- Asante kingdom, the, 62
- Bediako, 16, 151, 169
- colonialism, 70, 79
- education, 60, 64, 66–69, 70, 71, 72, 73, 74, 75, 76, 77, 80, 83, 106, 159
- history in Ghana, 60–64, 65, 69
- Moravian missionaries, 62, 63, 155, 156

Pietism, 15, 60, 61, 76, 159, 169, 193
Presbyterian Church of Ghana,
    69–70
Riis, Andreas, 61, 62, 63, 67, 155
salems, 63, 64, 68, 97, 188
translation, 60, 64–66, 193
See also Akrofi, C. A.; Christaller,
    J. G.
Bediako, Gillian Mary, ix, 10, 14, 18,
    128, 150, 154, 160, 162, 177,
    181, 184, 185, 186
Bediako, Kwame
    African Christian Scholarship, 3, 8,
        9, 21, 44, 54, 150, 151, 173, 195,
        196, 201, 204, 205, 207, 208
    Akrofi-Christaller Institute, xii, 37,
        149–64, 171, 188, 189
    critique of Bediako, as, 180–88
    Ebenezer, 9, 14, 83, 149, 153,
        154, 155, 156, 163, 186
    magnum opus, Bediako's, xii, 14
    Master of Theology in African
        Christianity, 164–80
    text by Bediako, reading it as, 9,
        13, 150–53, 156, 158, 188
    See also Akrofi-Christaller
        Institute
    atheism, 10, 53, 110, 123–24, 126–
        27, 130, 131, 139, 204
    Basel mission. *See* Basel Mission,
        Bediako
    biography, x, xiii, 10–11, 103–8,
        116, 124, 128–30, 139, 149–52,
        153, 192
        Aberdeen, 34, 37, 39, 139, 150
        Bordeaux, ix, 10, 14, 15, 53, 110,
            124, 127, 128, 149, 165
        London Bible College, 139
    Call to Glory, 10
    *Christianity in Africa: The Renewal
        of a Non-Western Religion
        (1997)*, xiii, 42, 43, 53, 54, 65, 66,
        67, 68, 81, 84, 91, 101, 102, 105,
        108, 203, 206
    controversy, 2, 5, 7, 12–13, 198
    conversion, x, 10, 11, 15, 104, 110,
        111, 125–29, 130, 139, 142, 143,
        146, 165, 175

Christology, 2, 4, 5, 10, 14, 102, 175,
    198, 203
    See also Fotland, *Ancestor
        Christology in Context*
criticism, 14, 186, 203, 204
Duff Lectures, 14, 21, 167, 168
identity (*see* identity, Bediako)
intellectual history, x, 3, 7, 10, 11,
    180, 192
*Jesus in Africa: The Christian
    Gospel in African History and
    Experience (2004)*, 11, 44, 154,
    176, 196, 199, 203
    apologia pro vita sua, Bediako's,
        129–32
legacy, 188–90, 197–202, 205–8
libation, 98–103, 163
methodology, 5, 44–45, 142, 147,
    149, 151, 158, 164, 180, 184,
    192, 194–95, 196, 198–99, 206–7
    historical-biographical
        approach, 7, 142, 146, 158,
        192, 194, 201
Négritude, lasting influence on
    Bediako, 11, 13, 17, 110–12, 121,
    126, 132–34, 137–39, 139–43,
    145, 146, 147, 166–67, 171, 188
    U Tam'si and, 14, 16, 110, 127,
        128, 131, 132, 144, 145, 146,
        166, 171
*Négritude et Surréalisme: Essai sur
    L'Oeuvre Poétique de Tchicaya
    U Tam'si [Négritude and
    Surrealism: A Study on the Poetic
    Works of Tchicaya U Tam'si]
    (1970)*, 124–25, 129, 138, 176
pioneer, as, xii, 3, 7, 9, 13, 187, 188,
    193, 197
politics. *See* politics, Bediako
poetry. *See* poetry, Bediako
Presbyterian Church of Ghana, and,
    ix, x, xii, 10, 104, 139, 150, 153,
    155
primal imagination, *See* primal
    imagination, Bediako
relevance for future scholarship,
    202–5

Bediako, Kwame *(continued)*
  theology
    grassroots, 107, 158, 160, 162, 178
    living church, theology of the, xii, 168, 172, 178
    mother tongue, as interpretative key, 2, 159–60, 172–80, 188, 203
    See also grassroots theology
  Theology and Identity: The Impact of Culture upon Christian Thought in the Second Century and in Modern Africa (1999), xi, xv, 4, 16, 102, 110, 139–43, 146, 151,167, 186, 192, 203
  L'Univers Interieur de Tchicaya U Tam'si [Interior Universe of Tchicaya U Tam'si, The] (1973), xiii, xvi, 9, 12, 13, 14, 15, 133, 139, 147, 204
  U Tam'si, areas of affinity with, 132–39
Black identity. *See* identity, African; identity, Négritude
Blyden, Edward W., 120
Bongmba, Elias Kifon, xiii, xvi, 10, 23, 26, 28, 30, 41, 47, 50, 56–57, 59, 173, 186, 197, 204, 205
British, 26, 76, 83, 86, 88, 93, 96
Busia, Kofi Abrefa
  African religions, the study of, 15, 60, 76, 77, 84, 86, 96, 99, 103, 105
  Nkrumah, in contrast to, 83, 95–96, 97
  politics, 103, 104, 186
  Position of the Chief in the Modern Political System of Ashanti: A Study, The (1968), 84–86, 91
  religion in Africa, African scholar of, 15
  sociology, 83, 95, 96, 97, 103
Césaire, Aimé, x, 112, 113, 114, 121
  Cahier d'un Retour au pays natal [Notebook of a Return to My Native Land] (1939, 1995), 114, 121

Chitando, Ezra, 24, 25, 28, 35, 53, 56
Christaller, J. G. [Johannes Gottlieb], 66
  Akrofi-Christaller Institute, connection to, 42, 156–57
  Basel Mission, 60
  Bediako, 157, 158
  translation, 65, 66, 74, 159, 193
Christian Council of Ghana, 84, 155
  libation, 98–102
  Nkrumah, 98, 103
  politics, 97–98
colonialism, 47, 83, 159
  British, 10, 11, 15, 16, 28, 29, 59, 60, 70, 71, 74, 79, 80, 98, 100, 116, 133, 151, 193
  education, 81
    See also Guggisberg, education
  French, 116, 133
    See also Basel Mission, colonialism; history, colonial
Congo. *See* Kesteloot, Lilyan; U Tam'si, Tchicaya
Cox, James L., 6, 31, 32, 33, 34, 37, 38, 39, 40, 42, 44, 49, 50, 51, 56
culture, gospel and, 64, 102, 141, 169

Damas, Léon, x, 112
Danfulani, Umar Habila Dadem, 20
Dedji, Valentin, 4, 102, 103, 112, 186
Dickson, Kwesi, 156, 161, 162, 205, 206

European Traditions in the Study of Religion in Africa (Ludwig and Adogame, 2004), 16, 30
Ezigbo, Victor, 4

Fotland, Roar, 3, 4, 10, 11, 124, 126, 127, 159, 160
  Ancestor Christology in Context (2005), 10, 11–12, 124
France
  Bediako, ix, 10, 14, 15, 53, 124, 149
  Négritude, 110, 116, 119, 176
  Paris, x, 76, 112, 113, 114, 119, 121, 125, 141, 177
  U Tam'si, Tchicaya, 122, 146

gender. *See* African Christian
scholarship, gender and
ethnicity
Ghana, history, 68, 70, 71, 79, 80, 83–84,
85, 86, 95, 99, 100, 102, 156, 188
Glover-Quartey, Alexander, xvi, 10, 96,
103, 104, 123, 126, 127
Gold Coast. *See* Ghana
grassroots theology, 107, 153–54, 158,
160, 162, 178, 202
Guggisberg, Sir Gordon, 97
colonialism, British, 60, 70, 79
education, 69, 70–72, 80, 88, 107
Achimota, 73–75
University College of the Gold
Coast/ University of Ghana,
75–77, 193

Hanciles, Jehu, 29, 46, 47, 60
Hastings, Adrian, 31, 47
history, 67, 106, 130, 142, 172, 180, 197
African, 80, 88, 107, 114, 115, 124,
125, 133, 142, 144, 147, 151, 155
colonial, 83, 116, 122
Christian/Church, 77, 84, 105, 106,
139, 143, 149, 150, 159, 163,
188, 198
African Christian, 156, 158, 170,
172, 188
missions, 67, 206
world, 67, 156, 162, 169, 176
See also Basel Mission, history;
Négritude, history
Horton, Robin, 48, 49

identity, 19, 78, 79, 106, 108, 120, 122,
123, 124, 125, 146, 182, 185
African, x, 4, 10, 13, 14, 16, 26, 29,
45, 53, 71, 79, 80, 86, 89, 94, 100,
110, 111, 115, 119, 132–34, 136,
143, 144, 150
African Christian, ii, xiv, 21, 28, 55,
84, 91, 93, 98, 144, 147, 167, 193
Bediako, x, xi, 20, 42, 44, 53, 155,
158, 164, 166, 167, 205, 206
Christian, 8, 128, 147
challenges, xi, 19–20, 21, 142, 144,
145

formation of, 16, 29, 87, 90
Négritude, ix, 13, 111, 113, 114, 115,
117, 118, 119, 125, 139–44, 147,
151, 167
See also Bediako, *Theology and
Identity*; Walls, identity
Idowu, E. Bolaji, xi, 7, 17, 29, 33, 34, 35,
51, 56, 100, 140
intellectuals, African, x, 7, 12, 54, 78,
112, 119, 120, 141, 176, 193
Irele, Abiola, 113, 114, 115, 117, 118
Isichei, Elizabeth, 18

*Journal of African Christian Thought
(JACT)*. *See* Akrofi-Christaller
Institute
July, Robert, 112, 114, 120

Kalu, Ogbu, 3, 37, 45, 161, 172
Kesteloot, Lilyan, 82, 83, 111, 113, 115
*Les écrivains noirs de langue
française: naissance d'une
literature [Black French Writers:
Birth of a Literary Tradition]
(1971)*, 113, 115
*Négritude et situation colonial
[Négritude and the Colonial
Context] (1968)*, 82, 111, 113,
114, 115
Kimble, David, 63, 64, 65, 70, 71, 79, 81

Laryea, Philip T., 73, 74
libation, xiii, 84, 98–103, 163

Maluleke, T. S., 6, 12, 78, 159, 174, 175,
181, 203, 206
Mbiti, John S., xi, xii, 7, 17, 24, 29, 33,
34, 35, 45, 49, 51, 53, 56, 74, 107,
120, 140, 168, 169, 172, 175,
196, 197
*African Religion and Philosophy
(1969)*, 29, 45
methodology, 35–57, 194–97
See African religions, the study of;
Bediako, methodology
Miller, Jon, 61, 69, 78, 79

INDEX

missionaries, xi, 24, 26, 35, 51, 52, 59, 60, 61, 62, 63, 64, 65, 67, 68, 69, 71, 72, 74, 75
  motivations, 77–81
  Scottish, 67, 69, 70
  See also Basel Mission
Moore, Gerald, 121, 122, 123, 132
Moravian missionaries. *See* Basel Mission
mother tongue theology, 159–60, 203
  See also Afua Kuma, mother tongue theology; Akrofi-Christaller Institute, mother tongue theology, as a center for; Bediako, theology, mother tongue

Nana Addo Dankwa III, 101, 102, 156, 163, 203
nationalism, x, 58, 81, 100, 113, 114, 115, 116
  Ghana, 26, 59, 60, 61, 70, 71, 92, 95, 103, 107, 111
  study of religion, and, 28–30, 52, 80, 83–87, 146, 151, 152
Négritude, 44, 45, 110–12, 119, 132, 136, 152, 165
  African identity (*see* identity, Negritude)
  anti-colonial, 15, 83, 114, 146
  colonialism (French), 110, 112, 114, 116, 117, 119, 120, 121, 134, 141
  criticisms of, 117–21, 146
  history, 112–15
  ideology, 110, 113, 116, 120, 124, 125, 142
  independence movements, 111, 116, 117
  literary movement, x, xi, 110, 114, 119, 124–25, 141, 177, 189
  politics, 112, 115–17
  religion, 13, 117, 121, 134, 141, 145, 151
  See also Bediako, Négritude, lasting influence of
Nkrumah, Kwame, x, 84, 95, 96, 97, 98
  African Personality, x, 45, 98, 99, 100, 157

Christian Council of Ghana (C.C.G.), 97–98
Convention Peoples' Party (C.P.P.), 90, 92
Department for the Study of Religions, establishment of, 93–95, 193, 194
independence (Ghana), 83, 86
religion in Africa
  scholar of, as, 15, 29, 87, 89, 92, 95, 96
  study of the, contributions to, 60, 83, 93
  religious beliefs, 11, 87–89, 90, 91, 92, 94
  See also Nationalism

Oduyoye, Mercy Amba, 16, 17, 20
Olabimtan, Kehinde, 18, 19, 40, 41, 42, 47, 54, 201, 204
Olademo, Oyeronke, 19, 20, 185
Olupona, Jacob, 25, 29

p'Bitek, Okot, 7, 34, 51, 52, 53, 54, 55, 56, 170
Parratt, John, 45, 46, 53, 54
Parrinder, Geoffrey, 26, 31, 32, 33, 34, 38, 59, 60, 72, 75, 76, 77, 93, 160, 193
Pentecost, Church of, 144
pentecostal, xiii, 3, 167
Philosophy, African, ii, 25, 33, 48, 83, 107, 116, 124, 133, 137, 141, 144, 168, 206
  See also Négritude
Platvoet, Jan, 24, 40, 41, 42, 43, 44, 49, 201
Pobee, John S., 29, 81, 91, 92, 93, 94, 95, 98, 99, 100
poetry, 16, 18, 112, 117, 199
  Afua Kuma, 144, 146, 176, 177, 178, 179, 188
  Bediako, x, 11, 110, 111, 116, 123, 124, 125, 126, 127, 130, 131, 132, 138, 139, 145, 166, 176, 188, 189, 207
  religion in Africa, as a source for the study of, 57, 147, 147, 180, 199

U Tam'si, x, xi, 11, 17, 29, 110, 120, 121, 122, 123, 124, 133, 134, 135, 142, 146, 166
  See also Négritude; U Tam'si
politics, x, 95, 107
  Bediako, 84, 103, 104, 105, 106, 108, 110, 183, 186, 197
  Ghanaian independence, 15, 59, 86
  Négritude, See Négritude, politics
  religion in Ghana, 45, 57, 85, 97–103
  traditional rule, 91
  See also Nationalism
Presbyterian Church of Ghana, xii, 69–70, 97, 155
  Scottish missions, 67, 69, 70, 73
  See also Basel Mission, Akrofi-Christaller Institute, Bediako
Présence Africaine, 140, 141
primal imagination, 145, 146, 171, 183
  Afua Kuma (see Afua Kuma, primal imagination)
  Akrofi-Christaller Institute (ACI), 163, 171
  Bediako, xiii, 17, 43, 125, 137, 138, 143–44, 145, 146, 163, 188, 192
  U Tam'si, 137, 142
primal religion, xi, 17, 18, 32, 33, 50, 51, 52, 53, 54, 64, 72, 98, 108, 133, 137, 161
  Afua Kuma, 176, 177, 178
  Bediako, xiii, 2, 3, 4, 5, 6, 14, 20, 37, 38, 105, 110, 134, 140, 145, 146, 151, 162, 171, 180, 192, 199, 205
  Ghanaian independence and, 87, 96, 98, 103, 108
  U Tam'si, 110, 134, 135, 136, 143, 144
  See also African Traditional Religion; Akrofi-Christaller Institute, primal religion
Proverbs, Akan or Twi, xv, 65, 90, 162, 208
Pym, David, 50, 51

Reindorf, Carl Christian, 62, 67, 68
Russell-Jones, Iwan, 192

salems
  See Basel Mission, salems
Sanneh, Lamin, 37, 62, 63, 69, 70, 71, 77, 78, 106, 107, 159, 174, 175
Sartre, Jean Paul, 109, 110, 113, 118, 119
Sawyerr, Harry, 152
Senghor, Léopold Sédar, x, 112, 114, 117, 118, 121, 137, 146, 176
Shenk, Wilbert R., 33
Stinton, Diane, 30, 112, 165
Surrealism, 116
  See also Bediako, Négritude et Surréalisme

Theology, 3, 5, 6, 24, 49, 130, 149, 189, 205, 206, 207
  African, ii, ix, xi, xii, 4, 5, 6, 9, 34, 35, 37, 42, 43, 44, 45, 46, 50, 54, 101, 111, 114, 117, 124, 138, 140, 141, 164, 168, 172, 181, 186, 195, 196, 198, 200, 204
  academic discipline, as an ix, 24, 28, 29, 30, 32, 35, 45, 47, 48, 88, 93, 148, 161, 162, 164, 200
  Akrofi-Christaller Institute, scholarship and, 153–54, 202
  methodological challenges, 13, 24, 26, 36
  Western, 9, 26, 34, 42, 50, 55, 145, 162, 192, 194, 195, 196, 198, 199
  Masters of Theology in African Christianity, 164–80
  See also Bediako, theology
Thomson, Alan, 2
Turner, Harold W., 31, 37, 171

U Tam'si, Tchicaya, ix, x, xi, 1, 16, 29, 121–22, 129, 130, 147, 194
  African religions, the African study of, 110
  atheism, 126, 135
  colonialism, 110, 170
  Congo, ix, 14, 17, 110, 121, 122, 124, 125, 133, 134, 140, 146
  Identity, African, 142, 144, 147, 166, 167, 177
  Négritude, 11, 14, 29, 116, 120

U Tam'si, Tchicaya *(continued)*
  religion, 134–39, 147
    African Traditional Religion/
      primal religion, 134, 135
    Christianity/Catholicism, 122,
      131–32, 134, 136, 145, 147,
      166, 170
    cosmic identification, 131, 132,
      138
    tensions with, 122, 135–36, 144
  primal imagination, 137, 138, 142,
    144, 151, 171
  Surrealism, xi, 17, 131
  themes, key, 122–23, 132–39
  See also Bediako, Négritude, U
    Tam'si
Ukpong, Justin, 46
University of Ghana, 15, 74, 103, 123,
  155
  Department for the Study of
    Religions, 107, 111, 161, 193,
    194
  See also Guggisberg, education,
    University College of the Gold
    Coast/ University of Ghana;
    Nkrumah, Department for the
    Study of religions, establishment
    of

van den Toren, Benno, 5, 175
van Rinsum, Henk, 34, 40, 41, 42, 44,
  201
Visser, Hans, 154, 174, 176

Walls, Andrew F.
  academy, Western, 163–64, 200
  African Christian scholarship, 13,
    35, 187, 189
  African religion and the academic
    study of, 26, 31, 33–34, 37, 38,
    48
  Akrofi-Christaller Institute, 148–49,
    161, 162, 169
  Bediako, 3, 7, 10, 18, 139, 143, 149,
    150, 190
  conversion, 125–26, 128, 167
  Enlightenment, the, 195, 200
  identity, 133, 194
  Scottish missions, 70
  Universities in West Africa,
    establishment of, 75, 76, 93, 193
West Africa, 17, 19, 22, 26, 45, 55, 163
  British colonialism, 116
  Christianity, 63, 102
  education, 59, 72, 75, 77, 93, 160,
    161, 162
  study of religion, 28–30, 31, 32
  See also Basel Mission, history
    in Ghana; colonialism;
    Ghana, history; Guggisberg;
    nationalism, Ghana; Parrinder;
    politics, Ghanaian independence
Westerlund, David, 26, 49
Wiredu, Kwasi, 29, 34, 51, 52, 55
World Christianity, ii, xii, 24–25, 187,
  198